# UNCOMMON
# GROUND

Leland Ferguson

# UNCOMMON GROUND

## Archaeology and Early African America, 1650 - 1800

**Smithsonian Institution Press**   Washington and London

Editor: Robin A. Gould
Production Editor: Eileen D'Araujo
Designer: Janice Wheeler

**Library of Congress Cataloging-in-Publication Data**
Ferguson, Leland G.
    Uncommon ground : archaeology and early African America, 1650–1800 / by Leland
Ferguson.
       p. cm.
    Includes bibliographical references and index.
    ISBN 1-56098-058-3. — ISBN 1-56098-059-1 (pbk.)
    1. Slavery—South Carolina.   2. Slaves—South Carolina—Social
conditions.   3. Plantations—South Carolina.   4. South Carolina—Antiquities.   5. South
Carolina—History—Colonial period, ca. 1600–1775.   6. Afro-Americans—South
Carolina—Antiquities.
I. Title.
E445.S7F37     1992
975.7′00496073—dc20                    91-52833
                                                       CIP

British Cataloguing-in-Publication Data available
Manufactured in the United States of America
98 97 96 95 94 93 92     5 4 3 2

∞The paper used in this publication meets the minimum requirements of the American Na-
tional Standard for Performance of Paper for Printed Library Materials Z39.48-1984
For permission to reproduce illustrations appearing in this book, please correspond directly
with the author. The Smithsonian Institution Press does not retain reproduction rights for
these illustrations.
Permission to use the lines from the Prelude to "Work Song and Blues" by Edward Kamau
Brathwaite from *Rights of Passage*, 1967, was generously given by the publisher, Oxford
University Press.

For my students and others who aim to become archaeologists

# Contents

# List of Figures

ix

# Acknowledgments

Making this book has been an adventure. In the middle 1970s I became interested in exploring the ways historical archaeology might illuminate African American history and, in turn, mainstream American history. Like most archaeologists of the time, I was trained not in history but in anthropological archaeology; as a graduate student I had done fieldwork on prehistoric Native Americans. Nevertheless, together with a few others, I found a leader in Dr. Charles Fairbanks. African American archaeology seemed to appeal to archaeologists who tried to understand American history from a non-Western point of view. The late Charles Fairbanks was such an archaeologist, and his papers on the Kingsley slave cabins in Florida introduced me, and many others, to the idea of an archaeology of African American history.

I had earlier discovered historical archaeology through my excavation of a British Revolutionary War fort for the Bicentennial celebration. I was fortunate in this project to have the advice and support of historical archaeologist Stanley South. So, I gained experience in historical archaeology, but still little in African American history; African American archaeology was a brand new field. As I joined the small group of archaeologists exploring African American sites, I had a big task ahead. These acknowledgments are for the people who have so generously helped me with this work.

Through more than ten years of research I have had the opportunity to exchange ideas with a wonderful variety of people including scholars from several fields, students with fresh views and new questions, and nonprofessionals interested in the African American past. While this book carries my name, and while I accept full responsibility for any mistakes, *Uncommon Ground* is the product of many people who have been willing to share their time, labor, ideas and, most important, their friendship.

Among professional colleagues I first want to thank Peter Wood and Elizabeth Fenn, friends of this project from the very beginning. They encouraged me to use archaeology, not simply to support written sources, but to learn something completely new about the African American past. I also want to express thanks to my colleagues in the Department of Anthropology and the Institute of Archaeology and Anthropology at the University of South Carolina for their support through the years. Special thanks to Stanley South, Karl Heider, Joan Gero, Stanton Green, James Michie, Albert Goodyear, and Gail Wagner for their generous help and encouragement.

Other colleagues who have guided my research with advice, criticism, and comments include Charles Joyner, Jerome Handler, Theresa Singleton, Charles Fairbanks, Kathleen Deagan, Gerald Milanich, Lesley Drucker, Roderick Ebanks, Marion Smith, Carl Steen, Roy Dickens, Mark Leone, Robert Schuyler, Douglas Armstrong, James Deetz, Merrick Posnansky, Winnie Owens-Hart, Gladys Fry, Alain Outlaw, Ivor Noël Hume, Thomas Funk, Joffre Coe, Michael Trinkley, Richard Polhemus, Larry Lepionka, Norman Barka, Elizabeth Reitz, Martha Zierden, Jacqueline Fehon, Thomas Wheaton, Patrick Garrow, Amy Friedlander, George McDaniel, and William Kelso.

Students come to college to learn, but they are also teachers. Over the years I have been blessed with many students—both undergraduates and graduates—who have contributed to my education. For the day-to-day help I received on this project from student research assistants I want to thank Stacy Gibbons, Joe Joseph, Ken Sassaman, Christopher Judge, Leith Smith, Melanie Cabak, Karrie Joseph, Elizabeth Haynes, Dianne Anderson, and Niels Taylor. My closest companions in this adventure have been my graduate students who chose to pursue research on African American sites for theses—David Babson, Elaine Nichols, Alexander West, Ronald Anthony, Richard Affleck, Cynthia Connor, James Errante, Natalie Adams, Leith Smith, and Jeffrey Jobe. Their help was invaluable and their camaraderie in the field made the work fun.

The early stages of this project were assisted by a research grant from the National Endowment for the Humanities, and my research in South Carolina lowcountry was partially funded by the South Carolina Department of Archives and History and the University of South Carolina. For direct assistance helping me find artifacts and notes, I would like to thank the South Carolina Institute of Archaeology and Anthropology; the Charleston Museum; the Department of Historic Resources, Commonwealth of Virginia; Colonial Williamsburg Foundation; North Carolina Department of Archives and History; Research Laboratories of Anthropology, University of North Carolina; St. Augustine Historical Foundation; the Department of Anthropology, College of William and Mary; Soil Systems Incorporated; Carolina Archaeological Services; Chicora Foundation, Inc.; and the African-Caribbean Institute of Jamaica. For their personal assistance at these institutions, I extend my thanks to Sharon Pekrul, Keith Derting, Nena Powell, Robert L. Stephenson, Bruce Rippeteau, Steve Smith, Charlie Rinehart, Jay Mills, Gordon Brown, Elaine Herold, Martha Zierden, Merry Outlaw, Beverly Bogley, Mary Ellen Norrissey, Charles Hodges, Keith Egloff, Audrey Noel Hume, Bill Pittman, Thomas Funk, Jaqueline Fehon, Linda Stine, Linda Nelson, Alan Albright, Christopher Amer, Ralph Wilbanks, and Marcel Dirk.

In contrast to most documentary research, archaeology requires teamwork. Students and colleagues form most of the team, but good archaeology also requires community participation. For their assistance, I extend thanks to Emory Campbell of Penn Community Services, Inc., the Max L. Hill family, Postell Smalls, Elijah Wigfall, Mary Huguenin, Tim Milling, Duffie Johnson, and Rodney Mooneyham.

This manuscript has benefited from the critical eye of several talented people. Carol Speight and Susan Jackson helped with editing and they have always been available for comment and advice. Charles Joyner emphasized to me that the world needed a readable book on African American archaeology and kindly commented on an early draft. Theodore Rosengarten also read my work in progress and gave me excellent guidance in the craft of writing. Karen Hess, John Adams, and Benjamin Dunlap read parts of the manuscript and offered advice on their fields of expertise. Rex Ellis, Elaine Nichols, Stephen Loring, David Babson, Stanley South, and Vennie Deas-Moore made suggestions on an early draft. I sincerely appreciate their efforts and hope they like the final product.

Beyond writing the text, producing this book required photographs, illustrations, word processing, and editing. Emily Short took excellent photographs; Bobbie May, Ruth Johnson, David Babson, Alexander West, Richard Affleck, and Gene Speer drafted the illustrations. Leith Smith laid out the rough draft manuscript and helped edit the Appendix. Dorothy O'Dell helped me keep the finances straight, Patricia Rhudy helped with typing, and Deannie Stevens worked magic with her word processing equipment. I also appreciate the interest and support provided by Daniel Goodwin, Robin Gould, and other members of the editorial staff at the Smithsonian Institution Press. As a guest editor for the Smithsonian, Dale Rosengarten offered substantive criticism as well as suggestions for adjusting words and punctuation. I sincerely appreciate her thoughtful and sensitive assistance.

My deepest thanks go to my family. Besides the essentials provided by parents, mine enriched my childhood by telling stories about the past; for me their suppertime recollections inspired a career. My older brother Adrian taught my first lessons in humor, imagination, and creativity. As always, I know he'll laugh at my mistakes; I also know that I won't mind. My wife Aline has tolerated and even encouraged my obsession with "the book"; and our new son Samuel, born as this project was reaching fruition, provided unimaginable joy.

So build build
again the new
villages: you
must mix spittle
with dirt, dung
to saliva and
sweat, making
mortar. Leaf
work for the
roof and vine
tendrils.
But square frames
crack, wood
rots, smooth mortar
too remains mortal,
trapped in its own salt,
its unstable foundations of water.
So grant, God
that this house will stand
the four winds
the seasons' alterations
the exploration of the worm.
Grant, God,
a clear release from thieves,
from robbers and from those that plot
and poison while they dip
into our dish.

Edward Kamau Brathwaite, from Prelude to
"Work Song and Blues" from *Rights of Passage*

Figure 1. Homes of freed slaves on an "old plantation street," St. Helena Island, South Carolina, circa 1900–1910 (see Dabbs 1970). (From the Penn School Collection, permission granted by Penn Center, St. Helena Island, South Carolina)

# Prologue

## AFRICAN AMERICAN PIONEERS

In 1740 blacks in South Carolina outnumbered whites by almost two to one, and one half of that majority had been born in Africa.[1] As slaves, they cleared trees to build plantations, and in some of those clearings they built their settlements. Research in history and folklore combined with recent archaeological finds help us imagine what those early homes were like:

• • • Linked by sandy yards, three small, two-room houses stand in the smoky shadows of tall pines and moss-draped live oaks. No little white cottages from "Gone with the Wind," these are more like African houses than the "slave cabins" we know preserved from the middle nineteenth century. Roofs of split planks and palmetto thatching top clay walls without windows.

In a sunny clearing behind the houses, saplings and stumps, the debris from clearing land, surround a garden; they keep the cattle out of the okra, corn, and sweet potatoes. Posts and poles, for this purpose and that, stand like sentinels in the well-swept yards. Near each house are two or three large holes. First dug for clay to build house walls, they now receive sweepings from the yard. These pits contain mostly sand and bark, wood shavings, and pine cones. Yet here also are fragments of broken pots, discarded bones, pieces of glass, metal, buttons, and other little things.

In front of one house a young mother goes about her late morning chores. They call her Benah, an African name for a girl-child born on Tuesday. She stoops to move the old basket holding her baby into the warm sunlight. The baby coughs and Benah quickly touches the single blue glass bead tied with a string around the baby's neck. Then she turns to stir a clay pot simmering on a hearth fashioned from three big bricks. Standing upright on legs bowed from childhood malnutrition, Benah deftly adjusts the skirt wrapped about her waist with one hand and slips the stem of her white clay tobacco pipe into the waistband. Beneath her bare feet lies the charcoal of hundreds of cooking fires kindled on this very spot since her mother and other black pioneers first built temporary thatched houses and began transforming forests and swamps into productive rice fields.

Scattered about are her cookwares. Three more pots sit near the fire—an iron one issued by Ben, the white planter's son, and two others of clay handbuilt by Benah. Clay pots are best for savory sauces. Although Benah uses the iron pot, her mother— one of the Africans with scars on her breast—never would. She always complained that the iron legs stuck into the ground and that the metal pot cooked too hot and fast. She preferred the slow cooking of her earthenware.

Benah's mother, now a spirit living near her grave in the pine woods, dug clay in the rice field ditch and taught her daughters to build pots and make spicy African sauces. Serving bowls for sauces are stacked on a split log. Two of these bowls, glazed and colored brown and yellow, were also given to her by Ben. Unknown to her, they were made by working women in Staffordshire, England. The others, like the cooking pots, were made right here in the sandy yard.

Benah's family usually eats morning and evening meals in front of the house beside the fire. Her family sits on the ground or planks while she serves rice or corn meal mush on large palmetto leaves. They dip handfuls of the stiff starch into piquant sauces made from okra leaves and other greens gathered from the woods and fields.

The small houses both have two rooms with separate entries. One room of Benah's house is reserved for her mother's brother, another African—a man who talks to spirits. Inside the other room Benah, her sister, brother, and three small children sleep. Benah's husband, a cooper and woodcarver who digs out cypress canoes, lives on a plantation across the river. Often on Sunday and sometimes at night he paddles the short distance between the banks to visit.

In the center of the earthen house-floor, an open hearth holds fires that fight the cold of winter and the devilish mosquitoes of the long hot months. In rainy weather Benah moves her cooking inside to this small fire. On the wall beyond the hearth, a leather bag and fishing net hang from a wrought-iron nail. Cow hides and woolen blankets that serve as beds are rolled up and piled in a corner. An empty wine bottle and a wooden bucket made by her husband and filled with water stand just beside the door. Outside, the young woman empties the pot of corn meal mush into a large gourd bowl, covering it with leaves to keep it warm. Then, gathering up her ailing baby, she balances the bowl on her head and walks off toward the place her relatives are clearing for new rice fields.

For thirty more years, Benah and her family and neighbors live in this settlement. In the last decade of the century, not long after the Revolutionary War, they move to some new houses closer to the rice fields along the river. The old settlement slowly settles into the ground. The heart pine posts reinforcing the clay walls rot in place but, hidden beneath the dark humus, the stains of these posts remain in the yellow sand of the subsoil. Wrought-iron nails used to hold the rafters together fall to the ground and begin to rust. The charred wood in the hearths is covered with blowing sand. Unless moved by some human or natural action, this charcoal will remain, preserved, in just this spot for thousands of years. The clay pits continue to fill with washings from frequent rains—broken pieces of pottery, buttons, fragments of glass and bone concealed within. Once a small village of pioneering African Americans, this eighteenth-century homeplace is now an archaeological site holding a retrievable story of early American life.


## FINDING THE "NEGRO HOUSES"

In the summer of 1986, students in my archaeological field class and I set out to find an eighteenth-century African American village. We were searching on Middleburg Plantation in an old rice-growing district about 25 miles north of Charleston, South Carolina (Figs. 2 and 3, see map in Appendix 1). This district lies near the center of the South Carolina lowcountry, the region of the largest black majority in colonial America. Our excavations were part of a bigger survey project aimed at learning more about early slave communities by finding the geographical pattern of settlements on the East Branch of Cooper River. Our summer research provides an example of the methods and techniques used in African American archaeology.

While the location of the slave quarters at Middleburg was not obvious, we could easily see other features of this antebellum rice plantation. The shining white "big house" of Middleburg still stands where it stood since at least 1699, nearly three hundred years. Here and there, other reminders of the plantation days remain. The avenue of oaks was established by the wealthy planter Jonathan Lucas sometime before 1831. Although Lucas is credited with "planting" the trees, they probably were uprooted, transported, set out, and cared for by slaves. The wide, nicely crowned road bed of the avenue certainly was graded with hoes and shovels in black hands. Behind the house a kitchen and decaying servants' quarters flank a formal garden, which is now more lawn than garden,

Figure 2. Middleburg Plantation house. First rooms built circa 1699. East Branch Cooper River, South Carolina. (The Historic American Buildings Survey, Library of Congress)

and two nineteenth-century Gothic-revival style barns stand about one hundred yards away in a grassy field.[2] A picture postcard of the scene might bear the caption: "The Simple Grace of the Old South is Well-Preserved at Middleburg Plantation. Middleburg is Located on the Cooper River in South Carolina's Lowcountry." Missing from the picture are the people in servitude who built this and other plantations and who left an abundant archaeological record underground.

Down the path behind the house lie the river, marsh, and rice fields. Now grown up in aquatic weeds, these fields are surrounded by more than a mile of earthen dikes or "banks" as they were called. Built by slaves, these banks are severely eroded now. Originally they were taller than a person and up to 15 feet wide. By the turn of the eighteenth century, rice banks on the 12½-mile stretch of the East Branch of Cooper River measured more than 55 miles long and contained more than 6.4 million cubic feet of earth.[3] This means that within approximately fifty years of tidal rice agriculture, Middleburg slaves, working in the water and muck with no more than shovels, hoes, and baskets, had built an

Figure 3. African American women threshing rice at Middleburg Plantation, circa 1900. (Photograph courtesy of John E. Gibbs)

earthwork approximately one-half the size of Monks Mound, the largest pre-historic Indian mound in North America. By 1850 Carolina slaves working on plantations like Middleburg throughout the rice growing district had built a system of banks and canals greater in volume than the Egyptian pyramid at Cheops.[4]

Near the Middleburg rice fields a brick smoke stack, almost 100 feet tall, stands amid the pines and live oaks like an ancient Mayan temple. At its base, slowly sinking into the junglelike growth, are the ghostly remains of a nineteenth-century steam engine and the brick foundation of a rice pounding mill.[5] Although we have yet to find the proof, local legend claims that ships left the Middleburg wharf loaded with rice, bound for England.

From early in the eighteenth century until 1861, Middleburg was a thriving rice plantation. A tour around the estate reveals much of the original layout, and the informed eye sees the skill and handiwork of African Americans everywhere—in the house, the roads, the fields, the mill (Fig. 4). From probate records we know that fifty-nine slaves lived at Middleburg in 1772 and ninety in

Figure 4. Dugout canoe discovered along the Edisto River in the South Carolina lowcountry. From the eighteenth through the early twentieth century African Americans carved cypress canoes for use along waterways connecting rice plantations (see Fleetwood 1982). (Photograph courtesy of the South Carolina Institute of Archaeology and Anthropology)

1790.[6] In fact, the majority of people who have ever lived at Middleburg were black. African American slaves built this plantation—they sawed the boards, drove the nails, laid the bricks, built the banks, and worked the crops. Yet there is no obvious evidence of their homes; the evidence is hidden within the soil.

Our archaeological strategy for finding the missing slave quarters was simple. We would search in the most likely places. The trick to this strategy was determining where the "most likely places" might be.

First we studied maps and talked to people. The land contours of the modern United States Geodetic Surveys and the sites of surviving plantation structures suggested to us that the quarters probably were situated on the same ridge as the "big house," overlooking the river or else adjacent to the marsh and near the rice fields. We thought these conjectures were good, but we wanted as much locational information as possible to minimize the amount of digging required to find foundations and floors. So we also looked for maps from the period when the plantation was operating. We knew from notes on early twentieth-century plats that there had been at least one plantation map made in the late eighteenth century and another in the middle of the nineteenth century. We even found a book, *Charleston Gardens*, which referred to an earlier map and described the "twelve cabins for the Negroes."[7] We searched archives and libraries as well as the personal collections of family and friends of the owners, but still we could not find the map or maps we thought existed. We had to be content with the written account.

In questioning local people we seemed to have more success. Mr. John Gibbs, a member of the white family that recently owned the plantation, thought he knew roughly where some quarters had stood until they were torn down early in the twentieth century. Black informants from the community remembered when people lived in the servants' quarters adjacent to the "big house," and they remembered some houses "across the hard road" about a mile from the plantation, but they could not recall old slave quarters on what is now Middleburg. Reasoning that quarters in the early twentieth century might well be in the same location as those two hundred years earlier, and that an eyewitness description should provide the most reliable information, we began our test excavations where Mr. Gibbs had thought some cabins should be, and we found nothing.

From this we went to Briggs's description in *Charleston Gardens* of a very old map of Middleburg: "This drawing. . . shows a forecourt with a square formal garden on each side. Beyond one garden are twelve cabins for the Negroes and beyond the other, a barn and machine house with other accessory buildings."[8] This description was pretty clear. The quarters were obviously located on one of two sides of the forecourt and garden, but what was the front of the house?

Eighteenth-century houses on important waterways such as the Cooper River often faced the water, and the present garden at Middleburg is on the river side of the house. The house now fronts the oak avenue away from the river, but it is one of those buildings that could be seen as "fronting" in either of two directions. We finally decided on the front as the side with the oak avenue, and we put in small test excavations on the western side of the yard. Here, we found a few artifacts—some glass, a few nails, and a brick footing—and concluded that we were in the vicinity of the barns. We moved our attention to the eastern side of the front yard, where we laid out a scattered pattern of eight 1 by 1 meter squares for our test excavations.

Cutting through the sod, we excavated with shovels in layers approximately 10 centimeters thick. We threw dirt into our mechanical sifters and collected everything larger than the quarter-inch mesh of the screens. As we watched the artifacts showing up in the screen baskets, there was the debris from the slave village! It wasn't spectacular—we didn't expect spectacular artifacts in our test pits—but it was there and it was substantial. The dark brown, almost black earth gave up hundreds of things; just the kinds of things we had hoped and expected to find around the quarters (Fig. 5). There was the slave-made pottery we call Colono Ware, imported English ceramics from the late eighteenth century, food bones of various kinds including birds and mammals, fragments of brick, hundreds of nails, pieces of glass, and other little things like buttons and fragments of imported white-kaolin tobacco pipes as well as locally made earth-colored pipes.[9] Rich with artifacts, the dark, charcoal and grease-stained soil looked like the sort commonly found around old houses. And this scatter of refuse—or midden as archaeologists would call it—was where we expected the slave quarters to be located. We had found it! Tens of thousands of the everyday things of slaves were still there, waiting to be excavated.

On the very weekend after we found the Middleburg quarters, we came upon a copy of the eighteenth-century map verifying our find. That Saturday evening, graduate student David W. Babson visited Mr. and Mrs. Thomas Huguenin at adjacent Halidon Hill to copy a nineteenth-century map of their plantation. Halidon Hill had been part of Middleburg in the eighteenth century, and we hoped this later map would provide clues to earlier features. This was the fourth time we had visited the Huguenins inquiring about maps and other historical sources, and they had willingly combed through drawer after drawer of maps and papers accumulated through the years. That evening David set up his drawing board and Mrs. Huguenin, as usual, searched for more things. Going through a drawer filled with modern maps she found a copy of the old Middleburg map hidden between some larger United States Geodetic Survey sheets. Drawn in

Figure 5. Artifacts from the Middleburg Plantation slave quarters. (Photograph by the author)

1786 by the well-known Charleston mapmaker Joseph Purcell, the map showed the entire Middleburg plantation: roads, fences, rice fields, barns, the "big house," and there, just where we had been digging, were twelve small squares labeled "Negro Houses" (Fig. 6).

The next week we continued our excavations in the dark earth around the "Negro Houses." Digging in one test pit, Elaine Nichols, another graduate student, noticed a disturbance in the soil—yellow sand mottled in the darker matrix stretched across the center of the square. After carefully cleaning the

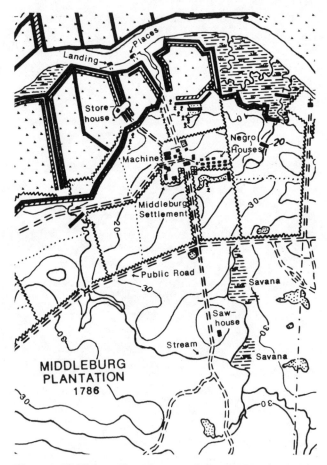

Figure 6. Middleburg Plantation map dating to 1786 showing "Negro Houses," Berkeley County, South Carolina. (Cartography by David W. Babson)

surface, Elaine photographed and drew this feature, then continued taking out another layer of soil. When she had come to the bottom of the midden, more than 50 centimeters below the ground surface, Elaine cleaned the top of the yellow, sandy subsoil. Here a band of dark earth about 25 centimeters wide crossed the bottom level of the excavation. Looking more closely we saw that the parallel edges of the feature were composed of the blurred arcs left by posts that had been set side-by-side and rotted in place in the ground.[10]

In 1710 Thomas Nairne advised prospective settlers that one of the first jobs on a new plantation was to "cutt down a few Trees, to split Palissades, or clapboards, and therewith make small houses or Huts to shelter the slaves."[11] Our excavation showed the bottom portion of a palisadelike wall, a wall set in the ground by slaves more than one hundred and fifty years ago. We would only have to follow the wall to find the outline of the entire structure.

As is often the case in archaeology, our first hypothesis wasn't supported. This palisade was apparently an early fence and not a house wall; however, these particular excavations led to the discovery of a late eighteenth-century house built by slaves. Although we know African Americans occupied this village in the early eighteenth century, we are still looking for the earliest houses.

# Introduction

## UNSUSPECTED TREASURE

By 1776 almost half a million Africans had arrived in the colonial South.[1] They cleared forests, planted crops, and built homes; together with a surprising number of Native American Indians, they comprised the slave population.[2] Their white masters, backed by military force, claimed ownership of everything—the rich land, the working people, and the crops they planted and reaped. Beyond claiming ownership, later planters gave their white ancestors almost total credit for the skills and even the labor of pioneering.

Early colonial slave owners needed the pioneering abilities of West Africans and Indians, and they might advertise slaves as "industrious and laborious in improving their Plantations" or "underst[anding] building mud walls"; on the other hand, more than a century later a South Carolina planter would simply refer to colonial slaves as having been "intractable negro men and women, but lately brought from the jungles of Africa."[3] Thus, through time the contributions of the South's African and Indian pioneers were hidden and forgotten, denying future generations of Americans full knowledge of their history and heritage.

This book is about the obscured settlers of the seventeenth and eighteenth centuries who labored to build plantations and who laid the foundation for African American culture; it is also about the recent beginning of African

American archaeology as a means for learning about that culture. In the following chapters I illustrate the kinds of artifacts left by slaves and now being found by archaeologists, and I show how archaeologists are using these artifacts together with contributions from history and folklore to learn new things about early African American lifeways.

The evolution of African American archaeology demonstrates how our view of the past is affected by the world around us, even for so-called objective social scientists like archaeologists. This Introduction traces the early development of African American studies in archaeology, and outlines my methods and guiding theory. In Chapter 1, I discuss Colono Ware—handbuilt pottery made and used in Indian villages, on plantations, and in colonial towns from Virginia to Florida. Broken fragments of this pottery frequently are found on early African American plantation sites, and Colono Ware has become a fundamental tool in interpreting these settlements.

Chapter 2 reviews African American lifeways along the south Atlantic coast, and Chapter 3 looks specifically at South Carolina, which had a black majority throughout most of the eighteenth century. Several early African American sites have been excavated in the South Carolina lowcountry. In the concluding chapter, I present archaeological evidence for African American religious ritual in eighteenth-century South Carolina and argue that by steadfastly struggling to create pots and houses as well as families, colonial African Americans created a subculture that became a source of power for responding to oppression.

But bear in mind that African American archaeology is brand-new: we are just beginning to discover what the buried record has to offer. So far we have learned most about pots and houses, and my interpretation of early African American life is based on these two artifact classes. Nevertheless, as I discuss pottery and architecture, I will also mention many other objects including tobacco pipes, buttons, glass beads, baskets, boats, hoes and shackles, preserved through time from the first days of African American settlement; we are truly discovering an unsuspected treasure.

What does this new field have to teach us about ourselves? Archaeologists are beginning to learn how easily we can fool ourselves into believing in our "objectivity" and how much we must struggle to break away from the power of commonly held and subtly racist views of history to find important truths about the past. Thus, this introductory book is wide ranging and speculative; not a review of completed research, but an offering of newly discovered awareness, ideas, and things. In the Prologue and Chapter 4, I have even offered fiction—a glimpse of my most abstract and far-reaching interpretations, also a promise of the kinds of things we have yet to learn. Readers may find this volume a little rough-hewn, less comprehensive and more tentative than books about well-established topics like political history or high-style architecture. I hope you also will find yourselves thinking in new ways about early African American history and asking questions you might not have imagined before.

## AFRICAN AMERICAN ARCHAEOLOGY

Prodded by the Civil Rights Movement, archaeologists in the late 1960s began excavating the buried artifacts of colonial African Americans. We have found, among other things, fire-charred pots last used for cooking eighteenth-century meals (Fig. 7), broken tobacco pipes decorated with African designs, food bones from wild animals brought home by African American hunters, slave cabins

**Counts of Artifacts from Two Eighteenth-Century Slave Quarters on the Santee River in South Carolina**

| Type of Artifact | Yaughan Quarters (1740s–1790s) | Curriboo Quarters (1740s–ca. 1800) |
| --- | --- | --- |
| *Cooking and Serving Artifacts* | | |
| Imported European ceramics | 1,627 | 445 |
| Locally made ceramics | 15,184 | 3,333 |
| Bottle and tumbler glass | 1,962 | 689 |
| Utensils | 27 | 13 |
| *House and Furniture Artifacts* | | |
| Window glass | 101 | 114 |
| Nails and spikes | 2,529 | 844 |
| Construction hardware | 10 | 4 |
| Keys and door lock parts | 3 | 5 |
| Furniture hardware | 12 | 4 |
| *Sewing and Clothing Artifacts* | | |
| Buckles | 6 | 2 |
| Thimbles and pins | 2 | 1 |
| Buttons | 38 | 13 |
| Glass beads | 20 | 3 |
| *Plantation Tools* | | |
| Construction tools | 15 | 14 |
| Farm tools | 6 | 8 |

(Adapted from Wheaton and Garrow 1985, table 11.2)

Figure 7. Fragment of a fire-charred jar used by slaves for cooking in colonial South Carolina. (Photograph by Emily Short)

with secret cellars and others with foundations for African-styled clay walls. Lying buried where they were used, these artifacts directly reflect the activities of daily life. With the exception of a few early slave narratives, this newly found archaeological record is as close to the slave's personal story as we have ever been.[4]

Two forces in the 1960s unintentionally pushed the African American past on the archaeological profession. One was the Civil Rights Movement, already mentioned; the other was a spinoff from "Lady Bird" Johnson's national beautification conference.[5]

In 1967 at the height of the Civil Rights Movement, the Florida State Park Service contracted with Dr. Charles Fairbanks of the University of Florida to conduct archaeological investigations of the still-standing slave cabins on Kingsley Plantation, a state-owned historic site (Fig. 8).[6] Located in northeastern Florida, Kingsley was at the southern end of a string of Sea Island cotton plantations that stretched from Charleston, South Carolina, down the length of the Georgia coast.[7] Fairbanks began digging to learn more about slave life. He called this fledgling practice "plantation archaeology,"[8] and soon the University of Florida became its intellectual center. For more than a decade, Fairbanks's

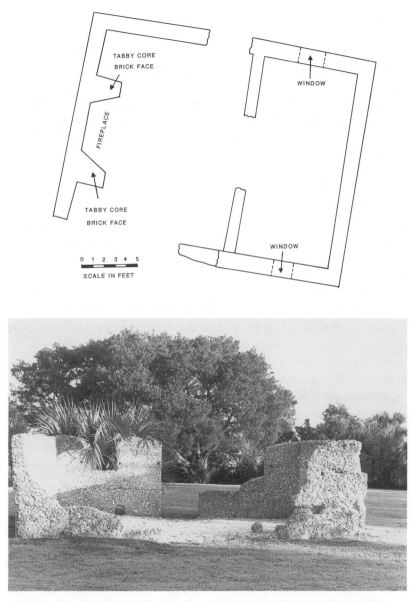

TABBY CORE
BRICK FACE

FIREPLACE

TABBY CORE
BRICK FACE

WINDOW

WINDOW

0 1 2 3 4 5
SCALE IN FEET

Figure 8. Floor plan from a Kingsley Plantation slave cabin excavated by Charles Fairbanks in 1969, the first excavation of its kind in the United States. Made of tabby, a concrete of sand and oyster shell, the Kingsley walls were similar to house walls built by freed slaves (*below*) on Daufuskie Island, South Carolina. (Adapted from Fairbanks 1972; photograph courtesy of Chicora Foundation, Inc.)

graduate program was the only place in the country where students were concentrating on African American archaeology.[9]

Fairbanks and the Florida State Park Service, it seems to me, were responding to the nationwide visibility of black activists and their demands for relevance in all aspects of American education, and not to any internal logic of social scientific research. Writing that the archaeology of slavery could "broaden and enrich the knowledge of our American heritage at a time when that tradition is in the midst of rapid and often baffling change," Fairbanks placed his work at Kingsley squarely in the service of a contemporary society struggling with civil rights problems and the war in Viet Nam. Though the avant-garde of the 1960s were arguing for a "new archaeology" aimed at improved scientific objectivity and more elegant and well-founded generalizations about human culture, Charles Fairbanks was not part of that movement.[10] Had the so-called new archaeologists of the late 1960s reviewed his paper on the Kingsley cabins they would probably have criticized him for being too particularistic and insufficiently scientific. No, in excavating the Kingsley cabins Fairbanks was not bowing to professional pressure or pleas for a new and more objective archaeology; he was addressing black demands for more attentiveness to black history, and without that political pressure African American archaeology would have developed much more slowly, if at all.

Pure serendipity connected "Lady Bird" Johnson's beautification conference to African American archaeology. In 1965 the First Lady assembled the nation's mayors for a conference on beautifying America.[11] This conference spurred a nascent movement concerned about the loss of the nation's historic buildings and sites to the rapid construction of the late 1950s and early 1960s. The mayors' conference established a committee to consider ways to mitigate this damage; the committee report, *With Heritage So Rich*, led to the passage of the National Historic Preservation Act of 1966.[12]

In keeping with the era's broadly based public ignorance of African American history, neither the mayoral committee report nor the National Historic Preservation Act said anything specific about African Americans, the preservation of African American historic sites, or African American archaeology. However, the structure of this law, together with the pressure of black social and political protest, changed archaeology and turned it toward the greatest single source of data about the history of early African Americans—their archaeological remains.[13]

The act emphasized that historic properties of local and state significance, as well as those of national significance, deserved listing on a National Register of Historic Places, and Section 106 of the act required that the impact of federally funded construction on any historic property be considered carefully and mitigating action taken where feasible. Moreover, when the regulations for the act were written they stated that any property that "had yielded or was likely to yield information important to history or prehistory" was significant under the law and worthy of protection.

Still, there was no official word about the historical and archaeological sites of black Americans or other minorities. But by the mid-1970s, the aggressive and vocal assertion of the significance of black history had reached bureaucrats and archaeologists alike and forced them to consider African American archaeological sites as sources of "information important to history." Ironically, the subjective interests and activities of black Americans had moved historical archaeologists, infatuated with their newfangled scientific objectivity, to lose some of their subjectivity and see tens of thousands of people they previously had ignored.

Digging with fresh interest on a variety of sites from isolated plantations to the streets of Williamsburg, archaeologists have been compiling an impressive collection of artifacts and notes on the everyday lives of colonial slaves. The data base is so large that if all our presently held notes and artifact collections were fully analyzed and interpreted, I believe we could more than double our knowledge of colonial slave life. As it is, data recovery has far outpaced analysis and the thoughtful development of direction and goals for African American archaeology.

As late as 1980 there still was no recognized subdiscipline of African American archaeology. A few papers had been written by Charles Fairbanks, his students, and a handful of others, but there was no articulated archaeological focus on the African American past—no regular symposia at national professional meetings, few journal papers, and no books on African American archaeology.[14] Yet, whenever significant historic sites were impacted by federally supported development, new preservation laws required that they be researched, the data analyzed, and reports published.


## GOALS AND PROBLEMS

With plenty of data and no relevant theory, archaeologists picked up goals as well as methods and theory from historical archaeology. Unfortunately they selected these goals at a time when mainstream historical archaeology was itself in the throes of an identity crisis—a complicated crisis that included differences between a minority of archaeologists primarily interested in the particulars of European American history and a large majority committed to the general social scientific goals of anthropology.[15] Although Charles Fairbanks and Robert Ascher had demonstrated that plantation archaeology could allow us to look at the lifeways of slaves, and thus to view the American past in a fundamentally different and more humanistic way,[16] most archaeologists working on African American sites took a different path. Following the social scientific majority, archaeologists working on African American sites typically applied the methods then in vogue: they constructed tabular lists of artifact frequencies to define slave or plantation "patterns," they measured the rate at which slaves picked up European traits, and they used artifacts to demonstrate the obvious difference in the economic status of slaves and their owners. Written primarily to fulfill contractual agreements for federally mandated archaeology, these treatments represented expedient applications of methods to newly recovered data without an orientation toward answering significant questions.[17] And, while these reports contain recovered data and interpretations of activities that are extremely valuable, the more general conclusions, with a few exceptions, are of little anthropological or historical interest.[18]

Bluntly, most archaeologists working with African American sites, even those working today, have had little academic background in African American history or the contemporary issues of social politics; we come from a different scholarly tradition. While historians like W.E.B. Dubois, cultural anthropologists like Melville Herskovits, and folklorists like the Works Projects Administration writers of the 1930s were busy piecing together black American history, our archaeological fathers, and a few mothers, were focusing on prehistoric Indians and wealthy or famous white people.[19]

During the 1960s and early 1970s, while archaeologists were preoccupied with building a new, more scientific archaeology, historians were writing books like Herbert Gutman's *The Black Family in Slavery and Freedom,* John Blassingame's *The Slave Community,* and Peter Wood's *Black Majority.* Approaching past slave life like ethnographers, they described social interaction and pointed out aspects of strength and stability in African American culture. In the midst of the raging debate about racial and social justice, they argued eloquently that the black family and community were stronger and black contributions to American life more important than most Americans knew. They showed that modern African American resistance exemplified by the Civil Rights Movement was part of a tradition of resistance to oppression that began with the earliest African slaves in the New World. Overall, they demonstrated that a significant portion of American history had been left out of our textbooks. In their work, questions of historical accuracy and social and political relevancy

became paramount, questions that social scientific theory and archaeology surely can help answer.[20] Future students with a keenly developed interest in early
African American life and a willingness to combine archaeology with other
research methods will embark, I believe, on an unparalleled adventure in
historical research.

## CREOLIZATION, SYMBOLS, AND POWER

Throughout this book I have tried to use theory and methods that allow a more
complete and accurate picture of early African American life as well as a
glimpse of the power base that African American pioneers accrued as they
crafted their culture under the constraints of bondage. Creolization, the guiding
theory, helps explain how African American culture developed, and in *Uncommon Ground* I use it primarily for that end. However, creolization theory also
allows for wide-ranging analyses of social and political interaction, studies
anticipated, but not included, in this presentation. Since the emphasis of such
studies is on the *process* of creolization, cultures need not be commonly known
as "creole cultures" for an analysis of creolization to be applicable.

According to Jamaican poet and historian Edward Kamau Brathwaite, slaves
and their masters were both involved in a multicultural adjustment he calls
"creolization," which entailed interaction, exchange, and creativity. In fact,
plantation colonies in the West Indies, on the northeastern coast of South
America, and along the southern coasts of North America witnessed settlements
so diverse culturally that in ordinary usage "creole" came to mean a cultural
and racial mixture created in the New World. Brathwaite writes that the word
creole "appears to have originated from a combination of the two Spanish words
*criar* (to create, to imagine, to establish, to found, to settle) and *colono* (a
colonist, a founder, a settler) into *crillo:* a committed settler, one identified with
the area of settlement, one native to the settlement though not ancestrally
indigenous to it."[21]

Although Indians were native to the New World, we may safely say that
neither Native Americans, Europeans, nor Africans were "ancestrally indigenous" to New World plantation settlements and, although creolization was more
than a plantation phenomenon, it was primarily on these plantations that the
African American subculture was built. Different demographic patterns, historical situations, and cultural mixes produced different creolized cultures in
various parts of the New World. Moreover, due to dramatic cultural differences
and especially due to the divisive character of racial slavery, most of these New
World colonies failed to develop single identifiable cultural norms. Rather, the

complex processes of creolization produced mixed cultures with divisions within the mixes, a series of interacting subcultures rather than a single creolized blend.

In his discussion of Jamaica as a creole society, Brathwaite describes a multiracial colonial plantation system where society is organized for the benefit of the colonizing power and the local European minority. "'Creole society' therefore is the result of a complex situation where a colonial polity reacts, as a whole, to external metropolitan pressures, and at the same time to internal adjustments made necessary by the juxtaposition of master and slave, elite and labourer, in a culturally heterogeneous relationship."[22]

Following Brathwaite, historian and folklorist Charles Joyner elaborated on the concept of creolization and applied it to the lifeways, including the material culture, of nineteenth-century slaves on Waccamaw Neck in coastal South Carolina.[23] Joyner's contribution was to use linguistic concepts to describe the process of creolizing culture. Transferring the linguistic concepts of grammar (rules of usage) and lexicon (words) to lifeways, he argues that while many of the "things" or artifacts of nineteenth-century slaves might appear American or European American, the ways they were used, that is, the "grammar" or structure of underlying rules of slave culture on Waccamaw Neck, remained principally African. "Such 'grammatical' principles," Joyner believes, "survived the middle passage and governed the selective adaptation of elements of both African and European culture."[24]

In this creolization model, material things are part of the lexicon of culture while the ways they are made, used, and perceived are part of the grammar or structure. This model is easily adapted to archaeological artifacts, and the eighteenth-century archaeological evidence presented in this book shows that at this early time both the "lexicon" and the "grammar," that is, many of the artifacts as well as the ways they were used within slave culture, were strongly African. Further, many of these artifacts were quite different in kind as well as quality from those used by European Americans.

Within creolizing culture, change can take place in either superficial features or underlying structure, or in both. John Otto, for example, shows that in the nineteenth century, slaves on Georgia's Cannon's Point plantation were eating from glazed and decorated English bowls; on the other hand the planter's family was using predominantly plates.[25] Otto argues that slaves may have been using these bowls for eating African-styled meals; Africans had been utilizing ceramic bowls as their primary serving dishes since long before colonial times. Thus, while the artifacts or "lexicon" of slave meals at Cannon's Point were European, the shape of those artifacts implies a foodways structure or "grammar" that was strongly African. An ignorant visitor might observe that slaves had adopted European tablewares but didn't know quite how to handle them, preferring bowls to plates; a more informed observer might see West African rules of etiquette employed with a new kind of bowl.

Conceiving of African American cultures as creolized helps us see the structure, that is, the cultural substance, behind the artifacts we find. It provides another important advantage in answering questions about the African American past and about the American past in general: within the bounds of this model we can look at relationships that cut across creolized subcultural groups as well as relationships within such groups. Archaeologist Charles Orser has postulated recently that by seeing plantation society as divided strictly by race and by using a simplistic concept of status based solely on economics, many plantation archaeologists have painted themselves into a corner. From this corner analysts cannot envision the complex social exchanges that made American plantations work—interactions between slaves and black drivers, field hands and house servants, black and white men who had been playmates as children, and between slaves and their white sexual partners. Rather than regarding plantation sites as laboratories for studying racially separated cultures, Orser suggests, archaeologists should examine the diverse human relationships that occurred on plantations. Taking a Marxian approach, Orser proposes that the most important social relations are occupational, those surrounding the slave mode of production, and that the most appropriate analytical categories for such studies are economics and power.[26]

I agree with Orser that these are excellent analytical categories for understanding how plantations worked, categories consistent with Brathwaite's "creolization." And, while I also agree that social and ethnic groupings on plantations were not defined strictly by biological race, I think that we can study the entire field of plantation social relationships more fruitfully by recognizing, as historian Sterling Stuckey has argued, that plantations do represent two distinct subcultures.[27] Throughout the plantation South, laboring slaves and their managers shared many aspects of culture; but for the most part, slave quarters and the "big house" were on separate ground.

Orser urges us to look closely at the social relationships of production and power. It strikes me that we already know a lot about southern American agriculture and slave labor, as well as the power base of plantation owners. The products of labor we don't know about are those things that slaves made for themselves, with or without their master's knowledge; and the power base we have difficulty seeing also belonged to slaves.

If we could magically return to the eighteenth century and poll members of an

African American community about their significant activities and relationships, we might find some people who truly believed that manipulating the system was the most important thing in life. I don't imagine, however, in spite of the awesome power wielded by planters, that plantation slaves typically would identify their most important activity as producing the master's crop; nor would they see their most important relationships as those between themselves and their overseer or master. Securing food, shelter, and clothing—by whatever means, including making or taking them as well as accepting their rations— surely would be classed as their chief activities. Similarly, I feel certain that the relations of husband and wife, parent and child, brother and sister, friend and neighbor, healer and patient would be considered by most people as their primary relationships. Through the competence exhibited in their ability to acquire and make things, as well as through the trust manifest in personal relationships, African American slaves would have derived power.

Unfortunately we cannot look directly at early African American communities. Historical documents help, but are heavily skewed toward the white side of plantation life. The archaeological record is more democratic. As British archaeologist Ian Hodder has argued, "the daily use of material items within different contexts recreates from moment to moment the framework of meaning within which people act."[28] Thus, fragments of pots, the outlines of houses, and so forth represent a past material world that not only provided tools for cooking and shelter, but also served as symbols that reinforced people's views of themselves as culturally distinct from others. Deciphering the meaning of those symbols teaches us about African American power.

To start we need to connect artifacts to people—not as simple a task as it sounds. Locating yards and houses by the dark stains of rotted posts and the scatter of lost and forgotten things requires careful exploration and research. Furthermore, we not only want to identify places, we also want to find out what people were doing on particular sites. This requires slow, painstaking excavation, days of sifting through soil, collecting and counting artifacts, filling notebooks, making maps and drawings, taking photographs, then analyzing the data with the same careful attention to quantification and description. No wonder archaeologists write highly technical and detailed reports, filled with broken artifacts and devoid of human beings. The result is that archaeologists communicate more easily with one another than with people outside the profession and miss the vitalizing effects of wider scholarly and public involvement. We not only need methods to link artifacts to specific activities, we also need methods to help archaeology find people—in both the present and the past.[29]

Historians and folklorists construct their picture of the past from written words, oral accounts, drawings, paintings, and photographs. Using verbal and visual sources, they often appear more intimate with people of the past than archaeologists do. In presenting their research, historians and folklorists have at their disposal verbatim quotes and individual names. In the 1930s, for example, a folklorist reported the testimony of ex-slave Ben Sullivan who lived on Sapelo Island, Georgia: "Old man Okra said he wanted a place like he had in Africa, so he built himself a hut. . . But Master made him pull it down. He said he didn't want an African hut on his place."[30]

Through folklore and history we can learn about specific people like Okra and his master; we can feel the tension between a slave who built his own African-styled house and a master threatened by this act of independence. In contrast, the people archaeologists usually study are anonymous and mute. Yet, where archaeology misses specific people, history misses things, as well as the breadth in time and space that archaeology affords.

If "Old man Okra" built a house, can we see it or one like it, and say to our children, "This is the kind of house built by early African American pioneers"? Can we find out when, where, and how many similar houses were built in the American South; can we compare the size, shape, and quality of Okra's house with that of nearby structures? These are questions archaeologists are specially trained to address. Through excavation we can find the decayed remains of thousands of houses built by Africans like Okra and their descendants across the American South. We may not know the builder's name but we can draw the floor plan, describe the construction, and assess the differences between the slave quarters and big houses. Combining historical, folkloristic, and archaeological data we may even learn the symbolic meanings that lodge in these things.[31]

# Chapter 1

# HANDMADE POTS

### REMEMBERING CLAY POTS

With his gray hair, fine features, and gentle eyes, Shad Hall of Sapelo Island, Georgia, was a proud-looking man (Fig. 9). He was a descendant of Belali Mohomet and his daughter Hester, both Africans.

Dressed in a denim jacket and blue work shirt buttoned neatly at the neck, Hall was eager to talk to interviewers from the Work Projects Administration. To him, his African heritage was no mystery. His grandmother Hester, her six sisters, and their father had come directly from Africa to the Georgia coast sometime in the nineteenth century. They wore beads around their waists and necks; kneeling on little mats they prayed to the sun three times a day. Hester had told Shad about Africa: the rich forest, yams, sugar cane, bananas, parrots, and clay-walled houses. She made a cake called "saraka" of water, honey, and meal or rice, and all the children stood still around a table while their mother prayed "Ameen, Ameen, Ameen"—only then did they eat the cakes.

As Shad Hall reminisced about his grandmother's stories of life in Africa, he casually recalled, "My grandmother Hester said she could remember the house she lived in, in Africa. She said the roof was covered with palmetto and grass, and the walls were made of mud. . . .I remember some pots and cups that she had made of clay. She brought these from Africa."[1]

1

Figure 9. Shad Hall of Sapelo Island, Georgia, remembered his grandmother's clay pots and cups. (WPA photograph by Muriel and Malcolm Bell, Jr.)

Other ex-slaves remembered clay bowls, and more. Maggie Black, who grew up on a plantation near Marion, South Carolina, said that "People this day and time don't have crockery like the people used to have. Honey, they had the prettiest little clay bowls then." And Albert Carolina, from Waccamaw Neck, reported that his grandmother had "a little bowl made out of clay." Carolina went on to describe how his "grandparents built a kiln of clay pots and baked them." (Unfortunately, no details of his description were included in the WPA narrative.) He told the interviewer that his grandmother was African and his grandfather was an Indian who wouldn't stay out of the swamp.[2] Their "kiln of pots" was probably the stack of pots´that traditional African and Native American potters build as they bake their pots on open fires. Albert Carolina clearly remembered his grandparents making pottery; and since people don't normally refer to "pots and cups" or "crockery" as clay unless they are familiar with the transformation of clay to ceramic, I suspect that Maggie Black and Shad Hall also remembered some lore of crafting pots.

Slavers carried Shad Hall's grandmother to America at the very end of the slave trade; his description of her pottery is one of the few direct historical references we have of the African contribution to American folk pottery. Whole clay pots were quite fragile, and I find it hard to imagine many such vessels surviving the stressful "middle passage" from Africa to the New World. Of course, Shad Hall may have been mistaken in thinking that Hester's pots were from Africa. She may have made them, years before he was born, on the Georgia coast. Whichever, Hester was one of the last of hundreds of thousands of African women who might have brought the skills of potting, if not whole pots, to their new American home.

Archaeological excavations of southern plantations and towns demonstrate that colonial slaves along the southern Atlantic coast often used homemade, handbuilt clay pots in preparing and eating their meals. And archaeological analyses show these pots can be used to learn about the foodways of slaves. Moreover, the contrast between these foodways and those of white owners and managers illustrates the integrity of colonial African American culture and the tension of cultural differences between African American and European American colonists.

While archaeologists now recognize the value of broken pottery in interpreting African American history, for a long time our cultural biases impeded our recognition of their importance. Thus, the following story and discussion of handmade pots is not only an archaeological interpretation of a colonial African American craft, but also an example of the ways the world around us molds our intellectual consciousness.


## WILLIAMSBURG AND COLONO-INDIAN WARE

Archaeologists first found fragments of the clay pots used by slaves at Virginia's Colonial Williamsburg and nearby plantations in the 1930s (Figs. 10–12).[3] In keeping with the times, however, early archaeological interpretations focused on the Europeans who settled Williamsburg. Almost half of the people who lived, worked, and left artifacts in this famous Virginia town during the eighteenth

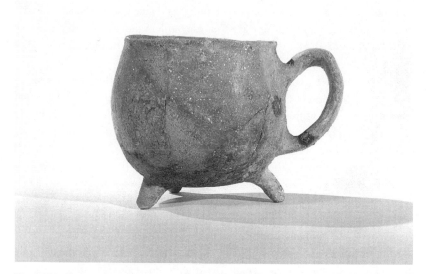

Figure 10. European-style cup found at Colonial Williamsburg, height: 9.5 cm. (Colonial Williamsburg Foundation)

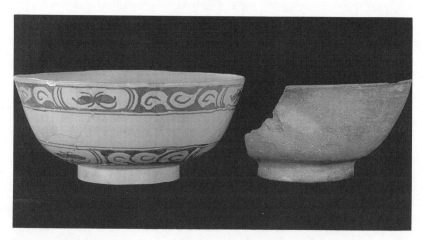

Figure 11. *Left,* English delftware bowl of about 1740; *right,* a locally made example of similar shape, height: 9.5 cm. (Colonial Williamsburg Foundation)

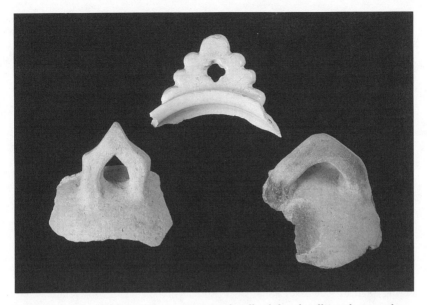

Figure 12. *Above,* English delftware porringer handle; *below,* locally made examples. (Colonial Williamsburg Foundation)

century were black.[4] But historians and archaeologists saw these black colonists dimly or not at all.

For practical purposes, we can say that historical archaeology began at Williamsburg—born in the 1920s as a search for house foundations. As a historical park and museum Colonial Williamsburg was founded with funds from the Rockefeller Foundation and, for more than forty years, the exhibits presented a view of American history emphasizing only the challenges and successes of colonial European Americans.[5]

As the attention of historical archaeology expanded beyond Williamsburg, it replicated European American colonization. Four "archaeological camps," regularly spaced along the Atlantic seaboard, recreated the pattern of early, successful European settlement in Virginia, Florida, Carolina, and Massachusetts. Archaeological excavations concentrated on the earliest sites: St. Augustine in Florida, Charles Towne in South Carolina, Jamestown and Williamsburg in Virginia, and Plymouth in Massachusetts—famous places of European American history. Research efforts spotlighted the villages and forts that established the colonial foothold in North America. Moreover, archaeologists not only emphasized European settlements, they more specifically emphasized Anglo-European settlements. Massachusetts, Virginia, and Carolina were English colonies and, although Florida was Spanish, it played a significant role in English colonial affairs and was coveted by the English from at least as early as the seventeenth century. In 1763 it was relinquished to the English by the Treaty of Paris. Not until encouraged by preparations for the celebration of the 500th anniversary of the Columbus expedition did archaeologists begin excavating Santa Elena in South Carolina, the earliest Spanish city in North America.[6] Likewise, neither the French settlement in Louisiana nor the Spanish settlement of California and the Southwest were strong centers for the development of historical archaeology.[7] The east coast, the area of Anglo-American activity, provides the standard version of American history; conforming to this popular focus, historical archaeology was created with a strong Anglo-American bias.

The bicentennial celebration of the United States stimulated an interest in the excavation of sites related to the American Revolution. Through the 1970s, archaeologists focused on Revolutionary War battlegrounds, while virtually ignoring African American sites. As historical archaeology evolved, archaeologists recreated the Anglo-American conquest of the New World for white twentieth-century Americans. Circumscribed by their disciplinary biases, historians and archaeologists at Williamsburg were slow to see Indian connections and even slower to see the importance of black colonists' participation. African Americans helped build and maintain the town and deposited many, perhaps most, of the artifacts uncovered, yet the official guidebook for Williamsburg states that slaves left "few material vestiges."[8]

In 1962, Ivor Noël Hume, Director of Archaeology at Colonial Williamsburg, published a paper on the sherds and vessels of handbuilt, unglazed earthenware pottery unearthed at the site. He pointed out that some of the vessels were clearly copies of European pottery such as porringers and skillets, but that "the vast majority of the vessels have only two features in common with any European ware, a flat bottom and a slightly everted rim."[9] Noting that both the clay and the pulverized shell temper added to the clay in manufacturing the pots were similar to those of prehistoric and historic Indian pottery in Virginia, Noël Hume concluded that the vessels had been made by free Indians. Calling the artifacts Colono-Indian Ware, he suggested the following association with slaves:

1. The unglazed ware is inferior to glazed wares of European and European American manufacture.
2. Glazed wares were within the financial reach of all but the poorest colonists.

3. That the unglazed ware is found in towns and wealthy plantation sites implies a common usage in both contexts.
4. Slaves would have developed European tastes in cooking techniques and tablewares.
5. Slaveholders likely would not have purchased glazed vessels for their slaves to use. [10]

Noël Hume concluded that "the astute Indians may have found a useful market amongst the slaves and would have tailored their wares to styles acceptable to these customers."

Noël Hume introduced his paper as a contribution to the "study of American Indian archaeology and culture." Entitled "An Indian Ware of the Colonial Period," it was published in a journal devoted to North American Indian archaeology. Thus, in presenting his seminal paper on handbuilt colonial pottery, Noël Hume chose to focus on the Indians who he thought made the ware, rather than on the slaves who used it or their European owners. Seven years later, in his well-known *Guide to Artifacts of Colonial America*, Noël Hume failed to mention Colono-Indian Ware even under the heading, "Ceramics, American." Apparently he did not regard this pottery as an especially noteworthy part of the history of Williamsburg.

Perhaps if Noël Hume were writing today, he would call his paper "Indian Pottery as a Key to Slave Life in Colonial Williamsburg" or "Indians, Slaves, and Handbuilt Earthenware in Colonial Virginia." But in 1962, he was not alone in his interpretation of the handbuilt pottery found on colonial town and plantation sites. Prominent archaeologists such as Charles Fairbanks, Lewis Binford, and Stanley South helped develop and nourish the narrow perception of Colono-Indian Ware as a tool for learning only about Indians and their trade relationships with whites. [11]


## CAROLINA DISCOVERIES

Conventional wisdom about Colono-Indian pottery remained unshaken until the middle 1970s, when archaeological discoveries in South Carolina and the sheer quantity of so-called Colono-Indian Ware being recovered forced some questioning and rethinking.

Working under the mandates of the National Historic Preservation Act and other federal statutes, archaeologists were excavating a wider variety of sites in South Carolina than ever before—plantation houses and kitchens, slave quarters, forts and jails—and finding thousands of sherds of handbuilt pottery (Figs. 13–14; Appendix 3, Table 1; see also map in Appendix 1).[12] South Carolina had a new underwater archaeology program and both amateur and professional divers were reporting countless sherds and many well preserved whole vessels near plantation wharves, ferries, and bridges. On many sites, Colono-Indian Ware was the most frequently found "type" of pottery; that is, more unglazed earthenware was found than, for example, imported British salt-glazed stoneware, creamware, or pearlware. Colono-Indian Ware was uncovered more frequently on plantations than in cities; in some cases, especially in the vicinity of slave quarters, the pottery was found in higher frequency than all other ceramic types combined! Clearly this ware was more than incidental evidence of contact between European or African settlers and Indians; rather it was a common feature of everyday life in Carolina towns and plantations—a key artifact for interpreting colonial culture, especially African American culture.

Figure 13. Colono Ware and European ceramics excavated at Drayton Hall Plantation on the Ashley River, South Carolina. Although only 15 percent of the ceramics from the Drayton kitchen were Colono Ware, this particular unit produced a large number of these unglazed sherds. (Photograph by the author)

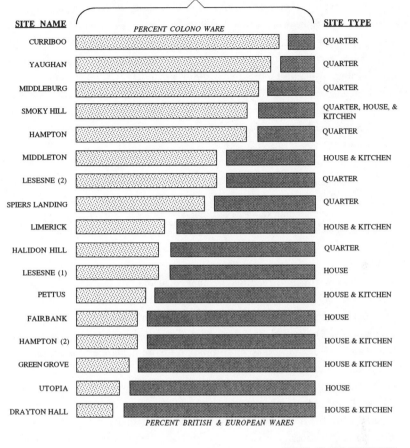

**100% OF CERAMICS FROM SITES**

| SITE NAME | PERCENT COLONO WARE | SITE TYPE |
|---|---|---|
| CURRIBOO | | QUARTER |
| YAUGHAN | | QUARTER |
| MIDDLEBURG | | QUARTER |
| SMOKY HILL | | QUARTER, HOUSE, & KITCHEN |
| HAMPTON | | QUARTER |
| MIDDLETON | | HOUSE & KITCHEN |
| LESESNE (2) | | QUARTER |
| SPIERS LANDING | | QUARTER |
| LIMERICK | | HOUSE & KITCHEN |
| HALIDON HILL | | QUARTER |
| LESESNE (1) | | HOUSE |
| PETTUS | | HOUSE & KITCHEN |
| FAIRBANK | | HOUSE |
| HAMPTON (2) | | HOUSE & KITCHEN |
| GREEN GROVE | | HOUSE & KITCHEN |
| UTOPIA | | HOUSE |
| DRAYTON HALL | | HOUSE & KITCHEN |

*PERCENT BRITISH & EUROPEAN WARES*

HOUSE= PLANTATION HOUSE
KITCHEN= PLANATION KITCHEN
QUARTER= SLAVE QUARTER

Figure 14. Colono Ware and European ceramics from plantation sites in South Carolina and Virginia. (See Appendix 3, Table 1.)

As we were marveling at the quantity of unglazed earthenware surfacing on Carolina plantations, a letter from Ghana and a water jug from a lowcountry river led me, quite unexpectedly, to a startling conclusion—African American slaves *made* as well as used a large portion of the pottery we called Colono-Indian Ware.

The letter from Ghana was the beginning. Richard Polhemus was the laboratory supervisor at the South Carolina Institute of Archaeology and Anthropology. Through his tenure there, Dick had the opportunity to work with the large collections from South Carolina archaeological sites of so-called Colono-Indian pottery as it was being washed and cataloged. While visiting his brother in Ghana, Dick traveled to museums and villages where local women continued a West African potting craft more than 3,000 years old. [13] His letter recounted his surprise at the similarity of the modern Ghanian ceramics to Colono-Indian Ware. I remember a small crowd gathering in the hallway of the Institute as Stanley South read Dick's observations. Restating his observations in 1977, Polhemus wrote:

> The Ghana vessels are flat bottomed, fine grit or sand tempered, plain burnished, and bear the incised "X" on the base which many "Colono-Indian" vessels from South Carolina also possess. Other than through a detailed analysis of the composition of the paste and temper the Ghana [pottery] could not be differentiated from vessels excavated in South Carolina. [14]

When Stanley finished reading, we looked at one another and then at the Colono-Indian vessels sitting atop a bank of file cabinets nearby. Could African Americans have made these pots? The seed was sown, but most of us didn't take it too seriously. The redoubtable Ivor Noël Hume had identified the pottery as Indian ware, and it would take more time and more evidence to overcome our faith in his interpretation.

In 1974, reporting on excavations at Revolutionary War Fort Moultrie at the mouth of Charleston Harbor, Stanley South identified 38 percent of all the ceramics excavated from both the American and British occupations as Colono-Indian Ware. Looking at a variety of possibilities, South argued that the pottery most likely was used by black laborers employed by American and British forces. Nevertheless, he subscribed to the thesis that "in South Carolina [Colono-Indian Ware] is primarily a Catawba Indian related phenomenon," adding almost as a postscript: "A suggestion to be considered in studies of Colono-Indian pottery is the high degree of similarity between it and pottery being made today in West Africa. The correspondence is so great that a consideration of African relationships is suggested."[15] South's afterthought was the glimmer of a new light on "Colono-Indian Ware." Almost three years later a large water jug prodded my imagination into action.

Although I had heard Dick's letter and read Stan's Fort Moultrie report, when I first saw the jug (Fig. 15) I had no thought of African American pottery. The

Figure 15. Jug from the Combahee River at Bluff Plantation, Colleton
County, South Carolina. (Photograph courtesy of the South Carolina Institute
of Archaeology and Anthropology)

jug was simply a mystery; a recreational diver had recovered the globular vessel
from the Combahee River in front of Bluff Plantation in Colleton County, South
Carolina.

Black slaves and their white managers had grown rice on Bluff Plantation for
almost one hundred and fifty years, and hobby divers—amateur archaeologists
with scuba gear—enjoyed drifting along the river bottom at such places, loading
their net bags with old bottles, dishes, and other "goodies" that disappeared
more than a century ago into the gently flowing tea-colored water. This jug was
one of hundreds of interesting artifacts retrieved from the plantation waterfront;

it was especially intriguing not for its beauty, although it was handsome, but for its uniqueness. I knew of no other vessel like it from the Combahee or any other site on the Carolina coast.

The jug looked similar to the American Indian pottery I had seen, but the shape was unfamiliar. It was handbuilt, without the use of a potter's wheel, by coiling and modeling the clay into a spherical body. A neck and sturdy handle had been added, and the entire surface below the neck had been textured with rectilinear lands and grooves by the carved surface of a paddle used to thin and shape the walls. The surface was a rich brown color without a glaze. I could tell that it had not been fired in a kiln but in the relatively cool temperature of an open hearth; potters and archaeologists call it "low-fired earthenware."[16] I knew about the manufacturing process, but the shape—I didn't recognize the shape.

"Is this an Indian pot?" the diver asked as I carefully turned the jug in my hands.

I replied, "I don't think so." Of course, his next question was: if not Indian, then what?

I searched for an answer, but I was unacquainted with this vessel form. Then, recalling the jug in the hand of the "woman at the well" in my childhood Bible, I ventured, "Well, it looks like it might have come from somewhere in the Mediterranean." I reached for an artifact I could identify and dropped the conversation about the jug.

Three years later my thoughts returned to the jug. I was sitting in on an introductory folklore class taught by my colleague Karl Heider. I wanted to learn to apply my archaeological training to my own culture, to the homes and lives of my Scottish ancestors in eastern North Carolina. Learning more about folklore was part of my "retooling" for this endeavor.

I had no thought of African American archaeology until Karl began to discuss the folk culture of blacks in the lowcountry. In Charleston's old market and at roadside stands along US Highway 17 north of the city, tourists can purchase coiled sweetgrass baskets from women whose ancestors worked the cotton and rice fields of antebellum plantations (Figs. 16–18). Karl ably demonstrated that these modern baskets descend from an ancient African craft tradition practiced continuously for three hundred years on the Carolina coast. In plantation days coiled baskets served a variety of purposes: wide winnowing trays called fanners helped remove chaff from rice after threshing; padded with blankets or quilts, fanners were also used as cradles for babies; "head tote" baskets carried produce to market; covered work baskets were used to store grain or sewing supplies.[17]

As I mulled over the idea that a craft like basketry had survived capture in

Figure 16. Sister Elizabeth Coakley's basket stand on U.S. 17 near Mt. Pleasant, South Carolina. (Photograph by Dale Rosengarten, courtesy of the McKissick Museum, University of South Carolina)

Figure 17. Adelaide Washington carrying a coiled basket to the field, St. Helena Island, circa 1900–1910 (see Dabbs 1970). (From the Penn School Collection, permission granted by Penn Center, St. Helena Island, South Carolina)

Figure 18. Fragments of eighteenth-century coiled basketry from excavations at the Heyward-Washington House privy, Charleston, South Carolina. (Courtesy of the Charleston Museum, Charleston, South Carolina)

Africa, the dangerous middle passage to the Americas, and the disorientation of slavery, my "archaeologist's mind" wondered about other artifacts as well. If basketry survived, then why not houses, pottery, wood carving, cooking hearths, tools? Pottery! All that pottery on plantation sites and in the rivers! Dick Polhemus's observations in Africa! If basketry survived, then it was not hard to imagine that the art of making pottery also survived. Along with South, Polhemus, and others, I had seen the evidence growing. I remembered the big jug; could that unusual pot from the Combahee have an African connection?

Within an hour I was in Thomas Cooper Library searching for information on West African pottery. Sylvia Leith-Ross's catalog *Nigerian Pottery* was one of the first books I pulled off the shelves and there it was. In central Nigeria, potters were still making globular jugs with strap handles that looked much like the one from the Combahee (Fig. 15). Later I learned that the stamped design and construction techniques used on this jug are those of San Marcos type pottery excavated from Indian villages and Spanish sites along the coast of Georgia and northeastern Florida. Showing the vessel to Charles Fairbanks and Kathleen Deagan, they both agreed with a San Marcos affinity but they too were unfamiliar with the shape. As I searched the library there was no sure way to know whether this pot was made by Indian or African American hands, but the similarity to African vessels was sufficiently tantalizing to keep me hunting for African connections to "Colono-Indian Ware."

Next I turned to Peter Wood's book *Black Majority: Negroes in Colonial South Carolina from 1670 through the Stono Rebellion*, looking, in vain, for references to pottery. Although it didn't mention pottery, the book provided a new way of seeing the history of Carolina. Beginning with the fact that the majority of colonial South Carolinians were black, Wood argued that many of the skills required to build the colony came from African traditions. In essence, he demonstrated that while whites dominated Carolina politically and economically, at the level of everyday life, Carolina was a black colony. Wood had set South Carolina history on its head. Rather than focusing on the activities of the well-known minority of white colonists, he revealed the obscured black majority.

Everything I read reinforced the notion that colonial African Americans, as well as Indians, were making pottery. Consider, for example,

1. that slaves were pioneers in America, carrying from Africa many agricultural and craft skills essential to daily life;
2. that the first slaves brought to Carolina came from plantations in the West Indies where they had established a pottery tradition;
3. that African slaves mixed with Indians captured in raids on Spanish domains of the Southeast (Indians comprised almost one third of the slave population in 1708) and could have shared elements of their material culture.

In my history courses, these facts were neglected in favor of the political maneuvering of colonial powers, the grand events of the American Revolution, and the birth of the nation. Most archaeologists working in South Carolina, myself included, were ignorant of crucial aspects of demography, culture, and social interaction. We were all victims of an education that dismissed the importance of blacks and distorted the role of Indians in American history, and we had carried these distortions into our archaeology.

While reading and following research leads from *Black Majority*, I was actively studying archaeological and ethnohistorical sources on the West Indies. Island blacks, I learned, were making pottery similar to Colono-Indian Ware from the earliest days of settlement and, what was more, they were still making it![18] A student, hearing of my interest, gave me a piece of contemporary handbuilt pottery from the island of Nevis, near Barbados, which she had brought home as a souvenir from a trip to the West Indies.[19] The little pot was built, burnished, and fired like those from Carolina (Fig. 19).

As soon as I finished Wood's book, I telephoned to thank him for writing it and to ask if, in the course of his work, he had come across any references to slaves making pottery. He hadn't, but he said he wouldn't be surprised if they were. Then *he* began to ask *me* questions—questions about pottery, architecture, wild foods, and other aspects of the domestic lives of slaves. He quizzed me about Charles Fairbanks's digs along the Georgia coast and about the potential for work in North Carolina. I responded as best I could and promised to keep him informed of future developments. I hung up the telephone feeling excited and surprised—excited that Wood so readily accepted the possibility of slaves making their own pottery, and surprised that such an authority on colonial

Figure 19. Contemporary vessel handbuilt by descendants of slaves on the island of Nevis, West Indies. (Photograph by Emily Short)

African American life was looking to archæology to learn about the domestic lives of slaves. I then realized what I think historian Peter Wood already knew: The key to learning about the day-to-day lives of colonial slaves—in essence, the key to describing the domestic foundation of African American culture— was not in the hands of historians but in the pockets of archæologists.

## COLONO WARE

Archæologists usually classify ceramic artifacts into groups called "types." Colono-Indian Ware, however, is not an artifact "type" and was never intended to be.[20] "Types" refer to objects of similar morphology, manufactured in a specific area and time period.[21] For example, describing Colono-Indian pottery from the Nottoway and Meherrin Indian villages in southeastern Virginia, Lewis Binford classified the ceramics into four types defined by morphology, geography, and time, and named them Courtland Plain, Courtland Burnished, Warekeck Plain, and Warekeck Burnished.[22] "Courtland" and "Warekeck" are place names, one a Virginia county, the other an Indian village in the region where the artifacts were found. The second part of the type names, "Plain" and "Burnished," refer to the most obvious aspect of morphology—the surface finish of the pottery. According to the type description, the major distinguishing difference between Courtland and Warekeck pottery is the temper added to the clay; fine sand was used in Courtland and finely crushed shell in Warekeck. Binford dated these artifacts between 1660 and 1760, with the Warekeck types preceding Courtland Burnished. He then grouped the related Courtland types into the Courtland Series, the others into the Warekeck Series. Noël Hume's broad category, Colono-Indian Ware, encompassed both series.[23] Thus, the hierarchical artifact taxonomy employed by Binford and commonly used in archæology is "type," "series," and "ware."

When prehistoric archæologists find a new kind of pottery, they usually classify it as a specific type within a larger, known series or ware, but in identifying Colono-Indian Ware, Noël Hume was in a different position. He had discovered a category much larger than a type, a wide range of pottery that extended, he claimed, from "Delaware to South Carolina—with variations of rim ornament and temper along the way."

Pondering the concept of Colono-Indian Ware, I knew that while Noël Hume was not entirely right in his perception, he was not entirely wrong either. There was no doubt that Indians made pottery, but the Carolina discoveries indicated that African Americans also produced low-fired earthenware. The suffix "Indi-

an" in Colono-Indian Ware denied the African American contribution, especially since the name was coined by the well-respected Ivor Noël Hume. We could
reserve the name Colono-Indian Ware for pottery made by Indians and come up
with something else for pottery made by blacks, I reasoned, but if Indians lived
with blacks on plantations and African Americans lived in Indian villages, it
might be impossible to ascribe pottery to one group or the other. We needed a
neutral term. So in 1978, in a paper entitled "Looking for the 'Afro-' in Colono-
Indian Ware," I proposed to expand Noël Hume's concept by dropping the suffix
"Indian" and calling the pottery, simply, "Colono Ware."[24] I considered Colono
Ware to be a very broad category on the order of "British ceramics," that would
include *all* low-fired, handbuilt pottery found on colonial sites, whether slave
quarters, "big houses," or Indian villages.

From my point of view, as soon as the non-European folk pottery of America
was affected, in whatever way, by European colonization, Colono Ware was
born; no doubt it happened with the first voyages of Spanish explorers to the so-
called New World in the early 1500s. The beginning may have been as simple as
an Indian potter using a newly acquired steel knife to carve a shaping paddle.
Or it may have been as complicated as the arrival, on a Spanish ship, of black
slaves and their pottery on the southeastern shore of North America. However it
happened, Colono Ware resulted whenever the colonial experience affected the
techniques of manufacture, the form, or the location of handbuilt pottery.

When I was a student at the University of North Carolina, my professor and
mentor Joffre Coe picked up a potsherd from a Cherokee Indian site in western
North Carolina, a site that had been occupied after the European invasion of
America. "See the wide lines and grooves in the complicated stamped design on
this sherd?" I nodded, and he responded, "Now look at how narrow they are on
this earlier prehistoric sherd."

Then he explained that he suspected the larger designs were carved with the
point of a knife; you could even see the undercutting of the knife point on the
edges of some of the grooves. The older sherds were carved with the narrow
point of a stone graver; it's easier to make a fine line with such a small tool, Coe
explained. I was impressed; on a potsherd that otherwise looked like southeastern prehistoric pottery, my professor saw evidence of people in contact.

He played a little trick on me and other unsuspecting archaeologists to prove
a point. His collection included a large rim sherd from the side of a cooking pot.
"Do you think this is historic or prehistoric?" he would ask.

The sherd had a plain finish and a little decoration on the rim. I thought it
came from about the time of contact, but I couldn't tell for sure whether it was
prehistoric or historic. Without saying a word, Coe turned the sherd sideways

and pointed to some fine scratches down the side. The scratches made the unmistakable outline of a musket! There was no doubt this pot was made by someone who had seen a European gun.

Not only did evidence of contact show up in techniques of manufacture and decoration, Indians also began to make pottery in the shape of European vessels.[25] In 1758 the French explorer Le Page du Pratz observed that among the Natchez, "women [make] dishes and plates like those of the French. I have had some made out of curiosity on the model of my earthenware."[26] From colonial times into the twentieth century, Native American potters have shown the influence of European ceramics in shapes ranging from plates to three-legged pots that resembled cast-iron cooking vessels (Fig. 20)—dramatic examples of ethnic interaction encoded in Colono Ware.[27]

However, Colono Ware does not have to be different from prehistoric pots in form, decoration, or manufacturing technique to be Colono Ware; it needs only to be found on a Colonial period site to furnish evidence of contact.[28] In seventeenth-century Virginia, colonists could buy Indian earthenware, paying for it sometimes with corn.[29] A visitor to a Rappahannock River Indian village wrote in 1686, "Christians buying their pots or vases fill them up with Indian corn and that is the price."[30] Such pots may have been cordmarked and shell tempered just like the prehistoric pottery of the Tidewater region. Nevertheless, Indian pottery bought by "Christians" and eventually deposited in colonial towns and plantations would not be found in those locations if it were not for the interaction between the variety of people fate brought together in the New World. The location of this pottery informs us about colonial life; hence, the pots and sherds are Colono Ware.[31]

By the same token, the pottery of colonial Indian villages is Colono Ware. From the earliest contact, Europeans influenced not only the shape and decoration of Indian pottery, but more important, the places Native Americans lived. Introductions like missions, the deerskin trade, European warfare, and new diseases all began to affect the location of Indian villages, and to this extent determined where pottery was made, broken, and deposited.[32] In the archaeologist's lingo, the spatial distribution of Historic period sites and of all the artifacts of those sites is a function of the colonial situation, and the pottery has a *spatial* attribute that makes it Colono Ware.

As Spanish explorers came into the Southeast, Indian villages ceased being purely aboriginal settlements, incorporating both black and white newcomers. On the Carolina coast, escaped slaves may have started living with Indians as early as the 1520s.[33] When Hernando de Soto arrived on the coast of Florida more than a decade later, he was greeted by a Spaniard who had survived the ill-

Figure 20. Tripod legs and flat bases on these Catawba *(above)* and Pamunkey *(below)* vessels from the nineteenth century show accommodations to the hard, flat surfaces of European-style hearths and tables (Holmes 1903, plates 127 and 136, Smithsonian Institution photographs).

fated Narvaez expedition of 1517 along the Gulf Coast.[34] The survivor was living with the Indians, spoke their language, and agreed to accompany De Soto as an interpreter. In the course of the journey, both black and white members of De Soto's party stayed behind with the Indians, becoming part of the nations that English settlers would encounter in later years. In 1751 South Carolina's Governor Glen advised a liaison looking for an interpreter to find the "free Negro that lives among the Catawbas, and is received by them as a Catawba, that Speaks both their Language and English, very well."[35]

The mingling of traditions from Africa, Europe, and America created three creole subcultures in southeastern America. The challenge, especially for Native and African Americans, was to find in the new situation strategies for individual, family, and community survival. The folk pottery of plantations, towns, and Indian villages was one response to that challenge. Interpreted as such, colonial earthenware could teach us important lessons from the past, but we needed a neutral term, like Colono Ware; otherwise our interpretations would become determined by terminology.

Some archaeologists were reluctant to accept the idea that slaves had made pottery. Others went to the opposite extreme and claimed that all of the pottery formerly called "Colono-Indian Ware" was made by enslaved African Americans and terms like "Colono-Black" and "Colono-African" began to appear. Some scholars applied "Colono-Indian" to the pottery they "knew" to have been made by Indians and "Colono Ware" to the pottery they "knew" to have been made by blacks. These archaeologists were seeking a simple interpretation of a complex historical situation. The older concept of Colono-Indian Ware reflected mid-twentieth century notions of a strictly segregated colonial experience: Indians made pottery and sold or traded it to white planters for their slaves—three separate groups, each with its own role. The new concept of Colono Ware took into account the more complex processes of colonial creolization: demography and culture varied from place to place within the colonies; some Indians worked as slaves on plantations and some blacks lived in Indian villages; both Africans and Indians were capable of making pottery and evidence suggests that both did. To complicate things further, designs for these folk-made pots could have come from European vessels as well as from traditional Native American and African patterns. The Colono Ware concept covers all these possibilities.

## FINDING POTS

In the winter of 1979 I began trying to find as many Colono Ware pots as possible. I expected that site-specific studies of African American settlements containing these artifacts would provide an astounding quantity of detail about slave life. I also believed that we needed a broad overview of the whole range of southern American Colono Ware from Chesapeake Bay to the St. Johns River. We needed to look at the big picture, keeping several important questions in mind:

1. What is the evidence of pottery manufactured by slaves on plantations?
2. How was African American pottery used?
3. How did form and function vary with different social and environmental situations?
4. How did the presence of objects slaves made themselves affect the way they viewed their world?

Armed with these questions and a grant from the National Endowment for the Humanities, I began my search. Among the tens of thousands of Colono Ware sherds already in archaeological collections, I decided not to look at small sherds, but to concentrate on whole pots or fragments of pots large enough for me to extrapolate the whole vessel's shape. I also would look at sherds showing evidence of forms not represented by the larger pieces, even if I could not extrapolate a complete pot shape from the small pieces. I intended to compile a catalog of the range of Colono Ware vessel shapes. To answer my questions of form and function, whole vessels would be more helpful than the smaller sherds.

Over the next two years, with the help of several patient curators, I pulled box after box of Colono Ware from the shelves of twelve institutional repositories— museums, universities, research centers—and I visited several archaeological projects to see materials as they were coming out of the ground.[36] Artifacts from slave quarters, plantation houses, town houses, jails, taverns, ferries, wharves, missions, fortifications, free Indian villages and a hospital were included in the collections. In all, I analyzed data on 117 whole Colono Ware vessels (See Appendixes 1 and 2; Appendix 3, Tables 2–4).

First I made scale drawings and photographs of the artifacts. Then I noted physical characteristics of each vessel such as signs of use, building methods, evidence of firing, details of decoration, and surface finish.

On colonial sites, most Colono Ware vessels are found in specialized contexts—trash pits, hearths, and cellars—that archaeologists call "features." In excavating features, researchers record information about the artifacts and the surrounding soil to assist in determining when the object was deposited and how it was used. To interpret the function of features, I depended on archaeological reports and sometimes talked directly to the excavating archaeologist. Techniques for discovering the time of deposition are exceptionally well developed for American historic sites, and the temporal ranges I was able to record for specimens, while not always as short as I would like, were usually good.[37] Indeed, the existing techniques for dating artifacts are so accurate that we do not need to rely on Colono Ware chronology to determine when sites and features were in use—industrially manufactured items such as ceramics, glass bottles, and nails serve much better in this capacity.

As I was collecting data, I was surprised, and gratified, by the shapes of pots and the signs of use. Archaeologists excavating in the southeastern United States generally find potsherds rather than whole pots. The opportunity to look at dozens of whole pots in a single project seldom comes along; two or three per major project is probably the average. I found that in looking at this large collection of vessels my perspective began to change. To quote the title of archaeologist David Braun's insightful paper, I began thinking of "Pots as Tools," and to see them the way the people who made and used the vessels saw them.[38] Bowls, jars, pans, bottles, and chamber pots, all served specific functions and evidence of wear provides clues to their use. Many vessels were charred from cooking fires. Residue from sealing infusions filmed the interior of some. Others were incised with so-called owner's marks. There was abrasion from stirring, wear from lids, cutlery marks, and in some vessels even the charred remains of food (Figs. 7, 21–25). The more I looked, the more convinced I became that archaeology could reconstruct the everyday lives of slaves.

Because all Colono Ware was originally thought to be "Colono-Indian Ware," I felt obliged to prove that this plantation pottery had African roots, so in beginning my research I looked for African examples of Colono Ware traits. But I was soon overwhelmed by the magnitude of the task. Slaves were drawn from a region of Africa approximately the size of the continental United States, which encompassed thousands of different communities and different cultures, ranging from the states and chiefdoms of the West African farming region to pastoral tribes and nomadic bands of hunters and gatherers. Within these different cultures, techniques of pottery building and decoration vary widely. Somewhere in Africa, I realized, we could find almost any trait showing up on American Colono Ware. Besides, direct comparisons would have to be made not to the African pottery of the recent past for which we have the best information, but to that of more than two hundred years ago—to archaeological specimens. And archaeological research on early colonial Africa is limited and scattered. It is no wonder that we can document Indian similarities to Colono Ware more easily than the African connections; prehistoric Southeastern Indian sites have been the focus of intensive archaeological research, while the African antecedents of Colono Ware are diffuse and barely explored.

Figure 21. Charring on jar from the South Carolina low-country. (Photograph by Emily Short)

Reevaluating the situation, I decided that, for the present, tracing the roots of Colono Ware in Africa was not my best goal. Rather, I set out to demonstrate that this well-preserved colonial artifact could tell us something we simply could not get from documentary history—details about the everyday lives of some of America's earliest colonists. Besides, if we could demonstrate that African Americans were making pottery on plantations in colonial America, we could explore an unknown feature of early American life and set the stage for establishing the African connection from this side of the Atlantic. Now the challenge was to find evidence of plantation pottery making.

Pieces of Colono Ware, particularly larger fragments, often show signs of the manufacturing process. The fractured edges of sherds allowed me to look at the sand or shell that was used as temper and to see the remnants of coils or the laminations of modeling left from building the pots (Figs. 26 and 27). Especially important to my search was evidence of "on site" manufacture; I wanted to demonstrate that at least some Colono Ware pots had been made on plantations.

Finding the firing locations for Colono Ware is not as easy as identifying the factories and workshops of European-style potteries. European and European American ceramics were fired in elaborate brick kilns that leave major archaeological evidence. Moreover, the high frequency of broken vessels or "wasters"

Figure 23. Lid wear on the rim of a bowl from near Williamsburg, Virginia. (Photograph by the author)

around the ruins of former kilns is a sure sign to archaeologists that they have found a pottery factory.

Colono Ware was not fired in an enclosed kiln; pots were stacked and fired on an open hearth, perhaps even in the cooking hearth. Once the pots were removed there would be little evidence of pottery firing. Hearth firings could take place anywhere, so large piles of wasters would not necessarily accumulate as they do around a more permanent kiln. We could not count on finding a specific firing location to demonstrate that pottery was being made on plantations.

Still, we might uncover other clues in our excavations:

1. Although piles of wasters would not be evident, pots must have broken during firing, and the occurrence of pots with distinctive firing breaks would be evidence of manufacture.

Figure 22. Marks on bowl bases found in the Cooper River, South Carolina. (Photographs by Emily Short)

Figure 24. Drip lines from a sealing infusion on a pot from
near Williamsburg, Virginia. (Photograph by the author)

2. Vessels sold or traded are usually good and serviceable. On the other hand, potters sometimes make poor quality vessels, and these should show up near the firing location.
3. Toys and other curiosities made by and for children would be found.
4. Local clay and temper sources would have been used.
5. The pottery made on plantations would be different from local Indian ware.[39]

In my collections research, I noted all these diagnostic traits: firing breaks, poor
quality vessels and toys, local materials, and distinctions between plantation

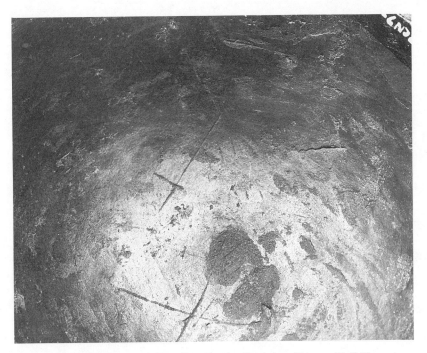

Figure 25. Cutlery marks in a bowl found in the Combahee River at Bluff Plantation, Colleton County, South Carolina. (Photograph by Emily Short)

and Indian village pottery. Spall fractures and related "firing clouds" were particularly important because they show direct evidence of firing.

When earthenware pots are fired, water is driven off as the physical structure changes from clay to ceramic. The rate and ease with which this water is released is a function of the type of clay, the temper, and the amount of water in the clay. When the clay is too "tight," that is, with insufficient pathways for the water to escape, the water turns to steam, pressure builds up, and disk-shaped spalls or flakes fracture off the vessel as the steam is rapidly released. Before firing, most potters carefully dry or "cure" their vessels in the sun or over low heat to help prevent spalling. After the initial firing, spalling seldom occurs, so it is a good indication that vessels were broken during firing rather than during use, that they are "wasters," in potter's jargon. [40]

When associated with firing clouds, spall fractures are even better indicators of firing mishaps. As vessels are fired in an open fire, it often happens that some

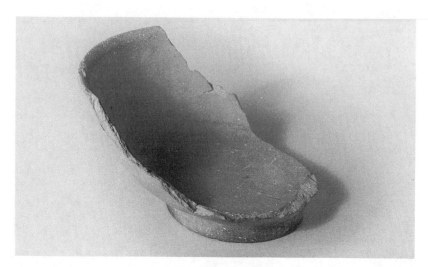

Figure 26. White flakes of shell temper speckle the surface of a bowl found in Williamsburg, Virginia. (Photograph by the author)

Figure 27. Bowl found in the Cooper River, South Carolina. A repair made before firing shows on the *left side* of the rim. (Photograph by Emily Short)

portions of the surface are oxidized while others are reduced, depending on the amount of oxygen at different locations around the pot. Areas of reduction turn dark colored, sometimes almost black, while areas of oxidation turn light. The result is frequently a particolored surface of firing clouds. When spalls come off and the vessel continues to fire, sometimes surface firing clouds will extend from the exterior surface of the vessel onto the newly exposed surface of the spalled area (Fig. 28). Combined, the two phenomena are firm evidence that a vessel was broken during manufacture. With this in mind, I was careful to record all evidence of spalling as well as associated firing clouds.

Most Colono Ware vessels are plain and undecorated, but all visual aspects of pottery, including minimal decoration, are potentially valuable in understanding the lives of the makers and users. I believe that, like other material items, pots carried "messages" about people and their culture. I recorded decoration, and I looked carefully at surface finish. Some finishes were primarily functional, for example, roughening of the surface to facilitate secure handling. Sometimes, however, surfaces were finished purely as decorative enhancement. In collecting information I used three categories of surface treatment—smoothed,

Figure 28. Colono Ware vessel with spall fracture and firing cloud, found in the Cooper River at Mepkin Plantation, Berkeley County, South Carolina, height: 12 cm. (Photograph by Emily Short)

burnished, and stamped. A smoothed surface results when the clay is smoothed with the hands, a piece of cloth, leather, or similar material while the vessel is still wet. When a partially dry vessel with a smooth surface is rubbed with a stone or other hard tool, the result is a burnished surface that shows small facets left by the tool. A carved paddle used in forming a vessel leaves a stamped finish.

As I collected data, I was aware of two biases in my research method. First, small pots are probably overrepresented, because when a small pot breaks it is more likely that fragments large enough to extrapolate the vessel shape will survive than when a large vessel breaks. I tried to minimize this bias by remaining keenly aware of large vessels in the various collections. Florida collections posed another problem related to the sherd size. There are very few whole pots, large or small, from Florida, because the primary site of St. Augustine was occupied so long and so intensively that sizeable sherds seldom survived. The second major bias is that my sample was geographically skewed; I studied pots from the sites archaeologists happened to have excavated, rather than from a representative survey over the colonial South. In Virginia more pots came from urban Williamsburg than from the plantations, and in South Carolina more specimens came from the rivers adjacent to plantations than any other location. However, as research continued, this uneven distribution became symbolic of the differences between slave life in Virginia's tidewater region and the Carolina lowcountry—in Virginia, slaves had more contact with European Americans than in South Carolina, where most African Americans lived relatively isolated lives in largely black communities along the shores of vast marshes and slow-moving rivers.

# Chapter 2

# NORTH AMERICA'S SLAVE COAST

## BLACK COLONISTS

Driving along the Colonial Parkway from Williamsburg to Jamestown, I suddenly saw in the beautiful scenery a confirming symbol of the dramatic differences in the lives of slaves in the different southern colonies. I was spending my days studying pots in the archæology laboratories at Williamsburg, and one evening after work I set out along the Parkway across gently rolling hills shaded by hardwood trees. The forest is mostly oak and hickory; here and there, brooks flow down the rocky ravines and beneath the road. To my surprise the landscape reminded me of the Blue Ridge Parkway winding along the top of the Appalachian Mountains. Of course, the hills were not as steep, the falls and cascades not as dramatic, and the forest was missing spruce and white pine, but somehow I felt closer to the mountains than to the Atlantic coast.

My point of reference was the flat land of the Carolina lowcountry, with its live oak trees draped by Spanish moss, its palmetto palms, and endless marsh. This Virginia landscape was worlds apart from the watery rice plantations of Carolina, where slaves cleared swamps, diked fields, and farmed the mucky soils that supported the South's richest aristocracy (Figs. 29 and 30). On Virginia's well-drained hillsides, slaves planted, hoed, picked, and cured tobacco. In the way they farmed the land and in the lives they led, slaves in Virginia

**33**

Figure 29. Creek and hills along the Colonial Parkway between Williamsburg and Jamestown, Virginia. (Photograph by the author)

Figure 30. Ben Brown and two companions in a tidal creek on St. Helena Island, South Carolina, circa 1900–1910 (see Dabbs 1970). (From the Penn School Collection, permission granted by Penn Center, St. Helena Island, South Carolina)

barely resembled those in Carolina. I remembered that in Carolina slaves worked by daily jobs or "tasks" under the direction of a black driver, while Virginia slaves commonly worked in "gangs" under the watchful eyes of white overseers.[1]

Land and crops partially explained the differences. Other contrasts between Virginia and Carolina included the time and character of European settlement, the ethnicity of slaves, relationships with Indians, demography and natural resources: all these affected slave lifestyle (Fig. 31). Florida, Georgia, and North Carolina also had distinct histories and plantation economies, and consequently different styles of life. As my research progressed, I began to relate

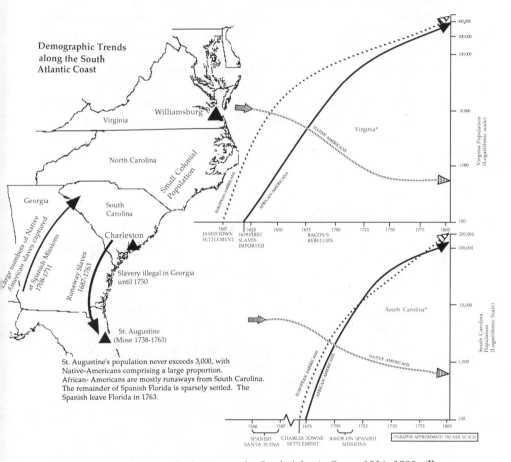

Figure 31. Demography and ethnicity on the South Atlantic Coast, 1526–1800. (Illustration by Alexander West, Richard Affleck, and Niels Taylor)

differences in pottery to differences in the lifeways of slaves from colony to colony. I now believed that Noël Hume's observation concerning "variations of rim ornament and temper" of the pottery along the coast was a gross understatement.[2]

Along the southeastern shore, Colono Ware varies in quantity, overall vessel shape, decoration, and evidence of use (Fig. 32). Taken together, these variables show that black slaves in the Carolina lowcountry led domestic lives much more African in character than those of Virginia. In Florida, Native American people and traditions significantly affected the lives of Europeans and African Americans who settled there. The domestic culture of slaves in North Carolina and Georgia evolved from these major cultural traditions.

Although the diverse collecting procedures used by archaeologists in different regions make direct comparison impossible, my impression from the available data (Appendix 3, Table 1) is that more Colono Ware has been found in South Carolina than in all other former colonies combined. Furthermore, the relative frequency of Colono Ware to European ceramics is greater in South Carolina and Florida than in other colonies, no doubt due to the large numbers of black slaves in South Carolina and Indians in Spanish Florida. In major

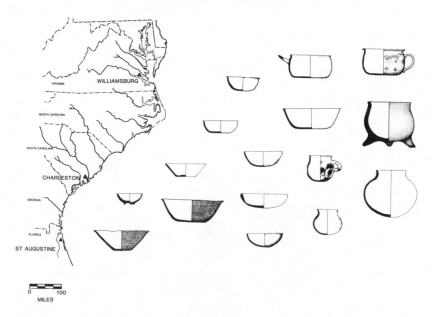

Figure 32. Colono Ware variability along the South Atlantic Coast. (Illustration by Alexander West, Richard Affleck, and Niels Taylor)

excavations, South Carolina archaeologists typically find thousands of Colono Ware sherds, while similar excavations in Virginia produce fewer than one hundred of these artifacts. At Corotoman Plantation, Virginia, for example, extensive excavations yielded only forty-four Colono Ware sherds.[3] In North Carolina collections, like those of Virginia, Colono Ware accounts for only a small minority of the ceramics. Colono Ware is even rarer on Georgia sites.[4] In almost two decades of careful recovery, archaeologists digging in Georgia have unearthed pitifully few pieces of Colono Ware.

Finding pieces of pottery is much easier than exposing the foundations of entire slave houses; therefore we know much more about early African American pottery than architecture. Nevertheless, after exposing more than twenty-five eighteenth-century slave houses, the evidence shows that contrasting landforms and settlement histories not only explain the variable incidence of Colono Ware but the style of housing as well. Slave houses in South Carolina are more like African houses than in any other place in the Southeast. Excavations of slave quarters in Virginia show house plans similar to the so-called earthfast houses of the early British pioneers; in the Carolina lowcountry the floor plan, small rooms, clay walls, and gabled roofs of slave houses are analogous to houses in West Africa. These house foundations, together with potsherds and other things we find, exhibit the diversity of African American lifeways along the south Atlantic coast.

## SPANISH SETTLEMENTS

Archaeologists generally associate Colono Ware with Virginia and South Carolina. Both Colono Ware and the colonial experience, however, are much older than these British colonies.

By the time the English settled in Carolina in 1670, Native Americans had been interacting with Europeans and Africans for almost one hundred and fifty years. In 1521 Spanish explorers kidnapped one hundred and fifty Indians from the Georgia coast and took them to the West Indies. Most of these Native Americans died in the Indies but, amazingly, one captive named Francisco de Chicora traveled to Spain and returned to his homeland in 1526. He came back with the ill-fated settlers of San Miguel de Guadalupe, apparently located near present-day Sapelo Island on the Georgia coast.[5] Thus, when Hernando de Soto and his legion traversed the region of Georgia and South Carolina in 1540 looking for riches, one of the natives had already been to Spain and back. In 1566, the Spanish frontier town of Santa Elena—much larger than the 1565 garrison at St. Augustine—was established on the southern end of present-day Parris Island, South Carolina, and for twenty years brought coastal Indians into contact with the aliens.[6] Both Santa Elena and St. Augustine were intended to provide the Spanish with a toehold in North America, to protect Spanish shipping lanes from New Spain (Mexico) and to promote missions for the Indians. Even after 1587 when Santa Elena was abandoned and the Spanish retreated to St. Augustine, the natives of the Carolina coast continued to have commerce with their neighbors to the south. Today we may forget the Spanish presence in Florida, but, as historian J. Leitch Wright has observed, "sixteenth century Southern Indians could not."[7]

The dramatic Spanish intrusion affected major aspects of Indian life. Tens of thousands of Native Americans died from disease. Spaniards and Africans came to live in Indian villages, and Indians moved near Spanish towns and missions. Native patterns of hunting, farming, settlement, trade, and warfare changed forever.

Everyday life for Indian people also was transformed. New objects like knives, cloth, and glass beads were brought in from the outside, and traditional pursuits like making pottery were altered from within. Native Americans did not begin by copying European vessels, but introduced new, and often subtle, variations on old themes. The rims of cooking pots, for example, became more flared, concealing the traditional decoration encircling the top of the vessel. Complicated stamps became larger and less carefully carved, perhaps, as Joffre Coe observed, because Indian carvers now were using knives rather than the traditional stone gravers. Red and black painting became more common. Bowls with carinated walls and elaborate incising on the rims became popular, and large, open, pan-shaped bowls—somewhat similar to Spanish forms—were made more frequently than in prehistoric times.

These developments were so subtle that they might have occurred in the normal evolution of Southeastern Indian pottery, whether or not the intruders had come along. However, since these changes happened quite rapidly just at the time of contact, I believe that the new pottery legitimately can be called Colono Ware, reflecting the impact of the colonial situation. Later, when large numbers of black slaves began to arrive, another foreign ingredient was added to the mix.[8]

Unlike the English farmers and traders to the north, the Spaniards who came to Florida brought with them few slaves and few women—their major goals were not settlement but establishing military security and Christian missions. Those Africans who did settle in the colony came as personal servants and laborers. Women who immigrated to St. Augustine usually came with their husbands;

most were Spanish-Indian women or descendants of very early New World Spanish families.[9] Once in Florida, single soldiers often married native wives, and both soldiers and Indians occasionally married blacks, forming creole households. Indian and black women also entered Spanish households as cooks, nurses, and housekeepers. Thus, St. Augustine became a town where Europeans dominated the political and military realm while Native American women prevailed in the home. This social division is visible in the archaeological record.

Archaeologists commonly find two types of Indian pottery in St. Augustine. St. Johns pottery, associated with the indigenous Timucua, comes from contexts between 1565 and the late seventeenth century; San Marcos pottery, associated with Indians who moved southward from the Georgia and southern Carolina coasts, comes from contexts dating between the mid-seventeenth century and 1763 when the Spanish ceded Florida to the British and the entire population left St. Augustine for Cuba. That these two types of Colono Ware are recovered more frequently in St. Augustine than any other pottery shows the influence of Indian women on domestic life (Fig. 33).[10] Contrasting Florida with the Caribbean and Central America, archaeologist Kathleen Deagan stresses the role of native women in preserving Indian foodways and pottery traditions.

> In the Caribbean and in parts of New Spain the colonists quickly organized native potters to produce ceramic forms suitable for Spanish tastes. This resulted in a ceramic tradition that combined Old World, New World, and newly synthesized traits. In Florida, however, the colonists simply adopted the traditional aboriginal ceramic forms and styles with few modifications. This was undoubtedly related to the absence of both *encomienda* [a type of Indian slavery] and European potters in the Florida colony and also to the immediate and continued role of native women in the households of the Spanish town. The wide-spread presence of Indian women in Hispanic kitchens could account for the incorporation of both native food-ways and native foodway technology into the Spanish town, and native cooks would not consider modification of the forms to be necessary.[11]

Pottery sherds excavated in the colonial houses and courtyards of St. Augustine show that the town's cooks used elongated pots with conoidal bases and flared rims set over open fires.[12] Both the vessels and cooking techniques were derived from American Indian traditions.[13] Surfaces of these pots were covered with complicated Indian-style stamping and the pot rims were decorated with clay applique strips and punctations common in southeastern Indian pottery. St. Augustine cooks also used San Marcos bowls and occasionally plates. Most

Figure 33. Fragments of San Marcos complicated-stamped cooking jars from St. Augustine, Florida. (Photograph by Emily Short)

bowls were shallow with flat bottoms, but recovered artifacts include Indian forms with incurving rims as well as bowls with European-looking ring bases. Often finished by burnishing and painting, these bowls and plates are tangible evidence of the continuation of traditional pottery form, decoration, and usage. Thus, archaeological analysis reveals the impact of Indian women and Indian culture on domestic life.[14] Barely visible in the written documents, Native American women emerge as major contributors to creolized St. Augustine society.

Black women, even less visible than Indians, probably had a hand in making some San Marcos pottery. Blacks entering St. Augustine from other Spanish colonies, Africa, or Carolina came from cultures with strong folk pottery traditions.[15] Perhaps, as they adjusted to a domestic system dominated by Florida Indians, black women began to make pottery imitating San Marcos designs. And they may have added some African or African American ceramic traits that archaeologists have yet to identify.

Although the Spanish brought few blacks into St. Augustine, after the English settlement of Carolina in 1670, the African American population began to increase. Through what has been called the "first underground railroad," fugitive slaves from South Carolina made their way by foot and dugout canoe across the swamps and marshes of coastal Georgia to freedom in Florida. In 1738 the Spanish governor gave these free people land, two miles north of St. Augustine, for a town and fort. Although officially named "Gracia Real de Santa Teresa de Mose," the adjacent components of this town are commonly known as "Mose" and "Fort Mose"; and whose location was recently identified and excavation initiated by Kathleen Deagan.[16] Undoubtedly, the site of Mose and Fort Mose is one of the most significant African American landmarks in the United States.

## TIDEWATER TOBACCO FARMS

### Slavery and Racism

In quantity and style, Colono Ware from Virginia contrasts sharply to the San Marcos pottery of St. Augustine. Virginia archaeologists find relatively fewer fragments than do archaeologists in St. Augustine, and the pieces they find are more European in style than the wares to the south. As a result of a general reluctance of Virginia historical archaeologists prior to the 1980s to quantify ceramic data, direct quantitative comparisons cannot be made. Nevertheless, my impression from reviewing reports as well as much of the primary data from Virginia is that the average proportion of Colono Ware to European and American industrially manufactured pieces may be as low as 5 to 10 percent. The excavation of an early Hispanic house in St. Augustine produced almost four thousand sherds of Colono Ware, comprising 64 percent of all the ceramics recovered.[17] The contrast is so great that after looking at Colono Ware from the entire southeastern coast I now understand why archaeologists at first chose to stress the similarity of Colono Ware to European vessels—they were looking at vessels from Virginia.

The shape of the pottery implies that something very different was going on in the kitchens of Virginia and Florida, and these domestic differences are consistent with the contrasting histories of people in the two colonies. In Florida, soldiers and priests exercised political control while Indian women held sway in the home. In contrast, English settlers in Virginia set the tone for both politics and domestic life. When African and Indian people came to live in Virginia towns and farms, they came as minor tributaries feeding a swelling river of European American culture.

Beginning in 1607, Virginia's English colonists cleared land and farmed tobacco utilizing their own labor as well as that of servants from the British Isles. As they needed supplies, these settlers and servants bought some of their food, tools, and utensils, including Colono Ware pottery, from Indians. In 1624 John Smith refers to Indian pottery in his *Generall Historie;* and in 1641 tobacco farmer Edward Bestwick's estate included, among other things, "3 old Indian bowles, 2 Indian trays and 3 earthen pottes." Bestwick was owed by John Davis for "two Indian bowles" and by John Cuttes for one.[18]

In all probability, Bestwick and his neighbors planted, cropped, and cured their tobacco with only the help of their families and perhaps a white servant or two. They built homes, sold their harvest, traded with neighboring Indians, and otherwise set the pattern of culture in the early seventeenth century. Virginia's African immigrants arrived later. According to Edmund S. Morgan, Virginia's foremost colonial historian, "Virginia developed her plantation system without slaves, and slavery introduced no novelties to methods of production. The seventeenth-century plantation already had its separate quartering house or houses for the servants. Their labor was already supervised in groups of eight or ten by an overseer."[19]

Black slaves came slowly into the white world of Virginia tobacco country, and as they came they were put to work side-by-side with a predominantly white labor force. The first Africans arrived in 1619 on a Dutch ship, which anchored off Jamestown for supplies, and for the next half-century they trickled in averaging only twenty per year.[20] In the beginning, both black people and the institution of slavery were fit into conventional cultural categories. Slaves were treated as servants whose indentures never expired; class distinctions, that is, the differences between free landholders and servants or slaves, were more important than race. Morgan asserts that servants and slaves "initially saw each other as sharing the same predicament. It was common, for example, for servants and slaves to run away together, steal hogs together, get drunk together. It was not uncommon for them to make love together."[21]

So, as black people became a part of Virginia society, they comprised a minority of a white-dominated servant stratum in which low status was as binding as race and ethnicity were divisive. Given this intimacy, there is no question that Virginia creolization, which started with Indian-European interaction, expanded to include features of African culture. In these earliest days, however, African traits were diluted by the greater numbers of whites at every level of society.

Slavery, and with slavery, African American culture, became entrenched in Virginia in the last half of the seventeenth century. Between 1650 and 1680, a complex set of economic and demographic events changed tobacco farming and dramatically increased the number of slaves. Small farms gave way to large plantations and black slaves became the primary source of labor (Fig. 34).[22] Virginia's African American population increased ten times, from no more than 300 people in 1650 to approximately 3,000 in 1680, outnumbering white servants, though still a small minority of the colony's 70,000 to 80,000 people.

During and after Bacon's Rebellion in the 1670s, Indians became both more subjugated and more enmeshed in Virginia culture. In their drive to extend tobacco cultivation, Virginians murdered and enslaved friendly Indian peoples. Bacon's Law of 1676 made Indian slavery official colonial policy.

Through their attacks on Native Americans, Virginians whetted their racism so that it became the primary tool for managing colonial society, including the lucrative plantations. Class differences became subordinate to racial differences, and white Virginians began to see both Native Americans and African Americans in the same way, as inferior people suitable for domination and exploitation. Although laws encouraging Indian slavery were repealed soon after the Rebellion, Indians captured in war continued to be sold in Virginia through the early eighteenth century, and free Indians began to be classed as servants. Even though Indians were never a large part of the labor force, Morgan says that "many more Indian slaves [were imported] than has usually been recognized,"

Figure 34. First European American servants, then African American slaves labored with iron hoes in Virginia tobacco fields. (Department of Historic Resources, Commonwealth of Virginia)

and historian Gary Nash reports that from the time of Bacon's Rebellion free Indians were "tenant farmers, day laborers and domestic servants."[23] Thus, from the late 1600s Indians lived and worked on some plantations with African Americans; we also know that runaway slaves and free blacks often sought refuge and acceptance in free Indian villages.[24] Obviously, the division between African and Native Americans in eighteenth-century Virginia was not a strict one.

### Virginia Colono Ware

The prevalence of Colono Ware in Virginia parallels the rapid rise of the black population and the beginning of Indian slavery and servitude. Although there is documentary evidence of Colono Ware earlier, the oldest sherds found so far in Virginia date from the 1670s.[25] These artifacts were recovered by archaeologist William Kelso of the Virginia Research Center for Archaeology, in the mid-1970s, from extensive excavations on the present-day Kingsmill Plantation tract near Williamsburg.[26] The first slaves in the Kingsmill region probably came to work for Colonel Thomas Pettus sometime after 1670. The Colono Ware Kelso unearthed from the sites of Pettus's house and a nearby cottage, called Utopia, had been lying underground some three hundred years (Fig. 35).

Examining the Colono Ware sherds from Pettus and Utopia on a research visit to Williamsburg, I became excited by the evidence of local manufacture. Much of the pottery was well fired, but some pieces had large spalls broken off the sides (Fig. 36) and others were so friable from poor firing that they were in

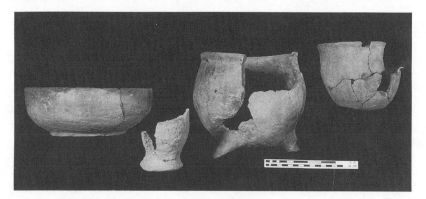

Figure 35. Tripod legs and flat bases on Colono Ware from seventeenth-century Virginia were made to be used on European-style hearths and tables. (Department of Historic Resources, Commonwealth of Virginia)

Figure 36. Spalling on a Colono Ware pot from the Pettus site near Williamsburg, Virginia. (Photograph by the author)

danger of coming apart in my hands (Fig. 37).[27] Small pieces of fossilized shell and rust-red hematite dotted the fractures and vessel surfaces. When I asked Merry Outlaw and Bly Bogley, researchers at the Center, about these inclusions they told me that shell and hematite occurred naturally in the clay matrix of the Yorktown Formation outcropping near Kingsmill.[28] I had no doubt that the vessels from Pettus and Utopia were plantation-made. Many of the pots were obvious rejects, not the kind of vessels that would have been brought to a plantation and sold, thus fulfilling my most critical criteria for determining on-site manufacture. Identifying the clay mixture from a nearby source confirmed my supposition. Here was clear archæological evidence that the pottery was made on the plantation.[29]

Once I deduced that Colono Ware was made on or near Pettus and Utopia on the Kingsmill tract, I turned my attention to the makers. Were they white, Indian, or black? Since European culture lacked a strong tradition of handbuilt, open-fired pottery, white people seemed the least likely candidates, and since black slaves always outnumbered Indians by a large number on Virginia plantations, the odds were in favor of the African Americans.

The pottery from Pettus and Utopia is thicker and more crudely fired than Colono Ware found on later eighteenth-century sites. My colleagues readily accepted my claim that the Pettus and Utopia pottery was produced by slaves,

Figure 37. Poorly fired bowl base from the Pettus site near Williamsburg, Virginia. (Department of Historic Resources, Commonwealth of Virginia)

but were reluctant to acknowledge the possibility that blacks made some of the finer pieces from later times. In fairness, I attribute only part of this reluctance to prejudice. Noël Hume and Binford had made a case that the majority of Virginia Colono Ware, different in both hardness and thickness from that at Pettus and Utopia, was made by Indians. On the other hand, I sensed that some archaeologists were willing to attribute the Pettus and Utopia artifacts to slaves *because* the ware was crudely made.

Of course, by showing my friends pictures of finely crafted ceramics from West Africa or exquisite examples of African domestic arts, such prejudicial views could be deflated, if not always removed.[30] Still, there remained a question of interpretation: Why did West African people, coming from a culture with a tradition of fine handbuilt pottery, make the poor examples excavated at Pettus and Utopia? So far, the best answer to this question hinges on the dislocations and stresses of slavery and frontier life (Fig. 38).

Ancient cultures like those in Africa, prehistoric America, or Europe had well-developed systems for producing and distributing necessary goods and services. In West Africa, for example, seventeenth- and eighteenth-century pottery generally was made by female specialists who sold or traded their wares to others, young girls from families who traditionally made pottery learned the craft, others did not. Although in recent times both men and women make

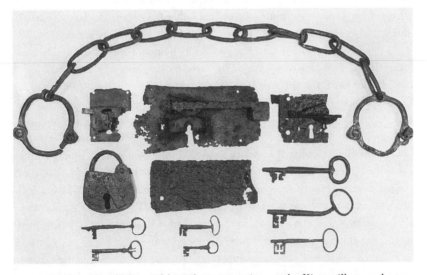

Figure 38. Shackles, locks, and keys from excavations at the Kingsmill tract plantations symbolize the rigid controls of slavery in colonial Virginia. (Department of Historic Resources, Commonwealth of Virginia)

pottery, males are associated almost exclusively with modern wheel throwing while women are associated with traditional handbuilding.[31]

In the pioneering situation of America, old African patterns of crafting and trading were broken up, and Native American patterns were, at least, strained. Some plantations probably had women who were excellent potters, though finding experienced craftspeople may have been difficult. On the other hand, while everyone was not skilled at making pots, the basic materials and techniques would have been widely known. Hence we might expect to find expertly produced pottery on some plantation sites; on others we may find the attempts of people who needed pots and had no way to get them other than to try their hand at manufacture. The crude vessels of Pettus and Utopia appear to be artifacts of this latter type of African American pioneering in Virginia. Over time skillful potters would become more widely known and novices would become more skilled, so that by the eighteenth century most Colono Ware in Virginia was well made.

While some Pettus and Utopia pots were poorly fired, others were serviceable and some showed evidence of having been used. The potters built their wares in generalized European shapes—bowls with flat and sometimes pedestaled bases, large jars with flat bases apparently used for storage, and other jars, like pipkins, with tripodal legs for cooking on a flat, hard hearth. In fact, like the Pettus and Utopia pottery, all of the whole vessel forms I found in Virginia dating through the eighteenth century had either flat or tripodal bases (Figs. 10 and 11; also see Appendix 3, Table 2 for data on Virginia vessels).

As Noël Hume pointed out, "simple [flat-bottomed] bowls that could be used either in the fireplace or on the table" were most common.[32] People living in houses with hard, flat surfaces like tables and brick hearths—in contrast to dirt floors and open, stone hearths—used these utensil shapes. The general shape of Virginia Colono Ware is so much like British serving and cookware that, as I examined the collections, I could easily imagine a housewife in eighteenth-century England putting the pottery to use. On the contrary, as I imagined the same woman encountering an elongated, conoidal-bottomed San Marcos cooking pot from St. Augustine, I could see her rolling it out the door and using it for a nesting box, or more accurately, a nesting pot. Thus, in Virginia, vessel shapes suggest that slave homes were more akin to those of poor white colonists than to traditional African or Native American houses.

The artifacts from Pettus and Utopia indicate that pottery was being made on this plantation in the last quarter of the seventeenth century, probably by slaves. Another little vessel, perhaps a toy, excavated at the eighteenth-century slave site of Kingsmill Quarter, had broken to pieces while being fired, and this artifact suggests that pottery-making continued in the Kingsmill area at least through the eighteenth century. If my supposition is correct that the potters at Kingsmill were African American, it is likely that slaves made pottery at other places in rural Virginia as well. Excavation of more plantation sites with particular attention given to this hypothesis should be enlightening.

To date, however, archaeological evidence indicates that the locally-made wares from Pettus and Utopia were the exception in Virginia. It appears that much, if not most, of the eighteenth century Colono Ware recovered in Virginia was made, as Noël Hume and others have suggested, by free Indians. Firing faults are rare in collections from eighteenth-century towns and plantations, in contrast to the pottery from Pettus and Utopia. Only one eighteenth-century vessel, among the whole pots I analyzed, shows a firing fault.[33] This negative evidence is consistent with the theory that Indian traders brought well-finished wares to both town and plantation for sale or trade. Moreover, the whole range of pottery from eighteenth-century Virginia resembles that found on Historic period Indian sites.[34]

But before we simply ascribe Virginia Colono Ware to Native American potters, several complicating factors should be taken into account. First, although demographic statistics are fragmentary, blacks lived in Virginia's Indian villages. Gary Nash comments that a considerable number of runaway slaves were given refuge by the coastal tribes,[35] and anthropologist John Swanton emphasizes the degree of miscegenation between blacks and Indians. Swanton reminds us:

> About 1705 the historian Berkeley reported that there were 12 villages [of Powhatan Indians], of which 8 were on the Eastern Shore and the only one of consequence, Pamunkey, had 150 inhabitants. Most of those on the eastern shore, who had meanwhile become much mixed with negroes, were driven away in 1831 during the excitement occasioned by the slave rising under Nat Turner. There are still in existence mixed-blood descendants of the Pamunkey, Chickahominy, Powhatan, Mattapony, Werowocomoco, Nansemond, Rappahannock, Potomac, Tapparanock, Wicocomoco, and Accohanoc, though only the first two are of any considerable size. . . .today the mixed-blood descendants still number several hundred.[36]

Analyzing Pamunkey pottery in 1951, Theodore Stern wrote that he thought African American influence on Pamunkey pottery was minor, but archaeologist Susan Henry demurred. "The role of African American influence in Pamunkey pottery manufacture," she insisted, "is unclear."[37] Henry's statement exhibits exemplary caution. Without carefully studying African American and Indian demography and craft history, no one can be sure of the African American contribution to Pamunkey pottery. Imagine a black-skinned woman making a European-styled pot using Indian technology in a Pamunkey village; she then sells the pot to a black slave household. Is the pot Indian, African, or European?

The second potential problem for our understanding the ethnic origin of Virginia Colono Ware is that we don't have a representative archaeological sample. Most Virginia Colono Ware comes either from Williamsburg or one of a few plantations near town. These plantations were owned by relatively wealthy families who had ready access to European goods; perhaps their slaves did not need handbuilt ceramics as much as those farther into the hinterland. Apart from the Pettus and Utopia artifacts, the single spalled vessel in my study of whole pots came from Flowerdew Hundred, the plantation farthest from Williamsburg in my sample. Archaeologist James Deetz, director of Flowerdew Hundred archaeology, has discovered a strong correlation between the incidence of Colono Ware at Flowerdew sites and the establishment, in the seventeenth century, of separate living quarters for African American slaves.[38] He suggests that once slaves were living on their own, away from intensive interaction with whites, they needed and began to make their own pottery. Further analysis may show that slaves were making Colono Ware on or near Flowerdew Hundred, and future excavations may show that slaves were making it on other remote plantations. The questions of who made eighteenth-century Colono Ware and where they made it are only beginning to be answered.

Like Colono Ware, the origins of locally made clay tobacco pipes commonly found on Virginia sites (Fig. 39) have puzzled archaeologists. Interpretations of the temporal and cultural associations of these pipes reflect the complex social situation of colonial Virginia. Ceramic pipes have been recovered from a variety of seventeenth-century sites including free Indian villages, plantations, and colonial towns; they date from the 1640s to about 1710. Made from local clays, some pipes were molded, others were handbuilt; and since archaeologists have found scant evidence of kilns, they were likely fired in open fires as Colono Ware was. Originally the molded forms, exhibiting more European technology, were said to have been made by white colonists, while the hand-modeled ones were attributed to Indians.[39] Henry also described most of the decoration on these pipes—abstract designs and figures comprised of small punctations and incisions—as Native American.

Until recently, no one raised the possibility that African American colonists

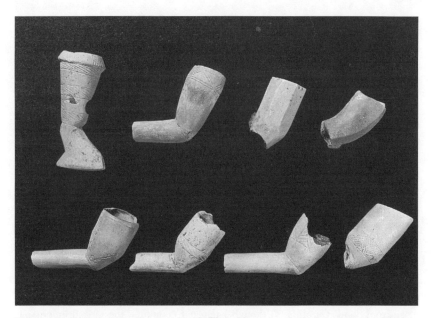

Figure 39. Tobacco pipes decorated with West African–style designs from the Kingsmill tract near Williamsburg, Virginia. (Department of Historic Resources, Commonwealth of Virginia)

made and decorated any of these pipes. Then, in the mid-1980s, Matthew Emerson, a student working with James Deetz at Flowerdew Hundred, began looking at these pipes from a new perspective. Analyzing 694 pipe bowls from fifteen sites, Emerson concluded that the details of pipe design and decoration exhibited evidence of all three ethnic groups; furthermore, he concluded, while some Native American influence was apparent, the shape of the pipes was predominantly European and the decorations predominantly African. Emerson found that most of the pipes had been made on Virginia's tobacco plantations during the last half of the seventeenth century, when whites and blacks lived in close contact with one another. Locally made pipes had declined and finally disappeared in the early eighteenth century, as plantation life grew more segregated and European pipes became more available.[40]

Identifying the West African region of Nigeria and Ghana as the homeland of most slaves imported to Virginia during the period of pipe making, Emerson looked to these areas for comparative examples of decorative art. He discovered that Chesapeake pipe makers decorated their pipe bowls with denticulate lines, stamps, dot impressions, and white clay inlays—design elements common in West African handicrafts. Moreover, these design elements frequently were formed into West African motifs and figures.

Occasionally African or Indian-style punctations and incising was used to decorate Colono Ware pottery from Virginia, but most vessel surfaces were unadorned.[41] Rather than covering vessel surfaces with cordmarked or stamped textures as might have been done traditionally, the surfaces were left smooth like those of glazed European ceramics. In the eighteenth century these smooth surfaces were enhanced by burnishing.[42] Virginia makers burnished their wares by rubbing the surface with a stone or hard stick when the unfired vessel was "leather hard." This burnishing produced a hard, reflective surface, resembling delicate, glazed European vessels.

During my quantitative analysis of Colono Ware, I discovered that the illusion of delicacy created by burnishing had fooled me. I studied collections first in South Carolina, where vessel surfaces generally were smoothed rather than burnished. As I drew and photographed the pottery from Williamsburg, I often remarked that the Virginia pots were thinner and more delicately made than those from South Carolina. Although I had not compared the measurements, I was sure my tactile impression was valid. Once I tabulated all the data, I calculated the average wall thickness from the two collections and discovered to my surprise that the Virginia specimens were thicker (Appendix 3, Table 4)! Even after I removed from the calculation the exceptionally thick pieces from the early sites of Pettus and Utopia, the Virginia ware proved to be the same thickness, on the average, as the South Carolina ware. It occurred to me that the illusion of delicacy may have been intentional, that Virginia potters burnished their vessels to make them appear more like the thin stonewares, earthenwares, and porcelains imported by white Virginians.

Besides burnishing, finishing pots often entailed adding appendages or decorations that made them even more similar to European crockery (Figs. 10–12, 40 and 41).[43] Handles on porringers, chamber pots, and cups were shaped like those on their European counterparts, and vessel rims were sometimes decorated similarly to English dishes. Bowls often were notched around the rim like English-made slipware plates, and other vessels had facets and scallops reminiscent of the rim treatment on salt-glazed stoneware and creamware plates. A few vessels in my sample were painted and at least one bowl was fluted, dimly recalling the ribbing seen on some English ceramics.

While the entire collection of Colono Ware from Virginia looks European, Noël Hume thought that "the chamberpot is probably the most 'European' of all" and I have to agree.[44] Colono Ware chamber pots (Fig. 40) often have large

Figure 40. Colono Ware chamber pot from Williamsburg. Flaking is from uric salts. Similar shape to the British "scratch blue" stoneware chamber pot in Figure 41. (Photograph by the author)

curving handles and out-turned rims like "scratch blue" stoneware pots of the middle eighteenth century. Flaking on the sides of the vessels shows evidence of use; the salts of urine have crystallized and damaged the burnished surfaces. Excavations at Wetherburn's Tavern, at outbuildings of the Apothecary Shop, and at several other Williamsburg structures have yielded pieces of these pots.

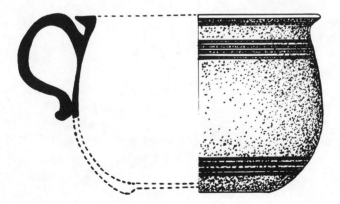

Figure 41. Imported "scratch blue" stoneware chamber pot. Similar shape to Colono Ware chamber pot, Figure 40. (Courtesy of the Charleston Museum, Charleston, South Carolina)

In colonial America, nothing could have been more European than "relieving" oneself in a special pot inside a house. The emphasis on individual privacy and separation from nature that characterized the developing Georgian ideology of eighteenth-century Virginia seems epitomized by these artifacts. Having no models from their own cultures, potters learned to make exact replicas of European chamber pots.

Although the shape and decoration of Virginia Colono Ware look British, the ware is definitely a creole product of mixed cultures. African and Indian potters, for example, employed their native technology.[45] The tempering, hand-building, and open-firing techniques that produced Virginia Colono Ware were alien to Europeans, who turned pots on wheels and fired them in enclosed kilns. Another practice used by both Native Americans and Africans was to coat the inside of some vessels with a vegetable infusion, to seal the surface and prevent leaking.[46] Several jars from Pettus and other sites were treated in this manner.

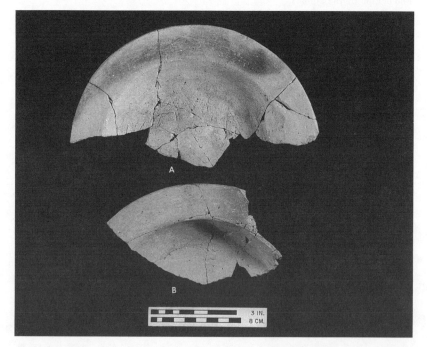

Figure 42. Nineteenth-century Colono Ware plates with cutlery marks, excavated on the Pamunkey Indian Reservation, Virginia. (Department of Historic Resources, Commonwealth of Virginia)

At first glance, technology seems to be the major traditional Indian or African feature of Virginia Colono Ware, but non-Europeans made a more subtle contribution as well. Responding to either their own preferences or the needs of their community, potters determined which vessel forms they would make, and how many of each. According to the archaeological record, their choice of shapes was not similar to that of European Americans. Most striking, for example, is that slaves in colonial Virginia did not use handbuilt plates. Colono Ware plates have been recovered from Pamunkey, Nottoway, and Weanock Indian sites (Fig. 42),[47] but no plates have been recovered from town or plantation sites. Why the difference? Had slaves wanted plates, they could have made or bought them. But instead, they used bowls. This decided African American preference for bowls holds for eighteenth-century Carolina as well as the Georgia and Carolina coast in the nineteenth century. Perhaps—as will be explored in a later section—even though Virginia slaves made a commitment to the superficial shape of European cooking and eating utensils, they maintained some of the culinary culture of Africa, an African structure or "grammar" we also find in their architecture.

## African American Earthfast Houses

Slave kitchens, the main places where Colono Ware was used, were scattered about the Kingsmill locality. In the early days of slavery in Virginia, blacks moved into already established servants' quarters wherever they might be—in the master's house or yard, or near the fields.[48] Thus, African Americans began their domestic life in the colony not in houses and kitchens of their own making but in structures built by Europeans. For some time slaves continued to live near white servants in the farm house and yard of their masters. However, after the economically troubled 1660s, serious tensions began developing between masters who expected obedience and respect and their white indentured servants who wanted independence and prosperity; this period of tension correlates with a trend toward building new servant's quarters further away from the master's house. With a rising black population and a declining number of white servants, these separate quarters soon became occupied primarily by African American slaves.[49] Reflecting the demographic and social dominance of whites, these houses and their kitchens resembled the dwellings of white Virginians, but like Colono Ware pottery, they show African American peculiarities.

Seventeenth-century slaves at Kingsmill lived in so-called earthfast houses: post and beam houses wherein the posts extended into the ground to form the foundation. Slaves' earthfast houses, like those of early European settlers, were constructed by placing posts in the ground in a square or rectangular pattern. These posts were then topped with beams; gabled roofs, and perhaps chimneys completed the structure.[50]

Later in the eighteenth century some quarters were built with brick foundations and chimneys, although earthfast houses remained customary (Fig. 43).[51] By the nineteenth century, earthfast houses seem to have been abandoned throughout the Chesapeake region and replaced by either frame buildings on brick foundations or cribbed log cabins.[52]

A confusion—or perhaps creolization—of styles is apparent, however, in runaway slave John Brown's description of his early nineteenth-century "log cabin" in Southampton County, Virginia: "It had a mud floor; the sides were of wattle and daub and the roof thatched over."[53] Normally, log cabins and wattle and daub houses are mutually exclusive: the former has cribbed horizontal logs for walls, while wattle-and-daub walls are built of upright posts through which

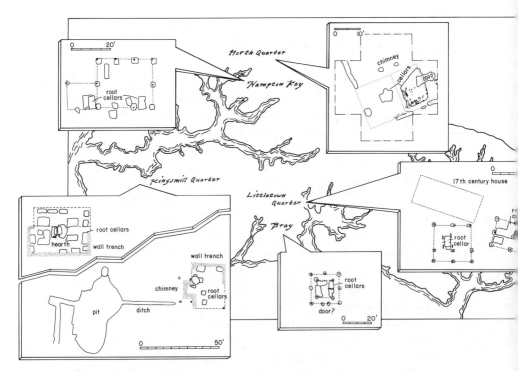

Figure 43. Plans of slave quarters found on the Kingsmill tract near Williamsburg, Virginia (Kelso 1984:103). (Printed with permission of Academic Press, Inc.)

thin sticks or wattle are woven and then plastered with clay daub. The mixture in Brown's account may have been an actual architectural hybrid, or perhaps there was faulty communication between Brown and the British transcriber of his narrative. Whatever, while log cabins were an exclusive European import, West Africans were quite familiar with prepared clay floors, wattle-and-daub walls, and thatched roofs.

Kingsmill's slave quarters varied in shape and size (Appendix 3, Table 5) and differed in construction from both the earthfast houses of the first settlers and the slave houses common in the nineteenth century.[54] The four earthfast houses excavated at Kingsmill were single unit buildings, averaging 308 square feet, similar in size but different in construction from log quarters for slaves from nineteenth-century Maryland and Virginia.[55] Three of the Kingsmill structures apparently had porches, one of which may have extended all the way around the house (Littletown Quarter #1, Fig. 43); the fourth shows signs of the addition of a large room.

Although one Kingsmill house (Hampton Bay) had a single post that might have helped support a stick and clay chimney, excavation revealed no clear evidence of a hearth and chimney for any of the buildings. However, beneath the floorboards of these houses slaves dug pits that Kelso has interpreted as root cellars; plentiful evidence of food storage, preparation, and consumption confirms that these were certainly domestic dwellings.

Dissimilarities between African American earthfast houses and those of white families reflect differences in culture and lifeways. Most earthfast houses belonging to white Virginians were somewhat larger, averaging about 18 feet square. They did not have either porch additions or root cellars, but did have brick or stick and clay chimneys.[56] Porches were rare in seventeenth- and eighteenth-century England; indeed, folklorist John Vlach has argued that American porch architecture stems from African antecedents.[57] The Kingsmill quarters support his contention. Though they looked European in basic design, they were changed and used in ways that suited African styles of living.

The absence of chimneys in the Virginia slave quarters may be another Africanism. Kelso believes the houses had stick and clay chimneys, and he explained his failure to find traces of stick and clay chimney supports, except at Hampton Bay, as a result of poor preservation. Archaeologists in both Virginia and Maryland, however, often find the post foundations of stick and clay chimneys on houses of white residents of the Chesapeake.[58] Another way to account for the complete absence of chimney bases from the earthfast slave houses of Kingsmill would be to assume that slaves cooked outside, an African trait that is substantiated by excavations in South Carolina. If outdoor cooking were the rule, then how do we explain the preponderance of Colono Ware vessels designed for flat hearths and tables? In a stable culture this would be a serious inconsistency, but in settlements undergoing active creolization, as in seventeenth-century Virginia, such variability might well have occurred. Clarifying this apparent inconsistency will require more digging.[59]

Kelso found the most distinctive African American features of the Kingsmill quarters inside the dwellings, underground. Beneath the floor of every slave quarter, he excavated at least one and sometimes several root cellars (Fig. 43). These root cellars were so common that Kelso identifies them as a distinguishing feature of Virginia slave quarters—a way of storing food "perhaps introduced to colonial society by the blacks themselves. The fact that these small pits do not appear on the preslavery sites may be more convincing evidence that they are indeed the product of black culture."[60]

An alternative hypothesis for these pits comes from a nineteenth-century planter who wrote that "Many persons, in building negro houses, in order to get clay convenient for filling the hearth and for mortar, dig a hole under the floor."[61] So, the pits could have remained from construction, adding support to Kelso's suggestion that the houses had stick and clay chimneys; they also could have been dug by slaves for clay to patch cracks around sills and in walls as well as to repair hearths. Regardless of why the pits were originally dug, how they were subsequently used is important. Within the pits Kelso found coins, usable tools, imported ceramics, and discarded food bones. Finds of such valuable items led him to conclude that "the earthen pits below the floorboards in the quarters played a vital role in a master-slave 'sharing system'."[62] Thus, beneath the English-style architecture of the Kingsmill quarters, African American slaves found a way to assert their culture, as well as supplement their rations.

In clay bowls and root cellars archaeologists see evidence of distinctive African American traits in the material world of Virginia slaves. Though subjugated by European culture, Africans and American Indians left their mark on colonial Virginia. The technology and probably the patterns of use of Colono Ware are non-European; features and usage of slave houses show subtle traces of an African past.

In future research, our knowledge of African American lifeways in the Tidewater region may be significantly expanded by excavating the camps and villages of maroons, that is runaway slaves. As a graduate student at the University of South Carolina, Elaine Nichols initiated this pioneering work with her discovery of a maroon site on Culpepper Island in the Great Dismal Swamp, located along the border of Virginia and North Carolina. As more such sites are found and excavated, we should begin to see beyond the subtle features of African

American architecture and lifeways on plantations to the homes that self-emancipated slaves built for themselves in their sanctuaries.[63]

## LOWCOUNTRY RICE PLANTATIONS

If history and demography assured that white culture would dominate the process of creolization in Virginia, the opposite was true in colonial Carolina. As Swiss immigrant Samuel Dyssli remarked in 1737, "Carolina looks more like a negro country than a country settled by white people" (Fig. 44).[64]

By 1700 the total population of the Carolina colony, founded in 1670, numbered only 7,000 people, of whom nearly half were slaves (Fig. 31). At the same time the Virginia population exceeded 50,000, including 10,000 slaves. Thus, though numerically smaller, the slave population of Carolina was proportionally much larger than that of Virginia, and this remained so throughout the eighteenth century.[65]

Carolina's pattern of settlement was also quite different from Virginia's. In Virginia, white pioneers established family farms, some of which later became plantations. In contrast, a large portion of Carolina's early immigrants were black. Many of the colony's founders were expatriate planters from Barbados,

Figure 44. An African American wedding in the South Carolina lowcountry, late eighteenth century. (Abby Aldrich Folk Art Center, Williamsburg, Virginia)

granted land by eight aristocratic proprietors whose main motive was profit. In place of family farms worked by indentured servants, Carolina's founders envisioned large-scale commercial plantations, endeavors fitting archaeologist Theresa Singleton's definition of a plantation as an "agricultural enterprise where workers of a subordinate class work together to produce a crop for someone else to be sold in a market, usually an international one."[66] Indeed, Barbadian planters brought their "subordinate class" with them to help open Carolina for international business.[67]

White settlers regarded the large southern Indian population, struggling in the grip of European colonialism, as an exploitable resource. They initiated an aggressive and lucrative trade with the natives for furs and skins, primarily deer skins. To expand this business into Virginia's trading territory and the Spanish mission realm, they encouraged internecine warfare among various southeastern tribes, and between 1700 and 1715 the Carolinians themselves fought three Indian wars rooted in commercial competition, colonial expansion, and international rivalry.[68] By selling Indians captured in these wars, several prominent Carolinians inaugurated profitable careers as slavers. According to historian Robert Weir, "South Carolinians were *the* Indian slave traders of North America."[69] Some Indian slaves were kept in Carolina to toil with blacks on local plantations, while thousands were sent to the West Indies to work and die on British sugar plantations.

Besides trading in slaves and skins, enterprising colonists employed their slaves in gathering naval stores from the pine forests, herding cattle on the natural savannas, and experimenting with various row crops. The most successful of these experimental crops was rice, most likely introduced from Africa in the 1690s.[70] Rice thrived in the warm, wet soils of the lowcountry. To expand its cultivation, planters stepped up their demand for slaves; both importations from Africa and raids on Indian villages increased. In the first decade of the eighteenth century, mission Indians on the Spanish borderlands in Florida felt the brunt of Carolina's craving for slaves. By 1710, slaves had become a majority of the colony's population, numbering 5,500, almost a third of them Indian. Between 1710 and 1715, wars with the Tuscaroras in North Carolina and the Yamassees at home contributed to the rising slave population and, together with disease, to the near annihilation of free Indian people in coastal Carolina.[71]

With the decline of the native population and the continuing success of rice plantations, the number of imported Africans grew rapidly. Indian slaves soon became physically and culturally integrated with the larger population of blacks, and from at least 1720 on, an African American majority prevailed in colonial South Carolina. Remarking on the strength of this African American slave presence, geographer D. W. Meinig recently observed that "the Low Country was becoming culturally and demographically a true African American region."[72]

Under frontier conditions, white Carolinians may have held the balance of political power, but black and Indian slaves possessed essential practical knowledge. Accustomed to heat, humidity, and luxuriant vegetation, many Africans would have found this subtropical part of America immediately familiar. Native Americans, of course, knew the Carolina environment intimately. Both were skilled at farming, hunting, fishing, and gathering. The chief domestic crops of the colony came from Native American and African agricultural traditions—corn, beans, and squash from America; rice, okra, and cow peas from Africa. Africans also grew indigo in their homeland long before their masters discovered its value as a cash crop. Besides providing skills as cultivators, slaves knew how to build earth-walled houses, carve canoes from cypress trees, make baskets, gather herbs for healing, and turn clay into pots. In the wilderness of America, African and Native American slaves were versatile pioneers and contributed materially to the economic success of the colony.

Slaves arrived from Africa with expertise in common skills like cooking and house building as well as more specialized crafts such as blacksmithing and woodworking. In 1765, South Carolinian Henry Laurens sent an African slave "reputed to be a blacksmith" to the governor of East Florida. Historian Peter Wood concludes that "Negroes shared and even dominated the cooper's art in South Carolina from the very beginning." Critically important to a colony where rice became the primary cash crop were African slaves from groups such as the "Malinke, Soninke, Serer, Joola, Balante, Kisi, Papel, Baga, Mende, Temme," people who historian Daniel Littlefield says were "conversant with numerous varieties of rice, both African and Asian, and with various methods of rice cultivation."[73]

In the nineteenth and twentieth centuries, planter-historians revised the pioneering past by diminishing the importance of skilled slaves and glorifying the role of the masters. Writing in the 1930s David Doar, one of the last Santee Delta rice planters, expressed awe and admiration for his forebears:

> As one views [banked and drained rice fields], he is amazed to learn that all of this was accomplished in the face of seemingly insuperable difficulties by every-day planters who had as tools only the axe, the spade and the hoe, in the hands of intractable negro men and women, but lately brought from the jungles of Africa.[74]

Doar also was impressed by the high-quality provisioning, health care, and religious ministrations provided slaves. He remembers the quarters as a street of sturdy six-room double-houses, each occupied by two families:

> The negro houses or quarters were generally built some distance from the planter's dwelling. They were double houses with a chimney in the center. In each half of the house were two sleeping and one living room and each house was occupied by two families. On some plantations the dwellings were single, and in any case they were built in rows with streets between. While they had no glazed windows they were comfortable, sometimes boarded up and shingled over the weather boarding. [75]

David Doar based his image of plantations, slaves, and slave quarters on the antebellum South of his parents' generation and their perceptions. By their era, the critical role of slaves in Carolina's frontier beginning, had been suppressed. Although Doar had a sort of nostalgic appreciation for African Americans who were "good handcraftsmen,"[76] by his generation stories of old-time slaves who built their own houses, found their own food, and taught their owners about growing corn, sweet potatoes, and money-making rice had passed out of the oral tradition. The houses of these African pioneers had fallen down, their skills had been demeaned, and their story had been forgotten; but their archaeological remains awaited discovery.

# Chapter 3

# CAROLINA'S AFRICAN AMERICAN MAJORITY

## GROUND HOUSES

Except for a few years after 1790, African Americans formed the majority of South Carolina's population from the early eighteenth century through 1922, when opportunities in northern cities began turning the balance.[1] No wonder then, when archaeologists began federally required excavation to mitigate the damage from various kinds of development they discovered African American sites almost every time they put their shovels in the ground. In South Carolina, more than in any state along the south Atlantic Coast, archaeologists have found reflections of Africa in early America.

In the mid-1970s, archaeologists working on colonial slave sites still had in mind the popular vision of little frame or log cabins, but in the lowcountry they encountered something quite different. Excavating at Yaughan and Curriboo, neighboring eighteenth-century plantations on the Santee River, Patrick Garrow and Thomas Wheaton found slave houses that resembled neither the log or frame cabins of the nineteenth century nor the earthfast houses of colonial Virginia.[2] Through archaeology they were looking into the dim past, before the glory days of the antebellum plantations, and in their digging they disclosed African-style, clay-walled houses.

The earliest of these houses (Appendix 3, Table 6), dating from the

**63**

mid-1700s, were narrow, single- and double-unit buildings without chimneys (Figs. 45–48). Trenches were dug into the ground to hold the foundations; then, according to the excavators, courses of clay reinforced with upright posts were laid in the bottom of the trenches and built to the desired height of the wall plate. An alternative interpretation has been offered by archaeologist Natalie Adams who argues that thin sticks called wattle were woven into the upright posts and then plastered with clay to produce "wattle-and-daub" walls.[3] Whichever, both interpretations describe clay walls similar to those built in Africa.

Near the houses archaeologists found several large pits dug deeply into the clay subsoil; these pits, later filled with trash, no doubt were used originally for extracting building clay. After removing the loamy topsoil, slaves probably loosened the clay subsoil with digging sticks or hoes, added water and mixed the clay with their hands and feet while standing in the pits. Then, taking moist lumps of clay from the pits, they either "daubed," that is, plastered, the woven wattle, or they built walls by laying lumps of clay like courses of bricks, a method common in West Africa and known as "cob walling."[4]

Through the last half of the eighteenth century, building foundations at

Figure 45. Excavated foundation of a clay-walled house at Curriboo Plantation, Berkeley County, South Carolina (Wheaton et al. 1983:156).

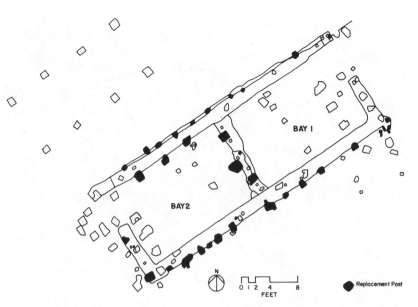

Figure 46. Foundation plan of a clay-walled house showing replacement posts; also shows adjacent structure. Curriboo Plantation, Berkeley County, South Carolina (adapted from Wheaton et al. 1983:169).

Figure 47. Archaeologist's conception of middle eighteenth-century slave house at Curriboo Plantation, Berkeley County, South Carolina (adapted from Wheaton and Garrow 1985:248).

Figure 48. Nineteenth-century Jamaican house similar to houses excavated in colonial South Carolina. (Courtesy of National Library of Jamaica)

Yaughan changed from wall trenches with posts set in the trenches to individual holes for posts (Fig. 49); and if walls had been cobbed with reinforcing posts, they probably changed to either wattle-and-daub or planking. The narrowly spaced wall plates presumably supported steep roofs with either gabled or hipped ends, covered by bark, split planks or, more likely, thatching (Figs. 50–52). In 1740 a school teacher at Yeomans Hall Plantation referred in his diary to "covering the old store with bark";[5] and split plank or shingle roofs were commonly used in the eighteenth century. However, the wall spacing suggests thatching: thatched roofs are most efficient when they are steep—water doesn't seep in through the thatching—and narrowly spaced walls reduce the required height of these roofs. In a 1763 letter, Henry Laurens cautioned his business partner about a "thatch'd House too near our Rice Store" on the Cooper River;[6] and outbuildings on St. Helena Island continued to be thatched with palmetto fronds well into the twentieth century (Figs. 50 and 51).[7]

Excavations at the Yaughan and Curriboo slave quarters were salvage projects conducted alongside clearing and earthmoving for a federally funded canal. Time constraints required that the archaeologists quickly strip the topsoil with heavy equipment and get to the job of excavating house foundations and other

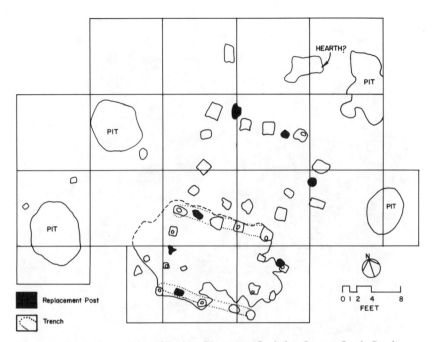

Figure 49. Post structure from Yaughan Plantation, Berkeley County, South Carolina (adapted from Wheaton et al. 1983:106).

features beneath. As a result of this rush, much information—such as clear-cut evidence of hearths and earthen house floors—was lost. Nevertheless, the archaeologists who excavated the sites believe that floors were bare dirt, and there was some evidence of an open hearth directly on the earthen floor in one of the buildings.[8]

The bottom of another hearth was found outside the houses, and the excavating archaeologists concluded that cooking was likely done on "exterior hearths, possibly only a few stones to set a pot on."[9] Over time, however, indoor hearths came to be used; the two latest buildings at Yaughan appear to have had stick and clay chimneys (Fig. 49). Project archaeologists interpreted post holes at one end of these houses as the supports for "porches" or "stoops,"[10] but after comparing these post patterns with the chimney bases on earthfast houses from the Chesapeake, I believe these two buildings had stick and clay chimneys.[11] These later buildings are similar to a supposed late eighteenth-century slave dwelling excavated farther up the Santee River at the Spiers Landing site. With its stick and clay chimney, raised floor and root cellar, the Spiers Landing structure is akin to those found by Kelso at Kingsmill (Fig. 53).[12] Thus, by 1800

Figure 50. Palmetto thatching on an early twentieth-century outbuilding, St. Helena Island, South Carolina. In the foreground, Mrs. Rebeccah Green winnows rice using a coiled "fanner" basket (see Dabbs 1970). (From the Penn School Collection, permission granted by Penn Center, St. Helena Island, South Carolina)

African American houses appear to have evolved from African-style structures to houses with some European features; nevertheless, dwellings continued to be small with most activities taking place in the yard—distinctive West African traits.

The clay-walled houses at Yaughan and Curriboo represent an aspect of

Figure 51. Animal shed thatched with palmetto fronds, St. Helena Island, South Carolina, twentieth century (WPA 1938:12).

African life not usually appreciated in the United States: the advantage of earthen-walled houses. Recently, while browsing in a large university bookstore, I watched a man casually pick up a book on African architecture. Perusing the cover, he murmured to his companion, "Hmmm—African architecture; if I'm not mistaken that's nothing but mud huts." Of course he was wrong; African architecture is highly variable and splendidly adaptive. From the brush shelters of the Kalihari Desert to the wooden palaces of Nigeria to the stone monuments of Egypt, African construction suits the physical and social needs of indigenous populations. In many places in Africa, clay walls, dirt floors, and thatched roofs served the people's needs for shelter, but to dismiss these dwellings as "nothing but mud huts" reflects an attitude rooted in the racial bigotry of the past and perpetuated by our ethnocentrism.

Ethnocentrism is a common, if dangerous, part of all culture. White America's cultural tradition is derived primarily from Britain and northern Europe, where cold weather encouraged people to live inside their houses. Our modern addiction to central heat and air conditioning has reinforced the tendency to think of living *in* our houses. In contrast, in much of Africa and other tropical and subtropical regions, people live *around* their houses as much as in them. In these regions, houses are used primarily for sleeping, storage, and shelter

Figure 52. Plank roof on a house with stick and clay chimney, St. Helena Island, South Carolina, 1909. In the foreground, Alfred Graham, an ex-slave and African, sews a coiled basket with his grandson at his knee (see Dabbs 1970). (From the Penn School Collection, permission granted by Penn Center, St. Helena Island, South Carolina)

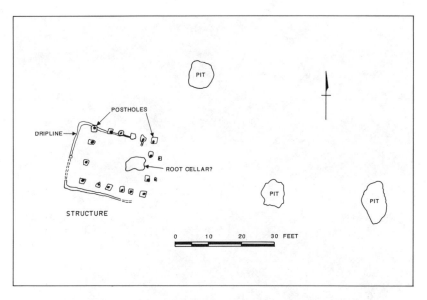

Figure 53. Plan of house excavated at the Spiers Landing site, Berkeley County, South Carolina (adapted from Drucker and Anthony 1979:91).

during short periods of inclement weather; working, cooking, eating, and socializing take place outside.

This pattern of living becomes real for students and for me when we're conducting fieldwork in the South Carolina lowcountry (Fig. 54). Indeed, the experience is shared by backpackers and campers all over America. On archaeological sites, we usually sleep in small tents and have a larger tent, a house, or a trailer for cooking and storing equipment. Through the day we work outside, then in the evening we eat and relax under giant live oak trees. Here tents become extensions of sleeping bags, and the open area around our tents and cooking quarters becomes our living room. Only mosquitoes and thunderstorms drive us inside. Thus, for a little while in the summer, we shift to a different style of life, away from rooms and roofs, and spend most of our time outdoors, as do many, perhaps most, of the people in the world. Usually, neither the students nor I want to leave.

People find many advantages to thatched and clay-walled houses. First, they can be built quickly using materials almost universally available, even in regions of severe deforestation. When circumstances call for families or villages to move, earthen houses can be left behind without great loss, and in the face of

Figure 54. Archaeology students excavating an early African American house on Middleburg Plantation, East Branch Cooper River, South Carolina. (Photograph by the author)

destructive disasters like storms or fire, they can be readily rebuilt. Houses infested with vermin might be intentionally burned.

Besides the relative ease with which they may be built and re-built, clay houses are also comfortable in hot climates. Earthen floors, thick insulating walls, and dark enclosed rooms trap the cool night air and guard against the penetrating midday sun. The smoke from small fires drives away mosquitoes, and when it is cold a well-stoked, centrally located hearth, radiating heat in every direction, can warm the whole house. Cooking fires might be brought inside on cold or rainy days and their coals and ashes literally swept out the door to provide more room when the weather improves. The early houses at Yaughan and Curriboo—small, earth-walled structures without formal fireplaces—exemplify this tropical technology as practiced in North America.

Colonial slave houses were in general small with only one or two rooms; in South Carolina rooms tended to be smaller than in Virginia where room size averaged 365 square feet. Of twenty rooms excavated in eighteenth-century

South Carolina slave houses (Fig. 55), the average room size is 209 square feet, much closer to the 10 by 10 foot size commonly considered by American folklorists to be the West African norm. Perhaps the small room size in many later nineteenth- and twentieth-century African American houses continues an African tradition in African American architecture.[13]

The shape of South Carolina houses also seems similar to those in Africa. Along the West African coast, the most common house is one with a gabled roof and a rectangular floor plan that is often divided into two chambers.[14] We believe the South Carolina houses had gabled roofs, and when room units were joined in double or multiple room houses at Yaughan and Curriboo, they were placed end-to-end like dominoes, in the customary West African pattern (Fig. 56). On the other hand, the small number of extant eighteenth-century slave houses in Virginia and neighboring Maryland, where relatively fewer blacks lived in more intimate contact with whites, were more like European American houses in both size and shape. Thus, while the archaeological and historical evidence from slave cabins in the tobacco colonies reveals similarities to European American houses in overall size and shape, archaeological sites in South Carolina show evidence of African-style architecture. Careful scrutiny of the documentary record supports this conclusion.

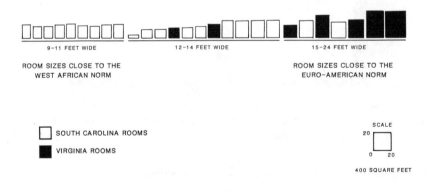

"ROOMS IN ANGLO-AMERICAN BUILDINGS AVERAGE BETWEEN 16x16 FEET AND 18x18 FEET, CONSIDERABLY LARGER THAN THE 10x10 FOOT AFRICAN NORM"[1]

9–11 FEET WIDE  12–14 FEET WIDE  15–24 FEET WIDE

ROOM SIZES CLOSE TO THE WEST AFRICAN NORM

ROOM SIZES CLOSE TO THE EURO-AMERICAN NORM

SOUTH CAROLINA ROOMS

VIRGINIA ROOMS

SCALE

20

0    20

400 SQUARE FEET

1. VLACH 1978: 124, 133

Figure 55. Room dimensions of African American houses, 1750–1800. (Illustration by Alexander West and Richard Affleck)

Figure 56. Earthen-walled houses in Nigeria typically have small rooms, rectangular plans, and clay walls similar to those found in colonial Carolina (Vlach 1978, figs. 67–68, with permission of the author).

Black men and women on the Georgia coast in the 1930s, just one generation removed from slavery, reflected that their grandparents lived in small, thatched, clay-walled houses—in both Africa and America. Shad Hall of Sapelo Island, Georgia, for example, remembered his grandmother's description of her house in Africa: "It was covered with palmetto and grass for the roof, and the walls were made of mud. They made the walls by taking up handfuls of mud and putting it on something firm, sticks put crossways so."[15]

Hall's neighbor Ben Sullivan, recalling his African-born grandmother Hettie, told WPA interviewers that "she said that in Africa she lived in a 'ground house.'"[16] The term "ground house" may have reflected Hettie's unfamiliarity with the English word for clay, but no doubt she remembered how such houses were built.

In nineteenth-century Georgia, according to Ben Sullivan's testimony, the desire to build a place like he had in African could put a slave in direct conflict with his master's view of things.

> Old man Okra said he wanted a place like he had in Africa, so he built himself a hut. I remember it well. It was about 12 by 14 feet, it had a dirt floor, and he built the sides like a woven basket with clay plaster on it. It had a flat roof that he made from brush and palmetto, and it had one door and no windows. But Master made him pull it down. He said he didn't want an African hut on his place.[17]

As late as 1907, a scholar photographed an African-style house in Edgefield County, South Carolina, that belonged to Tahro, a native Bakongo, one of the last slaves imported into the United States (Fig. 57).[18] This small house has narrowly spaced walls supporting a thatched roof and siding tied to upright posts. Except for the absence of clay plaster on the walls, Tahro's house is probably similar to one of the smaller one-roomed houses excavated at Yaughan.

An in-depth study of African contributions to North American architecture is long overdue. Besides the general neglect accorded African American studies in the past, this aspect of architectural history has suffered from particular misunderstandings. During the early twentieth century many scholars subscribed to the theory that slaves had completely lost their African culture. Eager to sever the connection between "acculturated" African Americans and the perceived "barbarism" of Africa, this view was supported by progressive scholars and Christian missionaries who overlooked or even suppressed African traits.[19] More recently, images like that of Okra's master exerting his authority may have reinforced the notion that African architecture was regularly destroyed; perhaps this perception has stymied research.

It is true that, in their efforts to dominate slaves and appease abolitionists, some nineteenth-century planters tried to erase African features, making their plantations conform to an "Anglo" ideal. But, in the pioneering days of the previous century, planters and overseers probably appreciated and encouraged

traditional African architectural skills. For example, an eighteenth-century Virginia planter advertised for a slave who "underst[ood] building clay walls. . .an Artist not a common Labourer";[20] and in 1819 Abriel Abbott, an English visitor to South Carolina, described a "servant building a house for himself in the style of an English cottage. The walls are formed with mud filled with straw."[21] True, this basic building technique was well-known in England and other parts of Europe, and it was used by early white settlers. Nevertheless, archaeologist William Kelso has written that "it is logical to assume that native Indians had a great deal of influence" on the early huts built by Anglo Americans on the Georgia coast, where slavery was illegal until 1750.[22] Given the demography of eighteenth-century Carolina, it is just as likely that construction skills and building design for slave quarters came from Africa, or perhaps Native America, as from Britain or Europe.

My colleague, Carl Steen, found an intriguing remark about clay-walled houses in a letter from a Revolutionary War partisan General Francis Marion to General Nathanael Greene. Describing the battle at Quinby Bridge north of Charleston, the Swamp Fox reported that General Sumter "Determined to Attack the Enemy posted in houses with Clay Walls which was very Difficult to penetrate without a field piece."[23] Steen and I agreed that the British soldiers must have been sheltered in the slave quarters of adjacent Quinby Plantation and that those quarters were built with clay walls (Fig. 58). Encouraged by this tidbit, I began searching for other references and soon came across two which left no doubt about the precedence of clay-walled houses over other forms of slave dwellings in South Carolina.

Jake McLeod was born in slavery about 1854 on a plantation near Lynches River in the coastal plain. He told interviewers, "My boss had four slave houses that were three or four hundred yards from his house, and I reckon he had about twenty-five slaves. One was a pole house [log cabin] with a brick chimney, and two rooms partitioned off; and the other two were clay houses." He went on to say that "they used to carry those with small pox by the swamp and build a dirt house for them."[24] Since McLeod would have been six years old in 1860, these earth-walled houses must have been standing in the late 1850s or during the Civil War. The sick house was probably similar to the semisubterranean "dugouts" used by early European settlers, while the clay houses were probably built with cob or wattle-and-daub walls.[25]

---

Figure 57. House built by Tahro, an African, in Edgefield County, South Carolina, 1907 (after Montgomery 1908, plates 42–43).

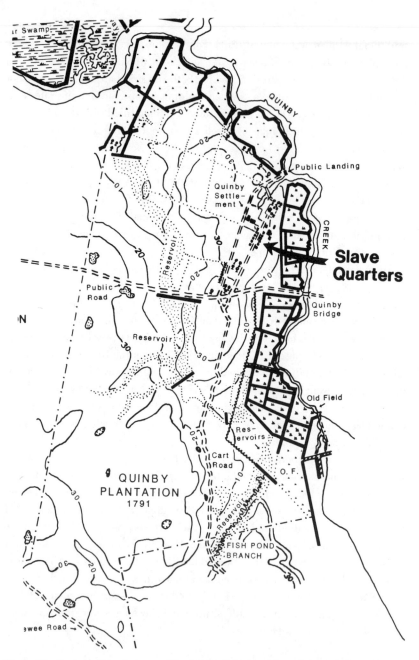

Figure 58. During a Revolutionary War battle, British soldiers defended themselves "in houses with clay walls," probably the line of slave quarters shown on this copy of a 1791 map of Quinby Plantation, South Carolina. (Cartography by David W. Babson)

The high frequency of descriptions of log cabins and frame houses in the narratives of other ex-slaves suggests that the "clay houses" mentioned by McLeod were rare in the mid-nineteenth century; a generation earlier, however, that was apparently not the case. In 1822 Robert J. Turnbull, a wealthy and prominent planter, penned a response to abolitionists in a volume entitled *A Refutation of the Calumnies*. Concerning the housing of lowcountry slaves, Turnbull said:

> Their dwellings consist of good clay cabins, with clay chimneys, but so much attention has been paid of late years to their comfort in this particu-lar, that it is now very common, particularly on the Sea Islands, to give them substantial frame houses on brick foundations and with brick chimneys. Many are of opinion that they enjoy more health in open tempo-rary cabins with ground or dirt floors. But this does not correspond with the experience of those who willingly incur the expense of better buildings.[26]

Reading this I looked carefully at my copy of the famous painting of slave quarters at Mulberry Plantation on the Cooper River (Fig. 59), and suddenly realized that the red-tinted walls and high pitched roofs of these slave quarters might represent clay-walled, thatched houses.

Figure 59. Painting of slave houses on Mulberry Plantation (1769–1811), West Branch Cooper River, South Carolina. (The Gibbes Museum of Art/Carolina Art As-sociation; Thomas Coram, *View of Mulberry [House and Street]*, oil on paper, 10 by 17.6 cm)

Turnbull distinguished between clay houses with clay chimneys and "open temporary cabins." The "open temporary cabins" may have been houses without doors and raised floors or they may have been open houses similar to eighteenth-century Creek Indian structures (Fig. 60) or to the more recent "chickees" of the Seminoles.[27] West African archaeologist Merrick Posnansky reports that in Ghana farmers often build low, open sheds with gabled roofs near their fields;[28] and a nineteenth-century Florida slaveholder wrote that "The dwellings of the slaves were palmetto huts, built by themselves of stakes and poles, thatched with palmetto leaf"[29] (see Fig. 51).

Another type of slave dwelling was observed by Carl Bauer, a Hessian soldier, during the Revolution: "Their quarters consist of miserable huts of beams piled on one another, in which there is neither chimney nor hearth."[30] Bauer noted that an iron pot stood "in the middle of the hut by the fire," but apparently he did not consider this a "hearth" in the European sense—that is, a fireplace vented by a chimney. Still, his description helps us picture the variety of slave

Figure 60. Open temporary structure with bark roof being used by Creek or Yuchi Indians on the border between South Carolina and Georgia, 1736. Present-day farmers in Ghana and other regions of Africa build similar structures, and slaves may have lived in such shelters in the eighteenth century (see Hvidt 1980). (Courtesy of the Royal Library, Copenhagen, Manuscript NKS 565, 40)

houses in colonial Carolina—open temporary cabins, clay walls, cribbed log walls, stick and clay chimneys, hearths in the middle of the floors—African and Indian traits combined with European elements in a new kind of architecture.

Later in the nineteenth century, abolitionists became vocally critical of the living conditions of slaves, especially their quarters. Sarah Grimke characterized South Carolina slaves as "wretchedly sheltered and lodged."[31] Citing reports from observers in the South, she described small, single-unit houses ranging from 12 to 14 feet square. Some were built of logs while others were "erected with posts and crotches" and covered with "coarse" boards. Most had dirt floors, and single openings that "serve[d] both for doors and windows." Some log houses had stick and clay chimneys, while in others the fire was built at one end of the floor or "made in the middle of the hut" with a "hole in the roof" or a "board or two off at the side" to let out the smoke. Grimke quoted Reuben L. Macy, a Quaker who lived in South Carolina in 1818 and 1819: "The houses for the field slaves were about 14 feet square, built in the coarsest manner, with one room, without any chimney or flooring, with a hole in the roof to let the smoke out."

Grimke regarded these houses as unfit for human habitation, and they may have been, but perhaps not for the reasons she thought. The field slave quarters Macy observed may have reflected African preferences in house design. No doubt many slaves suffered because they couldn't situate their houses where they wanted or because they didn't have sufficient time and materials to build and adequately maintain their houses, but they didn't suffer simply because dwellings did not resemble European American-style cottages.

Contrary to Grimke's view, slaves may have been doing the best they could in creating housing that combined their diverse African and Indian heritage with newly acquired ideas from Europeans. Log construction and roof planking likely were introduced by Europeans and willingly adopted by African Americans. Log cabins would have weathered the wet Southern winters better than clay houses; roof planking would certainly have lasted longer than thatching. On the other hand, slaves resisted some European practices. Ex-slave Charles Ball recounted that, "The native Africans. . .generally place little or even no value upon the fine houses. . .of their masters."[32] The penchant for living outside and having small houses with dirt floors, central fires, and few openings was part of the African architectural vocabulary. One planter admitted that "weatherboarded cabins are objectionable as being warmer in summer. . .and colder in winter" than log cabins.[33] Small rooms with central fireplaces on dirt floors may also have been warmer than the drafty raised floors and wall-end fireplaces built by whites. Small communal rooms and outdoor living fit the social needs of people who were not cast in the individualistic mold of the Renaissance and Enlightenment.

Ironically, some of the obvious European features of nineteenth-century slave architecture—frame houses, raised floors, and wall-end fireplaces—may have been forced on slaves by planters responding to abolitionists who abhorred the state of "savagery" in which black people lived. By making these changes planters could not only quell abolitionists' complaints but also reinforce their dominance.


## MAKING MOSOJO

> . . .my grandmother came by the Bahamas. She spoke funny words we didn't know. She would say 'mosojo' and sometimes 'sojo' when she meant pot. For water she would say 'deloe' and for fire she said 'diffy.' She would tell us, 'take sojo off diffy.'[34]

Calling pots "mosojo" or "sojo," Katie Brown's grandmother came to the Georgia coast sometime in the nineteenth century. A late arrival (the American slave trade officially ended in 1808), she is more representative of Africans debarking a century earlier than of those born in America. Whether slaves were "seasoned" in the West Indies, brought directly from Africa, or captured at the mission towns in Spanish Florida, once in Carolina they began exchanging not only words but also foods, crafts, and other traditional lifeways. Studying the Colono Ware found by archaeologists in South Carolina helps us distinguish the material components of that shared culture.

In his excavations of the original 1670 English settlement of Charles Towne, Stanley South found two kinds of Colono Ware: pottery from a nearby Indian ceremonial center and other pieces from within Charles Towne itself.[35] From the Indian ceremonial center site, abandoned a few years before English settlement, South recovered pieces of complicated stamped jars and burnished bowls typical of coastal Indian ware. Within the ditch of the defensive earthworks bordering the town, he found something different—plain pottery most likely made by blacks who had recently come from slave villages on Barbados or other islands in the British West Indies. South's excavation revealed the dual roots of eighteenth-century Colono Ware in Carolina.

As might be expected, given the large number of Indian slaves in early Carolina, much of the earliest Colono Ware found by archaeologists is similar to pottery made by free Indians. Although little archaeology has been conducted on these early sites, certain Indian styles—like painting and complicated stamping—stand out from the plainer features of later artifacts. From plantations along the rivers and sea islands as well as from the peninsula of Charleston, pieces of Indian-style Colono Ware have been recovered (Fig. 61). Considerable Indian-style pottery was found in the charred remains of the "big house" at Newington Plantation, on the Ashley River west of Charleston, which burned in 1715. Within a ground-floor hearth of this house, archaeologist Richard Polhemus recovered the lower half of a round-bottomed pot with a

Figure 61. Painted and check-stamped pottery from colonial South Carolina. (Photograph by Emily Short)

roughened surface. The surface was charred, showing that the pot was used for cooking, perhaps by an Indian slave.

Predominating the early Indian-style earthenware from Carolina sites are bowls with red painting and complicated or check stamping similar to artifacts found on the Spanish missions of the Georgia coast and in St. Augustine. However, although the artifacts from Newington and other sites show that such pots were used in Carolina, even in the kitchens of white households, these Indian-style pots were not as common as they were in Florida. Through time, the frequency of traditional Indian ceramics in Carolina diminished, and as the population of African slaves grew in the second quarter of the eighteenth century, small plain bowls and jars came to dominate plantation assemblages (Figs. 62 and 63). We do know, from archaeological excavations, that a great deal of handbuilt, low-fired pottery was made on plantations where the overwhelming majority of people were African American.

The most obvious evidence that pottery was made on plantations in South Carolina is the sheer quantity of artifacts found on these sites. The fact that hundreds of people who were capable of making pottery lived in just the location where it is abundantly found argues for their making it. Oral accounts from former slaves of pots their forebears built, makes a firmer case. The archaeological evidence from South Carolina is, however, even more direct. Lowcountry plantation pottery exhibits all the archaeological criteria for on-site manufacture: spall fractures, poorly built and fired vessels, toys, as well as use of local materials.

A teapot from Hampton Plantation that broke while being fired provides a good example of a spall fracture (Fig. 64). Perhaps the vessel fractured because the potter was not familiar with the imported clay. During firing large spalls broke away from the walls of the little pot. As firing continued, a portion of the newly exposed clay as well as the burnished surface of the vessel were darkened by a continuous firing cloud, showing that the spall came off during initial firing. Carefully examining the pot for evidence of use, I could find none—no wear on the base, no polishing on the handle and, most conclusively, no dark tea stain on the porous interior of the vessel. This teapot was a "waster," probably made and fired only a few feet from where the archaeologists uncovered it. Associated with it in the pit was a charred round-bottomed cooking pot, illustrating that while the teapot spalled and broke during firing, other vessels built at the site proved more useful. Although most of the Colono Ware from Hampton appeared to have been made from local clays, the light, buff-colored clay used for the teapot, according to the archaeologists' field report, "appears to be from outside the Hampton area and may have been intended to resemble

Figure 62. Vessels from the sites of Curriboo *(above)*
and Yaughan *(below)* Plantations, Berkeley County,
South Carolina. (Photograph by the author)

creamware or white stoneware."[36] Regardless of the clay source, fracture patterns show that the pot was fired at Hampton.

Distinctive spalling breaks often show up on pots from other South Carolina plantation sites.[37] Nine of sixty-seven specimens in the whole pot collection from the state have spalls, and in three of these cases surface firing clouds extend onto the exposed surface of the fracture (see Fig. 28). Moreover, in every

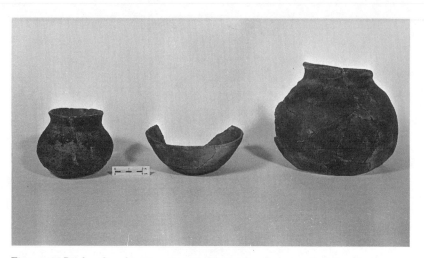

Figure 63. Bowl and cooking jars from the Spiers Landing site, Berkeley County, South Carolina. (Courtesy AF Consultants, Columbia, South Carolina)

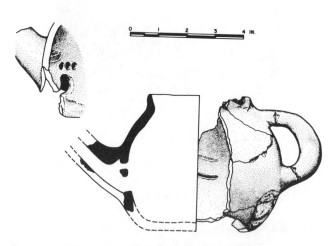

Figure 64. Colono Ware teapot from Hampton Plantation, Charleston County, South Carolina. Notice the spall fracture on the *lower right*. (Drawing courtesy the South Carolina Institute of Archaeology and Anthropology)

case the vessels with spalls come from plantation rather than urban sites, implying that more pottery was made on plantations, where the African American population was proportionally greater, than in cities. Archaeologists also find this spalling more frequently on South Carolina sites than on those in Virginia. From the whole vessel collection, only four or 8 percent of pots from Virginia have spalls, while 13 percent of those from South Carolina show spalling.[38]

Most Colono Ware from South Carolina is well-made, but the occasional example of poorly crafted pottery provides further evidence of plantation manufacture.[39] The broken teapot from Hampton is a case in point; besides being poorly fired, it was not skillfully made. The walls of the pot were nearly twice as thick as the base and this drastic difference in thickness probably caused linear fractures during firing, whereas the spall fractures resulted from incomplete drying or curing. A jar and two bowls from Yaughan also show evidence of poor craftsmanship. The excavating archaeologists reported that the jar "was very friable and crudely made, and it resembled a beginning potter's attempt at a cooking pot";[40] the thin walls and compound shape of the jar (Fig. 62, below) probably caused it to break during firing. The bowls from Yaughan show drastic variations in thickness. Their makers used a knife or similarly sharp tool to carve the outside of bowls to their desired shape (Fig. 65). This technique, shunned by most experienced potters, produced bowls with highly variable wall thickness, vulnerable to firing breakage. Bowls manufactured in this way also have been found at Lesesne Plantation near Charleston[41] and in collections I have examined from the Heyward-Washington House within the city. As in Virginia, these poor quality artifacts are suggestive of the dislocations of slavery and the need for pioneering people to make do with inadequate resources. Together with the much larger number of well-made vessels, however, they also testify to the perseverance and ingenuity of African American culture.

African skills and values continued to be passed down from generation to generation on American plantations. Children imitated their parents in aspects of work and play, including pottery making. Besides imitating their mothers in making real pots, children also apparently made toys—pinch pots, small pans, and funny little figures. Finding these toys in archaeological excavation offers more evidence that pottery was locally made.[42] Excavating the kitchen and grounds of Drayton Hall on the Ashley River, Lynne Lewis uncovered hundreds of pieces of Colono Ware. Most interesting, from my point of view, is a sherd with the incised initials "MHD" (Fig. 66).[43] Mary Henrietta Drayton lived at the plantation from the late 1780s into the 1840s and it seems reasonable to

Figure 65. Poorly crafted bowl (*above*) and sherd (*below*) from Yaughan Plantation, Berkeley County, South Carolina. (Drawing by Ruth Johnson)

speculate that she or one of her black playmates inscribed her initials in the moist clay before this pot was fired.

When slave potters first arrived from Africa, they had no way of knowing where to find choice potting clay in their new environs. In some cases they may have made unsuccessful experiments with local clays before finding the best material. The crude pieces from Pettus and Utopia in Virginia may be examples of such trial and error. But as newly arrived slaves learned about the natural environment, serious potters soon discovered where to find clay for their pots. Indians, both free and slave, probably were an important source of information. Native traditions included knowledge of where and how to find the best earth for making pottery, and no doubt Indian slaves carried this knowledge onto the plantations. Even without access to Indian know-how, however, slaves could have located sources of potting clay. Slaves lived close to the earth; they cleared and farmed plantations where clay was both a building material and a bane of

Figure 66. Colono Ware toys were made on plantations, and this little bowl had the initials MHD inscribed in the base, perhaps for Mary Henrietta Drayton (circa 1780–1840). (Photograph by Emily Short)

existence. Building walls and chimneys required clay. Moving earth to construct banks and canals, planting and hoeing in the rice fields of Carolina, slaves were mired in clay for most of their working lives.[44] Thus, finding the raw materials for making pottery would have presented no problem, and archæologists have reported that the "paste" or clay body of most pottery found on plantations is similar to the local clays.[45]

Yet not all the pottery found on plantation sites was made there; some was surely made in Indian camps and villages. When the estate of Mary Seabrook was sold at Ashley Ferry in 1753 it included a box containing "a few candles, 2 Indian panns, 1 funnell, and 1 equipage."[46] Since Indians made much of the Colono Ware in the early days of the Carolina colony, handbuilt earthenware may have been known generically as "Indian" pottery. Or, this identification may mean that Indians, either free or slave, produced or were thought to have produced the pottery. Archæologists have discovered striking similarities between pottery made by free Indians and a small number of eighteenth- and early nineteenth-century artifacts excavated on Carolina plantations (Fig. 67).[47] Moreover, the ratio of introduced to locally produced pottery changes over time.

From limited excavations of early eighteenth century sites, it appears that at that time a large proportion of Indian-style Colono Ware was being used on plantations. Then, through the remainder of the eighteenth century, and correlating with the rise in the African slave population, the quantity of Colono Ware increased; and it is from this period that we have the best evidence for plantation manufacture. From 1800 to the Civil War, the incidence of Colono Ware drops dramatically.[48] This decrease probably resulted from several factors: the outlawing of the African slave trade, the growing familiarity of African Americans with glazed and highly fired pottery, and the increased availability of industrially manufactured American ceramics.

River Burnished pottery (Fig. 68), a type of Colono Ware believed to have come from itinerant Catawba Indians, begins to show up in the late eighteenth century as a minority type on lowcountry sites. This pottery continued to be made and sold throughout the nineteenth century as plantation-manufactured pottery declined (Fig. 69).[49] Perhaps Catawba Indians, who were outside the mainstream of Carolina's plantation society, found a growing market among traditional cooks as plantation-made pottery began to disappear.

Living along the Santee River in mid-nineteenth century South Carolina, Phillip Porcher, "remembered frequently seeing the Catawba Indians in the days when they travelled down from the up-country to Charleston, making clay ware for the negroes along the way. They would camp until a section was supplied, then move on, till finally Charleston was reached. . . .their ware was decorated with colored sealing wax and was in great demand."[50]

William Gilmore Simms underscored the value placed on Indian pots, "considered by most of the worthy house-wives of the past generation, to be far superior to any other. I remember, for example, that it was a confident faith among the old ladies, that okra soup was always inferior if cooked in any but an Indian pot. . . .Certainly an iron vessel is one of the last which should be employed in the preparation of this truly southern dish."[51] Simms's "old ladies" were in the company of the famous Williamsburg cook Mary Randolph who called for her okra soup to be cooked in an earthenware pipkin and served over rice.[52]

Of course, okra is an African plant and rice was probably introduced to America from that continent, and they were traditionally cooked in earthenware pots; southern recipes for okra soup are clearly products of a creole culture. By now it is well-known that African people brought to America songs, stories, and language from their homelands. They also brought *things* and the ideas for

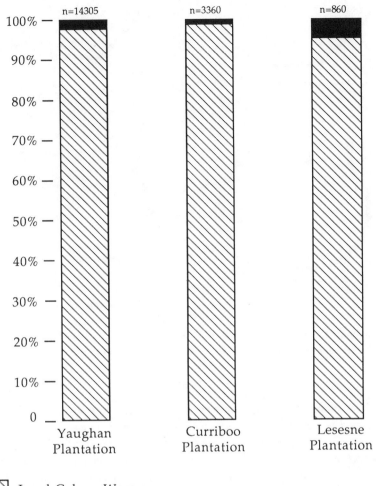

Local Colono Ware

Non-local Colono Ware

n=Total number of sherds

Sources: Yaughan and Curriboo: Wheaton, Friedlander, and Garrow 1983: 98-292;
Lesesne: Zierden, et al. 1986: 7-34.

Figure 67. Local and nonlocal Colono Ware on three South Carolina plantations.

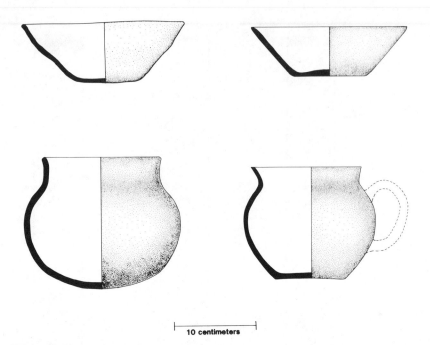

| 10 centimeters |

Figure 68. River Burnished type pottery found in the South Carolina lowcountry was probably made by Catawba Indians. (Drawings by Bobbie May)

making things: beads worn around the waist, prayer mats, baskets, boats, herbal remedies, earthen houses, pottery—the list could go on and on.

One might ask, how could fragile earthenware vessels survive the dangerous middle passage? Among the nearly one-half million people transported on perhaps two thousand ships who made this voyage, it seems likely that some were able, perhaps required, to carry utensils from Africa—gourds for drinking, vessels for holding rice or cooking, pots for urinating or defecating on the ships. People may have stowed away strings of beads, small woven mats or, in archaeologist James Deetz's words, other "small things forgotten." When slaves comprised only part of the cargo, they may have had more freedom of movement. Slaves may have been obliged to work on the ships, to cook, to slaughter and clean animals for food, to perform other routine tasks. Given all of the possibilities, there is reason to suppose that people kept with them some objects from home. These meager possessions, together with their ability to work and their wealth of knowledge—a knowledge that included how to make clay pots and okra soup—comprised the cultural equity of Africans arriving in America.

Figure 69. River Burnished pitcher bought by Samuel Cordes of St. Stephens, Berkeley County, South Carolina, from itinerant Catawba Indians in 1805. (Courtesy of the Charleston Museum, Charleston, South Carolina)

## FOOD FOR NYAM

"Nyam," the Gullah word for "eat," was common among the creole languages of both America and the west coast of Africa.[53] Of all the European and African words that meant the same thing, one African word, "nyam," came to stand for the basic human need for nourishment. Ninety-two-year-old Susan Maxwell, of Possum Point community on the Georgia coast, recalled that African slave Primus O'Neal would say "let me cook something for nyam" when he wanted to eat.[54] In colonial times—one or two generations before Primus O'Neal—slave foodways included many African and Native American "ingredients" that nourished a distinctive African American culinary style as well as the bodies of early African Americans.

Rice and corn, mainstays of early South Carolina economy and diet, were respectively, traditional African and Native American crops, both readily adopted by planter families. In 1758 Liza Pinckney wrote to a friend in England, "I have sent a large barrel of rice. . . .The children love it boiled dry to eat with their meat instead of bread."[55] Not only rice but sorghum also was brought from Africa to Carolina. In 1731 naturalist Mark Catesby commented that, sorghum "was first introduced from Africa by the Negroes." He described the grain as "Bunched Guinea Corn. . . being grown chiefly by Negroes, who make bread of it, and boil it in like manner of furmety"—a British dish prepared by boiling hulled wheat in milk.[56]

Sorghum bread probably was baked as pones on a flat griddle or in a covered pot while the boiled meal most likely was prepared in an iron or earthenware pot. Shad Hall recollected a recipe for boiled grain cakes that his African grandmother Hester used. She "made strange cake for us every month. She called it 'saraka.' She would make it out of meal and honey. She put meal in boiling water and took it right out. Then she would mix it with honey and make it in flat cakes. Sometimes she made it out of rice."[57]

Most West Africans ate little meat. In recent times as well as in the past, the common African meal consists of a starch such as rice, millet, or manioc served with a vegetable-based sauce or relish. These side dishes are made from boiled leafy and pulpy vegetables, mashed to a saucelike consistency. Vegetables and spices include beans, cowpeas, okra, eggplant, tamarind, baobab, onions, peanuts, sesame seeds, and red pepper. Several of these plants—okra, cowpeas, eggplant, and sesame, for example—were originally brought from Africa to become part of the African American diet. Other cultivated plants such as European brassicas—turnips, collards, and cabbage—and Native American squashes, pumpkins, and corn were also added to the vegetable diet. In the African tradition these foods were cooked for a long time and flavored by small pieces of meat—a style of cooking still popular among white and black southerners, who season their beans and greens with fatback and boil them for hours on end.

In contrast to most Africans, Native Americans were serious meat eaters. Deer, fish, and turkey, together with small animals like rabbits, racoons, opossums, and turtles were the primary sources of animal protein. These meats were usually cooked with cultivated vegetables such as corn, beans, and squash, or with wild plants like cattail, arrowroot, acorns, walnuts, and hickory nuts.

In the southern colonies native Indian corn or maize, well adapted to the hot, humid climate, became the primary foodstuff of most American slaves, even in the "Rice Kingdom" of Carolina and Georgia. To planters, rice was a valuable cash crop, whereas corn was relatively cheap, suitable food for slaves. As might be expected, American Indians prepared corn in a variety of ways. They boiled the young ears, simmered hominy with meat in soups, and steamed lumps of meal as dumplings.[58] Indian corn dishes were boiled in earthen pots, except for pones, which usually were placed in the bottom of a covered pot and baked. Considering the close contact between Native Americans and African Americans in the settlement period, slaves quite likely adopted many native cooking techniques, but they also prepared corn meal as mush, which was not an indigenous American dish. Catesby described eighteenth-century slaves preparing corn in three ways: as hominy, which he said was "generally more in esteem than any other preparation of this grain"; as pone, described as "sweet and pleasant"; and as mush, "made in the manner of hasty-pudding."[59] Made by boiling corn meal with water, mush does indeed resemble English hasty-pudding, but its probable origins are starchy dishes common in Africa.

By the nineteenth century, mush was surpassed in popularity by corn bread and hominy grits, both made from ground dried corn.[60] Hominy grits are quite different from hominy. To make hominy, corn is soaked in a mixture of water and wood-ash lye, which expands and loosens the hulls from the kernels. The hulls are then sifted away, usually in a special basket sifter; the swelled kernels that remain are hominy, ready to be fried or boiled for eating. Hominy grits, on the other hand, is ground corn. When dried corn is ground and sifted through sieves of different sizes, the finest product is corn meal, the coarse hulls are called bran, and the size in between is hominy grits. The bran usually is fed to livestock, while grits and corn meal are reserved for human consumption. Since the ground corn is separated by sifting, neither bran, grits, nor corn meal has the nutritional value of the whole grain.

The change from the African diet of rice, millet, and manioc to one based on corn was a step down in nutrition for African American slaves. Rice by itself is a nutritious grain, but corn without complementary vitamins and amino acids is nutritionally poor. Corn is low in niacin, a deficiency of which causes pellagra; corn also lacks certain amino acids making it only a partial protein.[61] To compensate for these deficiencies, corn must always be eaten simultaneously with legumes like beans. Native Americans maximized the food value of corn by cooking it with beans and protein-rich meat in soups or stews. Meat-eating Europeans also fared well with this grain. African slaves, however, with their predilection for vegetarianism, their tendency to cook corn as mush or bread, and their limited rations, must have suffered nutritionally as this grain became a staple of their diet. To make up for the inadequacies of corn, slaves needed to eat more animal flesh. Meat and fish, excellent sources of protein, could have compensated for corn's nutritional deficiency of amino acids.

Archaeological research and historical accounts from across the South show that by the middle of the nineteenth century, slaves consumed the flesh of a variety of domesticated animals, including beef, poultry, pork, sheep, and goat.[62] Among these, pork was the most important source of domesticated animal protein for slaves, according to historical reports. Nevertheless, this was not a sure solution to protein deficiency. Masters could be niggardly in providing meat, and they commonly handed out fatty bacon rather than cuts richer in protein. Thus, although meat appears to have generally increased in the slave diet, domesticated meat was probably an unreliable source of needed nutrition.

Along the South Carolina and Georgia coasts, meat sources for slave diets diverged from the general pattern. Excavation at many lowcountry sites, both slave and planter, has shown that beef became the principal domesticated meat source and that slaves supplemented their diet through hunting and fishing. The prominence of beef in this local area can be accounted for in several ways.[63] The lowcountry pinelands did not provide the mast of acorns and other nuts and roots necessary for the best pig foraging; on the other hand, the extensive savannas of the coastal plain afforded excellent grazing; cattle had been raised in Carolina since early colonial times. These facts of environment and history, coupled with the familiarity of many Africans with cows, encouraged the consumption of beef on lowcountry plantations.

Unfortunately, this prevalence of beef did not mean that slaves received sufficient rations of meat. Archaeological evidence shows that beef combined with other domesticated animals provided the bulk by weight of animal food; nevertheless, the largest number of individual animals butchered on lowcountry plantations were wild, showing that slaves were breaking some of the constraints of bondage and supplementing their diet significantly through hunting and fishing. Turtle and fish, racoons, rabbits, opossums, and deer—like Native Americans, nineteenth-century slaves on coastal plantations regularly consumed these animals, even using firearms to hunt deer, wild turkeys, and smaller game. In 1775 a British agricultural analyst wrote that in Carolina "one Indian, or dextrous negroe, will, with his gun and netts, get as much game and fish as five families can eat."[64]

## COOKING AND EATING

When I began surveying African foodways for comparison to those in the lowcountry, I expected to find a wide variability within Africa; I learned otherwise. On that continent different environments, languages, and experiences have produced cultures that differ in many ways, yet basic foodways throughout

Africa are astonishingly similar. And many of these shared eating habits were retained in the creolized foodways of American slaves.

In many regions of the world, customs involved in preparing and consuming food cross otherwise dramatic cultural boundaries. Wherever Western European culture has had a strong culinary influence, people sit down to eat in much the same way, each place set with a cup or tumbler, plate, knife, fork, and spoon. Food is brought to the table in common dishes and served onto individual plates for eating. These customs have their roots in the Renaissance and the subsequent Enlightenment when the medieval custom of eating from communal trays or trenchers gave way to an emphasis on individualism.[65] Today, across apparently firm boundaries of language and custom, these basic patterns of eating are shared. Far Eastern foodways exhibit an equally strong homogeneity: in the different cultures of Indochina, China, Korea, Japan, and the Philippines, chop sticks and rice bowls, woks and steamers are ubiquitous. Likewise, across vast regions of North America people appear to have conformed to a common standard when it came to eating.

Historical references to Native American foodways are more difficult to find than information on either Europeans or Africans. Perhaps this is because the southeastern natives, unlike Europeans and Africans, did not have special mealtimes. Early travelers reported that Indians kept a large pot constantly simmering on the fire. Whenever they felt hungry, people stopped by the steaming pots and dished out what they wanted into bowls; they ate with their hands or with spoons made from a gourd, a piece of wood, bison horn, or shell.[66]

In Africa the most common meal consists of a starchy main course, boiled or simmered in an earthenware or iron pot. Customarily it is served in a large container—a calabash, a ceramic bowl, or clean leaves. The serving dish is placed on the earthen floor where people sit to eat. Relishes, prepared in smaller pots, are placed in small bowls near the main dish. These relishes usually consist of well-cooked, sometimes spicy, vegetables; occasionally small pieces of meat or fish are added.[67] People eat with their hands, pinching off a portion of the starch, pressing a little hollow into it with the thumb, and dipping it into the relish. For drinking, a gourd or small bowl is used. In the archaeological record, this West African pattern of foodways would leave many fragments of small bowls as well as sherds of cooking pots. With some adjustments for predictable European influences, this is basically what we have found on African American colonial sites in Carolina—in contrast to the foodways of European American colonists.

Through the eighteenth century, the eating habits of Europeans and European Americans were changing. In seventeenth-century England foodways were simple, with much sharing of serving dishes:

Ceramics played a relatively minor role in food preparation and consumption. Cooking was usually done in metal vessels such as pots, kettles, and skillets. Food was served directly from the cooking pots, and eaten from trenchers—small wooden trays, usually with shallow depressions in their centers to hold liquid. Trenchers were communally used, with two or more "trencher mates" eating from a single one.[68]

Knives and spoons were used as utensils, though people often ate with their hands.[69] Trenchers were abandoned, in the eighteenth century, in favor of ceramic plates and bowls that held individual servings. Forks were introduced and eating with one's hands came to be regarded as bad manners. By the last quarter of the eighteenth century, plates and other individualized flatware had become so common, they show up as major components of archaeological collections from period sites. The archaeological and historical records indicate that while European Americans were adopting individualized plates and tableware, African Americans were creating a different culinary style that retained many traditional customs.

Eighteenth-century African American foodways combined elements of African, Native American, and European culinary culture. Utensils in a slave household near Charleston, observed Carl Bauer during the Revolutionary War,

> consist of a large iron pot and a few hollowed out dried gourds; and sometimes I have seen a bucket in their quarters. For his daily subsistence a Negro receives a quart of Indian corn or rice. The Negro crushes the corn on a handmill that is attached to the outside of the hut [Fig. 70]. The iron pot stands in the middle of the hut by the fire, and the crushed corn or rice is boiled in it.[70]

This account shows that within the cultural mixture, the chief ingredients were African and Native American—a pattern clearly supported by archaeological and historical research. Rice and corn, the basis of the slave diet, were African and Indian cereals. Gourds—used as bowls, bottles, dippers, jars, and even musical instruments—were common to both Africans and Native Americans.

The grinding stone, iron pot, and wooden bucket all were introduced from Europe, but each has non-European associations (Figs. 70–72). Native Americans ground corn in large wooden mortars with pestles, and Africans used the same technique for pounding rice, sorghum, and other foods. After colonization, European mill stones proved most efficient for grinding corn, and from Bauer's account we see that even the poorest slaves at times had access to hand-turned stones. On the other hand, stone grinding did not work for hulling and

Figure 70. Mrs. Rebeccah Green using a hand mill for grinding corn, St. Helena Island, South Carolina, 1909. Note coiled baskets containing whole and ground grain (see Dabbs 1970). (From the Penn School Collection, permission granted by Penn Center, St. Helena Island, South Carolina)

polishing rice; for this job the wooden mortar and pestle continued to be used into the twentieth century. Even when planters mechanized rice processing by harnessing water wheels and steam engines to threshing and pounding mills, the basic principle of the mortar and pestle remained in effect.[71]

The iron pot mentioned by Bauer is again of European origin, but the manner of using the pot was non-European and the maker of the bucket probably was

Figure 71. Using a wooden mortar and pestle to pound rice, St. Helena Island, South Carolina. (From the Penn School Collection, permission granted by Penn Center, St. Helena Island, South Carolina)

African American. Bauer describes the slaves cooking over a central hearth; their ancestors had done this for generations in Africa. Archæological excavations in both South Carolina and Virginia suggest that African Americans continued to use a central hearth, and oral testimony tells us that they retained the African custom of sitting on the floor to eat, in the manner of Shadwick Randolph's African grandmother who, "used to sit down in the middle of the floor of her house when she ate, and she always ate out of a wooden bowl. Sometimes she used a spoon, but most of the time she just ate with her fingers."[72]

Woodcarving has deep roots in Africa, where, for centuries before the arrival of Europeans, metal tools were employed to fashion both decorative and practical artifacts. Using stone tools, American Indians also had a well-developed wood carving tradition long before European contact. In colonial times African and Native American carving skills were often turned to economic gain by putting slaves to work as coopers, making staves and hoops for barrels (Fig.

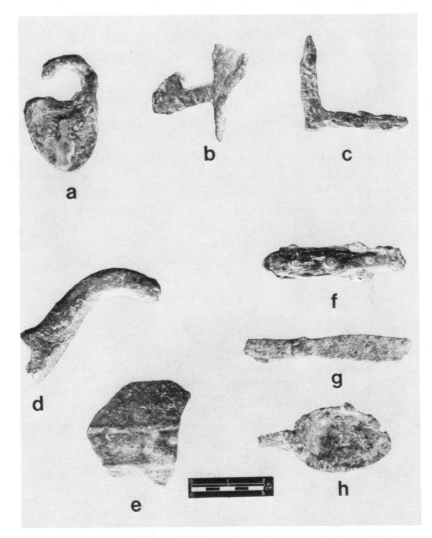

Figure 72. Metal hardware from the Spiers Landing site, Berkeley County, South Carolina: (a) padlock, (b) latch, (c) pintle, (d) kettle spout, (e) kettle fragment, (f) bone handled knife, (g) knife blade, (h) spoon. Note: these artifacts are as they appear during excavation; when rust is removed they exhibit more detail. (Courtesy AF Consultants, Columbia, South Carolina)

73).[73] Slaves used these same skills to make various domestic implements such as bowls for serving and eating and buckets, like the one Bauer observed, for carrying and storing water.

Grinding wheels, iron pots, gourds, wooden bowls and buckets—are the kinds of artifacts that because they were durable and seldom discarded, in the case of the pots and grindstones, or because they have been poorly preserved, are seldom found in archaeological excavations. However, the artifacts we regularly find—Colono Ware, imported European ceramics, glass bottles, and animal bone—are consistent with Bauer's glimpse of African American domestic life and significantly expand upon it. All of these things were part of a culinary system that included still other items like baskets, bags, knives, spoons, sticks, cooking fires and hearths, as well as the food itself.[74]

Although only a small number of fragments of iron pots have been found in slave-site excavations, the frequency with which they are mentioned in colonial records suggests they were common in slave households. The case for Colono

Figure 73. African skills in woodcarving were used in making water buckets. (Courtesy AF Consultants, Columbia, South Carolina and the Charleston Museum, Charleston, South Carolina)

Ware jars is converse to that for iron pots—we have no colonial records of slaves using Colono Ware cooking jars, but the high frequency with which charred jars have been found on the sites of slave villages shows that earthen jars were commonly used for cooking (Appendix 3, Table 3). From the relative frequency of large and small jars—very few large jars and many small ones—we can infer that large iron pots and small clay cooking jars complemented one another, and that large Colono Ware jars were seldom used.

The two large Colono Ware jars in the whole pot collection I looked at would have held approximately 4.5 and 6 liters. The more common smaller ones average a little over 1.5 liters (Appendix 3, Tables 3 and 4). Africans and Native Americans commonly used large jars for two purposes—cooking for families and other big gatherings and storing water, grain, or other foodstuffs. In Africa, large jars also may be used for specialized purposes like making beer or palm wine, but their most frequent function is storing water. In Carolina slaves might have stored food and water in large Colono Ware vessels, but so far we have found little evidence for large jars and no evidence of their serving this purpose. When found they are usually charred, indicating that they were used for cooking rather than storage.

Some reasonable explanations for these findings are as follows: in general, storage jars are not used as frequently as cooking and serving vessels; therefore they are not broken as often and leave fewer sherds in the ground. Perhaps the demand for storage jars declined in colonial times; slaves were issued food rations from plantation stores on a regular basis, thus reducing the need for household storage. The limited storage required could be accommodated by glazed, kiln-fired European and European American vessels, which were impermeable to water and generally less fragile than low-fired earthenware. For holding water and other liquids, I believe the large jars traditionally employed in Africa were replaced by slave-made wooden buckets and by glass bottles, which are commonly found on archaeological sites.[75] We can safely conclude, then, that in South Carolina the few large Colono Ware jars we find were used like iron pots, for cooking.

When planters issued pots required for boiling rice and hominy grits—say 2 to 3 gallons—for an extended household, these iron pots would have served the same purpose as large earthenware cooking jars in the traditional cultures. Native Americans would have used such large pots for simmering soups and stews, and Africans would have used them for boiling grains like rice and millet. For boiling meal, iron pots would have been preferable to earthenware. Quick boiling requires that vessels be brought to a high temperature, then allowed to cool. Small earthenware vessels may survive such drastic changes in heat, but larger vessels are likely to fracture. In contrast, metal pots can withstand intense heat and rapid cooling—perhaps one reason why slaves adopted these iron pots for cooking.

The smaller Colono Ware jars, making up 21 percent of the whole pots in my sample from Carolina, probably were used in preparing sauces and relishes to accompany starchy main dishes. These jars resemble those used in Africa for that purpose,[76] and nine of the total of sixteen (almost two-thirds) show thick charring encrustations—sure signs that they were cooking vessels. By contrast, only one of fifty vessels from Virginia was charred, showing that Colono Ware was more often used for cooking in South Carolina than Virginia.

The smaller cooking pots suggest that African Americans retained their customary cooking style, making the utensils they needed from materials at hand. Next to bowls, these small vessels are the most common form of Colono Ware excavated in South Carolina. They are simple pots with plain surfaces, everted rims, and rounded bottoms. Some have handles, which make them look somewhat like European mugs—a resemblance that led me to a curious misinterpretation.

Several years ago, before we had much of an understanding of Colono Ware, I became familiar with a small "Colono-Indian mug" sitting on top of a file cabinet in the South Carolina Institute of Archaeology and Anthropology. The cup was large, about 8 inches tall, with a rounded bottom and a handle on the side reminiscent of a coffee mug. Considering the piece to be Colono-Indian Ware, I thought it interesting and novel that a Native American potter had attached a European-style handle to a round-bottomed, Indian-style pot. Moreover, I halfway thought the potter had made a mistake; trying to imitate a European-style mug, she had made the pot too large. Later, when I had a context in which to put the piece, I realized the errors were all mine.

The little pot on the file cabinet had broken during firing. A large spall overlapped by a firing cloud pierced a hole in the vessel wall; the pot had never been used. Looking at other collections of Colono Ware, I began to see many vessels shaped like the "mug" on the file cabinet. I also noticed a consistent difference: most of the others were charred; they had been used for cooking. Some vessels of this class had handles and some didn't. All of a sudden the pot at the Institute made more sense—it wasn't an oversized mug put together by an Indian who didn't clearly understand the European style. It was a cooking vessel!

A review of the African literature showed that small jars like these—with and without handles—are used for preparing the vegetable sauces so popular in

West Africa. I realized that the "Colono-Indian mug" was most likely made by an African American for cooking a distinctive African dish.

The smooth lines and rounded bottoms of these cooking pots from Carolina carry a special elegance, an elegance that comes from the efficiency of the shape for cooking in an open fire. Smoothly curving, continuous, and spherical, the walls of the pots are resistant to thermal fractures. Archaeologist David Braun, an expert in analyzing earthenware vessel shapes, has determined that vessels with smooth, continuous lines, spherical bodies, and thin walls are less vulnerable to thermal fracture than thicker pots with flat bottoms and more angular forms and appendages.[77]

While we can easily understand that the earthenware jars from Carolina were ideal for distributing heat, still the rounded shape of the vessels seems unstable in comparison to European forms with flat bottoms or tripod legs. West African cooks easily solve this problem by constructing an open hearth with three stones or lumps of clay used to hold the round-bottomed vessels. Any vessel can be stabilized by adjusting the stones toward or away from the basal center of the pot. In open hearths like those described for Carolina slaves, earthenware and perhaps iron cooking pots would have been supported in the same way as in Africa. Since stones are hard to find in the lowcountry, slaves would have used bricks, lumps of clay or perhaps, near Charleston, the ballast stones from ships.

Another feature of unglazed earthenware is its permeability, which affects the ways vessels are used and the kind of cuisine they can accommodate. Because moisture seeps through the walls of earthenware pots and evaporates, such pots cook at lower temperatures than pots made of metal or more highly fired ceramics. This has implications for both handling and cooking. Since the rim of an earthenware vessel stays cooler than one might expect, cooks may pick jars up with their bare hands, careful to touch only the outcurved rim or handle. When jars are very hot, a forked stick, commonly seen around the hearths of West Africa, may be placed under the outcurved rim to lift the pot off the fire.

Cooking in earthenware means that foods are heated more slowly and over longer periods of time. Simmering is a common cooking technique in both West Africa and Native America, and it became an important technique in the American South. William Gilmore Simms's "old ladies" and cookbook writer Mary Randolph preferred earthenware for making okra soup, no doubt, because these pots were perfectly suited for simmering rather than boiling.

The archaeological evidence shows that colonial African Americans used Colono Ware jars and bowls more than any other form. Contemporary Americans might be surprised by the range of functions bowls and jars served. As we have seen jars were used for cooking. Bowls, too, had multiple purposes. Just after I started my research on Colono Ware I was shaken from my ethnocentrism by art historian Roy Sieber, well known for his knowledge of West African crafts and household objects. I showed Sieber a Colono Ware bowl and asked if it were similar to those he knew from West Africa. Taking it with both hands, palms up underneath the bowl as if afraid he might drop it, he replied, "Yes, a bowl like this might be used for drinking palm wine." And he lifted the bowl to his lips, pretending to sip that popular African drink. It would also be used, he said, to hold sauces at mealtimes. I was astonished and a little chagrined! When I looked at Colono Ware bowls, my first thoughts were of soups and stews. As I learned more about West African foodways, I understood that bowls commonly held the vegetable complement of a meal, but I hadn't thought that they might be used for drinking as well.

Colono Ware bowls, like the one I showed Sieber, are open and unrestricted. Most are hemispherical with a small flattened area at the base, while some have the shape of an inverted, truncated cone and others have ring bases. The bowls are the same size as those used in Africa for serving—about the same as a modern American serving bowl (Appendix 3, Tables 3 and 4). Burned-on grease on a few specimens show that they were occasionally used in the fire—an advantage they have over baskets or wooden or gourd bowls. Colono Ware bowls may have been used for warming food, and some of them show abrasion on the walls as if they served as pot lids, but none bears signs of intensive cooking as the earthenware jars do. Rather, bowls tended to be used for serving and eating—and drinking.

While there is no direct evidence that Carolina slaves ate food from these bowls with their hands, as both Africans and Native Americans were accustomed to do, there is little evidence of utensil marks or wear. The few cutlery marks we do see (Fig. 25) occur on Colono Ware vessels from the kitchens of "big houses" and from Charleston rather than from plantations' slave quarters. Like Shadwick Randolph's African grandmother, colonial slaves probably ate with their hands.

Thus, in the middle to late eighteenth century, while white colonists served food on platters and plates, slaves kept using predominantly bowls. At the slave quarters on Yaughan and Curriboo plantations, bowls not only continued to dominate serving ware but through the late eighteenth century their relative percentage was increasing. Moreover, if gourd and wooden bowls were added to the number of ceramic bowls, the relative percentage of bowls to flatware would be even higher. Slave potters were quite skillful; they could have made plates as easily as bowls or jars, but they chose not to make them. In the late eighteenth century both the structure and the artifacts of African American foodways were different from those of their white neighbors, and there is evidence that, through the nineteenth century, aspects of the contrasting structure persisted even as Colono Ware artifacts began to disappear.

By the middle of the nineteenth century, Colono Ware was rare. Here and there a few African Americans still made pots,[78] and Catawba Indians continued to sell their pottery in the towns and on plantations, but the heyday of handbuilt earthenware was over. This decline can be explained by a variety of factors:

1. The legal importation of African slaves ended in 1808, and with it regular infusion of African culture into plantation communities ceased;
2. European and American goods like iron cooking pots and ceramic dishes were becoming easier to acquire; and
3. In the face of abolitionist critiques, planters actively attempted to remove obvious "heathen" features from slave life.[79]

Nevertheless, though pottery manufacture was in decline, the "African culinary grammar" survived. Slaves still simmered their food, ate with their hands, and used bowls—albeit industrially manufactured, glazed ceramic bowls.[80]

# Chapter 4

# POWERFUL LEGACY

## SUMMER NIGHT

• • • In the dead of night a middle aged man, an African by birth, walks determinedly along a grassy rice field bank directly toward the river. His feet easily find the well-worn path. In daylight on this same path, laboring slaves watch carefully for cottonmouths, but on some nights both slavery and danger retreat. This confident traveler strides toward Africa's spirits.

In his left hand he carefully carries a small bowl containing a bundle tied in tattered cloth. If eyes could see through pitch dark they might find him touching the cloth as if his fingers talked to something trapped inside. From time to time one finger traces a cross inscribed on the bowl base. Evil may be stopped by working with this bowl.

Along his way night creatures disappear into the watery ditch beside the bank; ditch water gurgles as it flows toward the river with the falling tide. Otherwise there is silence. Treading steadily for more than a half mile, his feet finally reach the tall grass at the river's edge. He stands perfectly still and gazes at the broad expanse of river flowing powerfully yet quietly toward the sea. Darker than the cloudy sky, the black river carries rafts of matted grass, debris from rich men's fields. Beneath these rafts of waste, beneath the surface of the river, beneath the entire watery world, his ancestors live as spirits.

Staring intently toward the floating weeds, he imagines Benah's baby, thin and

**109**

breathing weakly in her arms. Soft coughs rattle from a chest too weak to cry. Who attacked this child? Witch? White men? The alien spirits of this foreign land?

As he dreams, his thoughts flow from cause to cure. In the moist earth of the rice dike, he scratches a cross and stands upon it. Soon his dreaming journey takes him to another time. The sickly baby fades into a strong young man, a leader, sitting down beneath a live oak tree. He talks to other men, and as he talks he holds a healthy baby on his knee. Keeping this image in his mind, the African hurls the bowl as far as he can into the river.

Slowly turning in his trance, the healer lies down upon his cross. Minutes pass, and soon the new rice gently bends as a sweet breeze begins to blow. Beyond the fields, this cool wind flows through a clay-house door, across the mother and her child. The healing wind becomes the air he breathes.

With the first gray light of morning the African rises and walks through morning fog along the rice field bank toward Benah's house. In the slave quarters those who felt the nighttime breeze find new hope that Benah's child will survive another troubled day. With the changing tide, the small clay bowl settles gently to the river bed.


## MAGIC BOWLS

In modern Cuba when African American priests make a special charm called *zarabanda,* they begin by "tracing, in white chalk, a cruciform pattern at the bottom of an iron kettle"; and when they make another called *prenda* they also draw "a cross, in chalk or white ashes at the bottom of the kettle."[1] Art historian Robert Farris Thompson has argued that these and other examples of crosses and circles in certain African American rituals are derived from depictions of the cosmos traditional among Bakongo priests from the southwest coast of Africa. The basic form of this cosmogram is a simple cross with one line representing the boundary between the living world and that of the dead, and the other representing the path of power from below to above, as well as the vertical path across the boundary (Fig. 74). Marks on the bases of Colono Ware bowls found in river bottoms and slave quarter sites in South Carolina suggest that more than one hundred and fifty years ago African American priests used similar symbols of the cosmos (Figs. 22, 75–77).[2]

While cataloging thousands of Colono Ware sherds, South Carolina archaeologists began noticing marks on the bases of some bowls (Appendix 3, Table 7). Most of these marks were simple crosses or "Xs." In some cases a circle or rectangle enclosed the cross; in others, "arms" extended counterclockwise from the ends of the cross, opposite from the direction of the Nazi swastika. On one

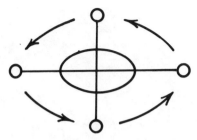

Figure 74. Bakongo sign of the cosmos
(after Thompson 1983:109)

there was a circle without a cross, and on a few others we found more complicated marks.

Initially we called these "maker's marks" since the first ones discovered had
been incised on the vessel bases before firing (Fig. 22, top; Fig. 76, bottom),
and bore a resemblance to maker's marks on European and Oriental pottery.
Similar marks, however, were soon found inscribed on interior bottoms, and still

Figure 75. Marked Colono Ware bowl from South Carolina. (Photograph by Emily
Short)

Figure 76. Marks on bowls from South Carolina. *Above,* engraved mark on the interior of a flat-bottomed bowl from slave quarters at Curriboo Plantation on the Santee River. *Below,* incised mark on the exterior base of a bowl from the Cooper River adjacent to Mepkin Plantation. (Photographs by Emily Short)

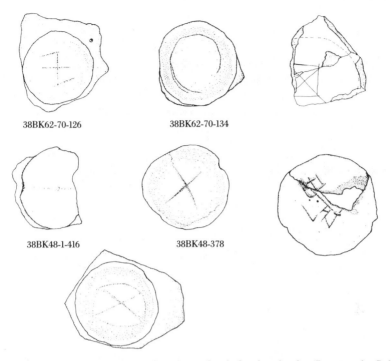

38BK62-70-126       38BK62-70-134

38BK48-1-416       38BK48-378

Figure 77. Schematic diagrams of marks on South Carolina bowls. (Drawings by Bobbie May)

others were scratched into the bowls after the vessels were fired (Fig. 22, bottom; Fig. 75; Fig. 76, top). Some archaeologists argued that they were "owner's marks," but there was too little variety in the marks to suggest different owners. Besides, most Colono Ware vessels are distinctive enough in shape and coloring to be easily identified. Interpreting the marks as either "maker's" or "owner's" had serious flaws.

Although we could not explain what these marks meant, over a period of several years a strong pattern emerged linking the marks to earthenware bowls collected underwater from lowcountry rivers. What we knew was this:

1. The majority of marks were a cruciform or some variation of a cross or X.
2. All marks were on Colono Ware bowls, none on the Colono Ware cooking jars we commonly found. Also, there were no such marks on imported European bowls, although slaves were using large amounts of European ware as well as Colono Ware.
3. Marks always were located at the very bottom of the bowl, either on the inside or outside. Sometimes they were made before firing and in other cases after firing.

4. Marks were more commonly found on bowls with ring bases than on those with rounded or flattened bases, even though ring-based bowls comprised only a small proportion of the total number of bowls recovered.
5. Although marked pieces have been found around former slave quarters, most were picked up in rivers adjacent to old rice plantations. This was true in spite of the fact that many more Colono Ware sherds had been recovered from terrestrial sites than from those underwater.

Clearly the marks were associated with bowls and with water, but what did they signify? In February 1987 at a Williamsburg symposium on African American culture, I showed slide illustrations of the marked pots from South Carolina and mentioned that while we believed these bowls were in some way associated with the water, we really didn't know how to interpret them. After the presentation, two members of the audience called my attention to the similarity of the marks to Bakongo cosmograms.[3]

The Bakongo are a numerous and powerful people located in the southern portion of modern Zaire near the Angolan border. Their homeland is in the area identified in discussions of the Atlantic slave trade as the "Congo-Angolan region." Bakongo culture has been so influential that many non-Bakongo people in Zaire and northern Angola have adopted Bakongo practices, especially in religion. During the time when traders brought slaves to North America, almost half of those arriving in South Carolina came from the Congo-Angolan region, the region of Bakongo influence.

According to Bakongo religion, an almighty God, *Nzambi*, emanates power that may be controlled for either good or evil by living human beings, people who make sacred medicines or *minkisi*. Minkisi control the spirits of the Bakongo cosmos connecting the living with the powers of the dead. Making an African *nkisi* (plural: minkisi) involves packaging a variety of "spirit-embodying materials," which might include cemetery earth, white clay, stones, and other items. Nkisi containers include leaves, shells, bags, wooden images, cloth bundles, and ceramic vessels.[4] "In Kongo mythology, Ne Kongo himself, the progenitor of the kingdom, prepared the primordial medicines in an earthenware pot set on three stones above a fire. Clay pots have therefore always been classical containers of *minkisi*."[5]

Bakongo philosophers explain the earth, the land of the living, as a mountain over a watery barrier separating this world from the land of the dead beneath. Each day the sun rises over the earth and proceeds in a counterclockwise direction, as viewed from the southern hemisphere, across the sky to set in the water. Then, during earthly nighttime, the sun illuminates the underside of the universe, the land of the dead, until it rises again in the northeast. The cycle continues incessantly, representing the continuity of life: birth, death, and rebirth.[6]

Historian Sterling Stuckey points out that circularity, especially counterclockwise circularity, pervades West African ideology from the area of Bakongo culture all the way to Gambia and Senegal on the Windward Coast. The circle, he argues, proved equally important in African American slave culture: "The circle imported [to America] by Africans from the Congo region was so powerful in its elaboration of a religious vision that it contributed disproportionately to the centrality of the circle in slavery." So consistent and profound was the slaves' use of the circle, Stuckey suggests, "that it gave form and meaning to black religion and art."[7]

The watery barrier, which in West and Central African cosmology separates the corporeal and spirit worlds, also found a weighty role in African American ideology. Stuckey quotes Melville Herskovits's assertion of the significance of water spirits and river-cult priests among African American slaves:

> In all those parts of the New World where African religious beliefs have persisted. . .the river cult or, in broader terms, the cult of water spirits, holds an important place. All this testifies to the vitality of this element in African religion, and supports the conclusion. . .as to the possible influence such priests wielded even as slaves.[8]

Considering the ubiquitous West African emphasis on water spirits and circularity, and the dominating influence of Bakongo cosmology and ritual in the Congo-Angolan region, it should not be surprising that early African American religion would bear these same characteristics. The marks on bowls picked up from river bottoms in the Carolina lowcountry strongly resemble Bakongo cosmograms. The association of marks with earthenware vessels, ring bases, and underwater sites also fits the general West African model.

South Carolina's marked bowls were made and used by American descendants of the mythical Ne Kongo who cooked medicines in earthenware pots. Although no marks have been found on Colono Ware cooking jars or pots, some marked bowls show charring from use over a fire. Overall, the traditional African association of medicines or charms with earthenware vessels, and the exclusive archaeological association of marks with handbuilt earthenware bowls, and not with imported European ware, suggests an interpretation of the bowls as receptacles for minkisi or for use in a ritual similar to those involving minkisi.

As Africans came to the Americas they arrived with a belief in water spirits and a profound respect for the cross and circularity as symbols of life and death. Again, we can read these tenets in the archaeological record: two-thirds of the marks are unquestionably cruciform and three out of four marked bowls have been recovered from underwater sites, bowls that embody circularity. Not only are the bowls themselves segments of spheres, and circles the dominating lines of spheres, but the ring bases add even more circles to the vessels, which apparently were made especially to be marked and put in the water. Ring bases are not common on Colono Ware, and the ring bases found on marked bowls often seem to have been quickly pinched-out circles rather than carefully formed rings. Nevertheless, when they are attached to spherical bowls, the ring bases appear as circles attached to circles; when marked they appear as circles enclosing the Bakongo cosmogram.

Overall, the archaeological pattern fits the West African model quite well. The combination of marks, handbuilt earthenware, circles, and underwater context suggest that African American priests performed traditional rituals passed from Africa to the South Carolina lowcountry.


## ARCHAEOLOGY AND AFRICAN AMERICAN RESISTANCE

Analyzing modern African American religion as well as scraps of evidence from earlier times, historians have concluded that as the earliest Africans came to this country they brought African notions of religion, ritual, and supernatural power.[9] In the first half of the nineteenth century an abolitionist who had formerly owned slaves wrote that on his Florida plantation "the guinea negroes had sometimes a small inclosure for their 'god house.'"[10] This rare reference probably represents hundreds, if not thousands, of never-mentioned 'god houses' and shrines built by Africans and their descendants on southern plantations. In his excavation of a mid-nineteenth-century village on the Texas coast that was occupied by slaves smuggled directly from Africa, archaeologist Kenneth Brown has discovered a room that contained many artifacts similar to those used to fill minkisi.[11]

Here and there on other sites archaeologists have found artifacts suggesting African-style charms and rituals. All along the south Atlantic coast archaeologists have reported finding small numbers of predominantly blue glass beads on slave sites, beads similar to those used as charms in Africa and Near Eastern countries to ward off the "evil eye";[12] and while excavating near an early African American cemetery on Parris Island, South Carolina, Stanley South recovered a cache of 4,000 glass beads that may have been part of an African American religious ritual.[13] From Garrison Plantation near Baltimore, Maryland, archaeologist Eric Klingelhofer has reported glass, ceramic, and wooden objects that he thinks may have had ritual uses. Klingelhofer also has called attention to the similarity of engraved pewter spoons from Garrison and from the Kingsmill Plantations in Virginia to spoons decorated by the African American Maroons of Surinam. Designs on these spoons may be purely decorative; on the other hand, the patterns of lines and crosses from both Garrison and Kingsmill (Fig. 78) resemble the marks on South Carolina bowls.[14]

While objects like engraved spoons and African-style shrines seldom were mentioned in written documents, artifacts excavated on plantation sites, coupled with our discoveries of Bakongo-style marks on bowls from lowcountry sites suggest that the preserved remains of many shrines and rituals must lie buried underground across the South. Archæological evidence of African-style religious practice in America reinforces and makes tangible our sense that slaves brought to the Americas not only a variety of practical skills, but also elements of their African spiritual beliefs.

Figure 78. The design engraved on the third spoon from the right is similar to the Bakongo cosmogram. Spoons from excavations at Kingsmill tract near Williamsburg, Virginia. (Department of Historic Resources, Commonwealth of Virginia)

As Africans began to become Americans they started with a world view and value system quite different from whites. Newly imported slaves understood European culture no better than Europeans understood Africa, and most of them probably approached their captors' way of life with suspicion and caution. Recall that runaway Charles Ball observed that "The native Africans. . . generally place little, or even no value upon the fine houses and superb furniture of their masters." He went on to say that "They are universally of the opinion. . . that after death they shall return to their own country."[15] Cultural anthropologists would find Ball's observations of the native Africans familiar. One of anthropology's firmest conclusions has been that throughout the world people believe their way of living—from the way they get their food to their beliefs about the cosmos—is the best way.

African slaves knew African ways of planting crops, cooking food, rearing children, building houses, and worshipping God; European ways must have seemed strange and awkward. In spite of the demoralizing effects of their enslavement, African Americans must have retained a strong belief that African ways were best. Thus, in digging slave sites, we should expect to find evidence of African traditions carried over in colonial America. Moreover, given the social isolation of racial slavery and the physical isolation of remote plantations, it should come as no surprise that African Americans did not disappear into the so-called American melting pot but used their African inheritance together with newly encountered things and ideas to create a distinctive creolized African American culture.

In her treatise on African American religion and culture on the South Carolina and Georgia sea islands, Margaret Washington Creel concludes by observing that we must recognize the truth in the assertion that "insofar as people develop their own culture they are not slaves."[16] Interpreted more actively, this assertion implies that insofar as people create their own culture in the face of slavery's oppression they resist slavery. Can this be true? I believe it is, once we understand the intrinsic power of culture.

So far, archaeology has been of little value in expanding our knowledge of overt expressions of African American resistance to slavery such as sabotage, flight, and violence. Although William Kelso has uncovered caches of apparent contraband beneath the floors of slave houses in Virginia, archaeologists ordinarily cannot find and identify more abstract actions like theft, pretended illness, or conspiracy to revolt. Archaeology does show, however, that early African Americans along the Atlantic seaboard from Virginia to Florida created a distinctive material culture.

Throughout their lives most slaves lived in African American villages separated from white people and the white subculture. The majority of adults may have seen an overseer or planter every day, but most slaves were not intimate with white people; white people must have been more like parts of their environment than key figures in their social lives. On the other hand, while white people and European American culture were "foreign" aspects of most African American lives, slaves interacted intimately and continuously with their families and neighbors. Children grew up surrounded by African American culture, sleeping in African American-style houses and sitting down to meals served in handmade earthenware bowls. In South Carolina and Georgia, slaves even spoke a distinctive African American language. Material things were concrete components of their everyday experience. Besides the rations they received from the planter, slaves ate food secured by their kinsmen through hunting, fishing, gathering, gardening, and stealing. Youngsters paddled canoes and carried buckets carved by African American craftsmen. They heard stories of the awesome power of magic and religion, and they probably saw artifacts like bowls and tobacco pipes with mysterious marks scratched into their surfaces. Following Ian Hodder, I believe that such material symbols, everything from houses to art work, operate in the same way that oral tradition does—creating identity and molding values. The power to create identity and mold values is deeply significant, if often overlooked.

In offering his model for analyzing plantation society, Charles Orser has stated that the slaves' power was manifest in the planter's desire for their labor; if slaves could withhold labor, they could sabotage plantation activities or negotiate with the planter; if they could manage to withhold their labor permanently, they would be free. Orser approaches plantation social relations from a relatively simple Marxian perspective—sufficient power may control economy by controlling labor.[17] Unfortunately, in describing plantation society, most archaeologists have failed to see African American ideological power.

In a careful consideration of the bases of social power, social theorist Michael Mann has outlined three types: economic, militaristic, and ideological power.[18] Even though some slaves found a modicum of economic power and a few rose up in armed revolt against their masters, colonial American planters held the overwhelming balance of economic and militaristic power. Planters, however, could not control the beliefs and values of their slaves as easily. While masters could whip, torture, confine, and break up slave families, they had difficulty in forcing their rationalizations of slavery and other aspects of their world view on African Americans. As planters tried to manipulate slaves, they came up against cultural boundaries that proved elusive as well as alien. While many slaves may not have overtly resisted their enslavement on a day-to-day basis, most did ignore European American culture in favor of their own, and in doing so they also ignored and resisted the European American ideology that rationalized their enslavement. Archaeological research helps us see the contrast between the world the slaves built and the one they rejected.

# EPILOGUE

My introduction to the legacy of America's black pioneers came long before my training as an archaeologist. When I was eight, in August of 1949, my buddy Don and I slid down the red-clay cut behind our houses to watch a "gang" of men working on the railroad. Standing beside the water buckets, we watched as fifteen or twenty black men lowered a long steel rail in to place. Visible waves of heat rose from the gravel and cross-ties, and I remember beads of sweat and shouted orders from a gray-haired boss as the men adjusted the track, pushing and prying with long iron bars. For some time the noisy work went on, and then, in the midst of that heat and effort, I heard music. A rich, melodious voice sang out; a loud clap followed. I heard the voice again and this time looked up to see a line of hammers fall. The gray-haired man was singing! Again the song, the hammers fell. Soon I felt the rhythm and heard the different hammers as they hit. As those men drove the spikes that held the track, Don and I watched spellbound and envious.

We heard and felt that workday performance in ignorance, unaware that both music and dance were parts of these men that went far beyond the railroad track. During this time, before the Civil Rights Movement and after most southern families had moved from farms to town, the separation of the so-called races was perhaps more severe than ever before or since. Although I saw "colored people" daily—the janitor in our school, people downtown, and workmen, like those on the railroad—I had few black acquaintances and no black friends. We had no

**121**

opportunity to meet and know African Americans. Don and I saw the railroad men through the rigid fence of statutory segregation. How were we to know that they had learned to sing in homes and churches from brothers and sisters, parents and grandparents, that the songs were part of an oral tradition surviving from a distant past and place? We had no idea that similar songs were sung as black men swung the axes that cleared the fields in pioneering days. In our white world, the only pioneers were men like Daniel Boone and Davy Crockett. More than twenty years later I learned that songs with leaders and unisoned responses stretch ultimately across the Atlantic and back to the griots of western Africa who led people in repeating the verbal lore of their ancestors. Don and I only knew that we wanted to be like those men, to sing and lift those big hammers and drive the railroad spikes.

Finished with the track, the gray-haired singer walked toward us and reached for the water dipper. He was big and neat as if he didn't feel the summer heat. The sleeves of his blue workshirt were rolled evenly to his upper arms, his overalls were buttoned at the side, and a leather fob disappeared into the little pocket on his bib where I could see the faded outline of his railroad watch. He wore a soft striped cap with an embroidered patch, "SR" for Southern Railroad.

We watched him drink, like watching a quarterback on the sidelines between possessions; and, like a quarterback, he looked serious, as if the next set of plays, or plans for work, occupied his mind. Other workers milled around the water buckets, talking and laughing, but we only saw the singer. Finally Don found the courage to speak, "Do only niggers get to do that?"

I cannot recall his words, but I definitely remember his response. "Colored people or Negro!" he almost shouted at us. "*Never* say nigger!" We were crestfallen. I vaguely remember some kind words following his reproach, but they were no consolation. We slowly climbed the red bank feeling rejected and confused.

Through my teenage years the alienation continued, and I alternately and somewhat arbitrarily enjoyed, scorned, and admired "colored people," without ever knowing a single African American. Then, a little more than a decade after that day in the railroad cut, my confusion was rekindled and a mystery was added.

The summer of my second year in college, 1962, I was working in an engineering office in Winston-Salem, North Carolina. On one lunch hour, while eating alone at the K & W Cafeteria, a young black man, about my age, dressed in a coat and tie, came in and started to go through the line. The woman behind the standing roast beef spoke to him and the line stopped. People started going around him and finally the manager came up. The men exchanged words and then the young man turned and came to sit at the table next to mine. The manager followed and began to raise his voice in anger at the now silent demonstrator. Uncomfortable to be so close to this confrontation, I folded my newspaper and ducked out under a brass railing to keep from walking by his table.

That afternoon as I sat at my drawings, I pored over those lunchtime events. I had never thought much about either segregation or where black people ate, and those social issues were not the focus of my reflections. No, I kept seeing that young man, my own age, sitting calmly at the table while people stared and the manager shouted at him with threats to call the police. It was his courage that held my attention; I had never before had "colored people" and courage in the same thought. He had been so calmly defiant of authority; where did he find that courage? Was I that courageous?

The confrontation continued. Through 1962 more sit-ins were staged; black leaders led marches and made speeches quoting from both the Bible and the Constitution. Many whites I knew were blindly furious at having the status quo disturbed by "uppity niggers." Others were forced to reflect; black leaders were touching a tender nerve, exposing contradictions between our clearly stated Christian and American values and our actions. We struggled to rationalize away the guilt of imposing or accepting an inequality so familiar that most had never perceived it as unjust. Slowly we began to change: I remember my father saying, "I don't like Martin Luther King, but some of the things he says are true." My family shared the pain as we heard the tragic news of black children being bombed as they attended their Sunday school. Thinking people could not deny the dignity of black leaders who held hands and marched from Selma to Montgomery. I came to see that the movement was reinforcing justice and compassion as basic American values, and I remember a surprising sense of personal American pride at seeing justice prevail with the Civil Rights Act of 1964.

However white Southerners and others responded to the Civil Rights Movement, one thing was true: it commanded respect. Black leaders were courageous, dignified, and articulate. But where did their strength come from? How was it created? Most whites could not say. Consciously or unconsciously, we were forced through the movement to question at least one set of commonly held beliefs. How could American Negroes—supposedly primitive at worst and poorly educated at best—gather the strength to fight the establishment and win? The answer, of course, was that beyond the eye and mind of the white majority, African American culture was vibrantly alive, and had been alive for more than three hundred years. Through that span, African Americans combined African legacy with American culture, and along the way they left stories in the ground.

# Appendix 1.

# PROVENIENCE OF COLONO WARE VESSELS FROM SOUTH CAROLINA AND VIRGINIA BY COUNTY

In this listing and others in this appendix the initial alpha-numeric designation is the identifying specimen "number" associated with data on file for this project at the South Carolina Institute of Archæology and Anthropology. In some cases, for example the "Herbert Pitcher" belonging to an individual or BIN-65-80E designating a specimen shown in Binford (1965:80), I created the specimen number; in most cases the specimen number is the repository catalog number. For artifacts from the South Carolina Institute of Archæology and Anthropology the first six digits of the catalog number are also the site designation. Plantation names are those used in the seventeenth and eighteenth centuries. Provenience information comes from the referenced publications or from repository notes.

**Abbreviations:**
SCIAA = South Carolina Institute of Archæology and Anthropology
CM = Charleston Museum
DHR = Department of Historic Resources, Commonwealth of Virginia
ACW = Department of Archaeology, Colonial Williamsburg
AWM = Department of Anthropology, College of William and Mary
FDHF = Flowerdew Hundred Foundation
WF&G = Wheaton, Friedlander, and Garrow 1983
D&A = Drucker and Anthony 1979
L&H = Lewis and Haskel 1980
L = Lewis 1978

K = Kelso 1984
B = Baker 1972

## South Carolina
### *Berkeley County:*
1. 38BK62-69-20: Pimlico Plantation, Cooper River, underwater. SCIAA.
2. 38BK62-69-39 (II or B): Pimlico Plantation, Cooper River, underwater. SCIAA.
3. 38BK62-70-130: Pimlico Plantation, Cooper River, underwater. SCIAA.
4. 38BK62-70-128: Pimlico Plantation, Cooper River, underwater. SCIAA.
5. 38BK62-70-132: Pimlico Plantation, Cooper River, underwater. SCIAA.
6. 38BK62-1-2: Pimlico Plantation, Cooper River, underwater. SCIAA.
7. 38BK62-75-72: Pimlico Plantation, Cooper River, underwater. SCIAA.
8. 38BK62-68-22: Pimlico Plantation, Cooper River, underwater. SCIAA.
9. 38BK62-69-32: Pimlico Plantation, Cooper River, underwater. SCIAA.
10. 38BK62-69-39 (I or A): Pimlico Plantation, Cooper River, underwater. SCIAA.
11. 38BK62-69-40: Pimlico Plantation, Cooper River, underwater. SCIAA.
12. 38BK62-75-74: Pimlico Plantation, Cooper River, underwater. SCIAA.
13. 38BK51-2-1: Childsbury Village, Cooper River, underwater. SCIAA.
14. 38BK51-2-1: Childsbury Village, Cooper River, underwater. SCIAA.
15. 38BK48-WW-1: Mepkin Plantation, Cooper River, underwater.
16. 38BK48-WW-2: Mepkin Plantation, Cooper River, underwater.
17. Cooper River 1: unknown provenience, Cooper River, underwater. SCIAA.
18. Cooper River 2: unknown provenience: Cooper River, underwater. SCIAA.
19. 38BK76-F2-1: Yaughan Plantation, clay extraction/trash pit near slave house (Structure 76C). WF&G; SCIAA.
20. 38BK75B-F2-3: Yaughan Plantation, clay extraction/trash pit near slave house (Structure 76C). WF&G; SCIAA.
21. 38BK76-F14-1: Yaughan Plantation, clay extraction/trash pit near slave house (Structure 76L). WF&G; SCIAA.
22. 38BK75-F31-1: Yaughan Plantation, clay extraction pit near slave houses. WF&G; SCIAA.
23. 38BK75B-F2-13: Yaughan Plantation, clay extraction/trash pit near slave houses (Structures 75B1 & 2). WF&G; SCIAA.
24. 38BK75B-F29-6: Yaughan Plantation, clay extraction/trash pit near slave houses (Structures 75B1 & 2). WF&G; SCIAA.
25. 38BK75B-F29-5: Yaughan Plantation, clay extraction/trash pit near slave houses (Structures 75B1 & 2). WF&G; SCIAA.
26. 38BK245A-A10: Curriboo Plantation, cellar of plantation office? (Structure 245A). WF&G; SCIAA.
27. 38BK245A-A7: Curriboo Plantation, cellar of plantation office? (Structure 245A). WF&G; SCIAA.
28. 38BK245-F6-2: Curriboo Plantation, irrigation ditch near slave houses. WF&G; SCIAA.

Some important African American archæological sites along the South
Atlantic Coast.

29. 38BK160-8D-9-I: Spiers Landing. D&A; SCIAA.
30. 38BK160-10B-12G13: Spiers Landing. D&A; SCIAA.
31. 38BK160-8E-10G9: Spiers Landing. D&A; SCIAA.
32. 38BK160-10C-4: Spiers Landing. D&A; SCIAA.
33. 38BK160-8D-9-2: Spiers Landing. D&A; SCIAA.
34. 38BK160-8G-5: Spiers Landing. D&A; SCIAA.
35. ETN-124, 17224-B: Purchased in 1805 from Catawba Indians at Yaughan Plantation. CM.

### Charleston County:

1. 38CH241-78B-1: Hampton Plantation, pit associated with slaves on basis of high
percentage of Colono Ware. L&H; SCIAA.
2. 38CH241-77C-1: Hampton Plantation, pit associated with slaves on basis of high
percentage of Colono Ware. L&H; SCIAA.

3. DH41D: Drayton Hall, between main house and kitchen flanker. L; CM.
4. DH28Q/IQ: Drayton Hall, behind kitchen flanker of main house. L; CM.
5. DH28QQ-I: Drayton Hall, behind kitchen flanker of main house. L; CM.
6. DH28QQ-II: Drayton Hall, behind kitchen flanker of main house. L; CM.
7. HWNII8: Charleston, Heyward-Washington House. CM.
8. HWN#9: Charleston, Heyward-Washington House. CM.
9. 38CH201-ARL 200: Charleston, 28 St. Phillip St. CM.
10. ARL 10,15: Charleston, Meeting and Holbeck Streets. CM.
11. "Herbert Pitcher": Charleston, privy at 107 Church St.

### Colleton County:

1. 38CN7-1-196: Bluff Plantation, Combahee River, underwater. SCIAA.
2. 38CN7-1-254 (A): Bluff Plantation, Combahee River, underwater. SCIAA.
3. 38CN7-1-254 (B): Bluff Plantation, Combahee River, underwater. SCIAA.
4. 38CN7-1-254 (C): Bluff Plantation, Combahee River, underwater. SCIAA.
5. 38CN7-1-254 (D): Bluff Plantation, Combahee River, underwater. SCIAA.
6. 38CN7-1-109: Bluff Plantation, Combahee River, underwater. SCIAA.
7. 38CN7-19-5: Bluff Plantation, Combahee River, underwater. SCIAA.

### Dorchester County:

1. 38DR15-20A-56: H = 4.0 cm, W = 9.7 cm. Newington Plantation. SCIAA.
2. 38DR15-200F-21: Newington Plantation. SCIAA.

### Georgetown County:

1. 38GE57-1-37: Brown's Ferry vessel, Black River, underwater. SCIAA.
2. 38GE57-79-4: Brown's Ferry vessel, Black River, underwater. SCIAA.
3. 38GE62-2-1: Keithfield Plantation, Black River, underwater. SCIAA.

### Greenwood County:

1. 38GN2-I: Cambridge, cellar of house. B; SCIAA.
2. 38GN2-III: Cambridge, cellar of house. B; SCIAA.

### Virginia
### James City County:

1. KM402C: Kingsmill Plantation, slave quarter. K; CW.
2. KM751E: Kingsmill Plantation, north quarter. K; CW.
3. KM404C: Kingsmill Plantation, slave quarter. K; CW.
4. KM54C (1): Pettus Plantation. K; CW.
5. KM54G: Pettus Plantation. K; CW.
6. KM55C-1: Pettus Plantation. K; CW.
7. KM55C-2: Pettus Plantation. K; CW.
8. KM312M-I: Pettus Plantation, Utopia Cottage. K; CW.

9. KM312M-II: Pettus Plantation, Utopia Cottage. K; CW.

10. KM312G,K,M (1): Pettus Plantation, Utopia Cottage. K; CW.

11. KM314A (1): Pettus Plantation, Utopia Cottage. K; CW.

12. GL223-A: Governors Land. CW.

13. GL449-A: Governors Land. CW.

14. GL462-A: Governors Land. CW.

### Prince George County:

1. PG3/577F2A3-16C: Flowerdew Hundred. FDHF.

2. PG3/508B3CD8-54: SPL=0: Flowerdew Hundred. FDHF.

### Williamsburg County:

1. ER386A-15A: Williamsburg, post office. CW.

2. ER378-15A: Williamsburg, post office. CW.

3. 10C-136-29A1: Williamsburg, First Theatre (Gilmer). CW.

4. 18H: Williamsburg, Virginia Gazette/Hunter's Store/Hunter's Tenement. CW.

5. 10C-71-16B: Williamsburg, president's house. CW.

6. ER600C-14G: Williamsburg, Travis house (lots J & K). CW.

7. NH62-10-9(17J3): Williamsburg, Nicholson shop kitchen. CW.

8. ER1745-G-4C & ER1700-A-4C: Williamsburg, public hospital. CW.

9. ER1779L-61-4C & ER1779L-62-4C: Williamsburg, public hospital. CW.

10. ER1779S-II-4C: Williamsburg, public hospital. CW.

11. ER1779F-4C: Williamsburg, public hospital. CW.

12. 17J4: Williamsburg, apothecary shop outbuilding. CW.

13. ER1165W-9N: Williamsburg, Weatherburn's tavern. CW.

14. 5348 ER1165W-9N: Williamsburg, Weatherburn's tavern. CW.

15. 10C-58-10B: Williamsburg, Brick House tavern. CW.

16. 10C-107-20A 19: Williamsburg, Palace (west court outbuildings). CW.

17. 10C-112-20A 21: Williamsburg, Palace kitchen (SW corner of terraces). CW.

18. ER22: Williamsburg, corner of Henry & Duke of Gloucester Streets. CW.

19. TL807C: Williamsburg, Trebell's Landing. CW.

20. CL118J,L,M: College Landing. CW.

21. CL118H,L,M: College Landing. CW.

22. WS277: Mathews Manor. CW.

23. ER1570B-2P & ER1570D-2P: Hubard Site. CW.

24. ER797D-4B & ER797G-4B: Custis Site. CW.

25. 10C-54-9D1. W&M.

# Appendix 2.

# SPECIMEN NUMBERS FOR WHOLE VESSELS SHOWN IN FIGURES

Figure 10. 10C-58-10B.

Figure 11. 10C-112-20A21.

Figure 15. 38CN7-19-5.

Figure 21. 38BK62-70-12.

Figure 23. KM751E.

Figure 25. 38CN7-1-254B.

Figure 26. 10C-112-20A21.

Figure 27. 38BK62-75-72.

Figure 28. 38BK48-322.

Figure 35. Left to right: KM312G, no data, KM312M, KM55C.

Figure 36. KM54G.

Figure 40. ER797B.4B.

Figure 62. 38BK245A-A10.

Figure 63. 38BK160-10C-4, 38BK160-8D-9-I, 38BK160-10B.

Figure 64. 38CH241-77C-1.

Figure 65. 38BK75B-F2-13.

Figure 68. From top left: Cooper River 1, 38BK75B-F2-3, ETN-124, ARL-8630, Herbert Pitcher.

Figure 69. ETN-124.

Figure 75. 38BK48-JT-5.

# Appendix 3.

# COLONO WARE AND ARCHITECTURAL DATA

Table 1. Ceramic Frequencies from Colonial Sites, Ranked by Percentage

| Site Name | State:[1] Type[2] | Colono Ware | % | Imported Ceramics | % | Total |
|-----------|-----------|-------------|---|-------------------|---|-------|
| *Rural Sites* | | | | | | |
| Curriboo | SC:SQ | 3,333 | 88.22 | 445 | 11.78 | 3,778 |
| Yaughan | SC:SQ | 18,024 | 87.19 | 2,649 | 12.81 | 20,673 |
| Middleburg | SC:SQ | 2,095 | 79.42 | 543 | 20.58 | 2,638 |
| Smoky Hill | SC:H,K,SQ | 196 | 74.24 | 68 | 25.76 | 264 |
| Hampton (1) | SC:SQ | 430 | 74.14 | 150 | 25.86 | 580 |
| Lesesne (2) | SC:SQ | 895 | 61.94 | 550 | 38.06 | 1,445 |
| Middleton | SC:H,K | 3,383 | 61.79 | 2,092 | 38.21 | 5,475 |
| Spiers Landing | SC:SQ | 1,230 | 55.91 | 970 | 44.09 | 2,200 |
| Limerick | SC:H,K | 4,818 | 38.54 | 7,684 | 61.46 | 12,502 |
| Halidon Hill | SC:SQ | 141 | 36.62 | 244 | 63.38 | 385 |
| Lesene (1) | SC:H | 7,738 | 36.20 | 13,639 | 63.80 | 21,377 |
| Pettus | VA:H,K | n.d. | 29.00 | n.d. | 71.00 | n.d. |
| Hampton (2) | SC:H,K | 94 | 26.86 | 256 | 73.14 | 350 |
| Green Grove | SC:H,K | 4,182 | 26.68 | 11,491 | 73.32 | 15,673 |
| Fairbank | SC:H | 1,137 | 22.27 | 3,969 | 77.73 | 5,106 |

(*continued*)

**Table 1.** (*Continued*)

| Site Name | State:[1] Type[2] | Colono Ware | % | Imported Ceramics | % | Total |
|---|---|---|---|---|---|---|
| Utopia | VA:H | n.d. | 17.00 | n.d. | 83.00 | n.d. |
| Drayton Hall | SC:H,K | 1,600 | 16.18 | 8,290 | 83.82 | 9,890 |
| Wormslow | GA:W | 6 | 4.51 | 127 | 95.49 | 133 |
| Kings Bay (Cabin A) | GA:SQ | 6 | 0.90 | 664 | 99.10 | 670 |
| Total rural | | 49,308 | 47.81 | 53,831 | 52.19 | 103,139 |
| *Urban and Fort Sites* | | | | | | |
| De La Cruz | FL | 8,359 | 93.73 | 559 | 6.27 | 8,918 |
| SA-7-4 | FL | 3,523 | 65.43 | 1,861 | 34.57 | 5,384 |
| Ft. Moultrie | SC | 758 | 37.99 | 1,237 | 62.01 | 1,995 |
| Ninety Six Jail | SC | 100 | 17.06 | 486 | 82.94 | 586 |
| Rutledge House | SC | 117 | 4.00 | 2,808 | 96.00 | 2,925 |
| Gibbes House | SC | 10 | 3.60 | 268 | 96.40 | 278 |
| Camden | SC | 386 | 3.02 | 12,410 | 96.98 | 12,796 |
| Edenton | NC | 324 | 2.28 | 13,863 | 97.72 | 14,187 |
| Meeting Street | SC | 90 | 1.48 | 5,971 | 98.52 | 6,061 |
| Brunswick Town | NC | 243 | 1.03 | 23,427 | 98.97 | 23,670 |
| Cambridge | SC | 62 | 0.70 | 8,751 | 99.30 | 8,813 |
| Long Bluff | SC | 0 | 0.00 | 710 | 100.00 | 710 |
| Total urban/fort | | 13,972 | 16.19 | 72,351 | 83.81 | 86,323 |

[1]GA = Georgia, FL = Florida, NC = North Carolina, SC = South Carolina, VA = Virginia
[2]SQ = Slave quarter, H = Plantation house, K = Plantation kitchen, W = Water well
*Sources:*

| Site | Source |
|---|---|
| Brunswick Town | South 1977:126–127 |
| Cambridge | South 1977:128–129 |
| Camden | Lewis 1976:158–168 |
| Curriboo | Wheaton et al. 1983:219–222, 241 |
| De La Cruz | Deagan 1983:113 |
| Drayton Hall | Lewis 1978:63–65 |
| Edenton | Foss et al. 1979:97–107 |
| Ft. Moultrie | South 1974:181 |
| Gibbes House | Zierden et al. 1987:48–59 |
| Green Grove | Carrillo 1980:75 |

(*continued*)

**Table 1.** (*Continued*)

| Site | Source |
|------|--------|
| Halidon Hill | Affleck 1990:114–123, 160–164 |
| Hampton | Lewis and Haskell 1980:72–78, 69–90 |
| Kings Bay (Cabin A) | Adams 1987:179, 196 |
| Lesesne | Zierden et al. 1986:4.108–4.109, 7.27 |
| Limerick | Lees 1980:130 |
| Long Bluff | Lewis 1975:26–27 |
| Meeting Street | Herold 1981:74 |
| Middleburg | Affleck 1990:103–114, 149–159 |
| Middleton | Lewis and Hardesty 1979:76, 79 |
| Ninety Six Jail | Holschlag and Rodeffer 1977:98 |
| Pettus | Outlaw et al. 1979, fig. 2 |
| Rutledge House | Zierden and Grimes 1989:62–69 |
| SA-7-4 | Shepard 1983:77 |
| Smoky Hill | Affleck 1990:91–102, 143–149 |
| Spiers Landing | Drucker and Anthony 1979:66 |
| Utopia | Outlaw et al. 1979, fig. 2 |
| Wormslow | Kelso 1979:161–162 |
| Yaughan | Wheaton et al. 1983:219–222, 241 |

**Table 2. Whole Colono Ware Vessels from Virginia**

| Catalog Number[1] | Type | Height (cm) | Major Diameter (cm) | Wall Thickness (cm) | Charred | Spall | Date Range[2] |
|---|---|---|---|---|---|---|---|
| BIN-65-80E | Bowl | 7.50 | 26.00 | n.d. | n.d. | n.d. | 1670–1760 |
| BIN-65-80F | Bowl | 3.50 | 29.00 | n.d. | n.d. | n.d. | 1670–1760 |
| NH-62-10-4 | Bowl | 6.30 | 20.30 | n.d. | 0 | 0 | 1763–1772 |
| ER1779L-62-4C | Bowl | 7.70 | 17.00 | 0.80 | 0 | 0 | 1705–1750 |
| VGAZETTE 18H | Bowl | 5.30 | 15.90 | 0.80 | 0 | 0 | 1650–1825 |
| WS-277 | Bowl | 6.10 | 16.20 | 1.10 | 0 | 0 | 1650–1850 |
| NH-68-5-13 | Bowl | 8.80 | 22.80 | n.d. | 0 | 0 | 1730–1740 |
| KM54C-1 | Bowl | 13.20 | 41.00 | 1.40 | 0 | 0 | 1650–1700 |
| ER1779F-4C | Bowl | 7.60 | 20.30 | 0.70 | 0 | 0 | 1705–1750 |
| ER386A-15A | Bowl | 5.60 | 16.50 | 0.60 | 0 | 0 | 1770–1775 |
| KM404C | Bowl | 4.70 | 10.50 | 0.70 | 0 | 1 | 1735–1780 |
| KM402C | Bowl | 8.40 | 20.70 | 1.10 | 0 | 0 | 1650–1780 |
| 10C-107-20A19 | Bowl | 9.30 | 27.40 | 0.70 | 0 | 0 | 1650–1825 |
| GL223A | Bowl | 2.70 | 7.30 | 0.45 | 0 | 0 | 1650–1780 |
| 10C-71-16B | Bowl | 5.40 | 16.30 | 0.70 | 0 | 0 | 1650–1825 |
| 10C-16-2B1 | Bowl | 5.00 | 23.90 | n.d. | 0 | 0 | 1690–1800 |
| 10C-112-20A21 | Bowl | 8.50 | 19.20 | 0.70 | 0 | 0 | 1690–1800 |
| GL449A | Bowl | 3.00 | 8.00 | 0.30 | 0 | 0 | 1750–1775 |
| KM312G,K,M-1 | Bowl | 9.30 | 26.20 | 1.20 | 0 | 0 | 1680–1710 |
| 10C-150-44B | Bowl | 6.50 | 20.30 | n.d. | 0 | 0 | 1690–1800 |
| 17J3 | Bowl | 7.30 | 19.70 | 0.80 | 0 | 0 | 1690–1800 |
| ER1779S-11-4C | Bowl | 7.50 | 24.10 | 0.70 | 0 | n.d. | 1705–1750 |
| PG3/577F2A3-1 | Bowl | 9.70 | 25.50 | 0.65 | 0 | 0 | 1700–1750 |
| ER1700A-4C | Bowl | 6.30 | 15.80 | 0.70 | 0 | 0 | 1750–1800 |
| GL462A | Bowl | 7.20 | 19.00 | 0.55 | 0 | 0 | 1780–1825 |
| KM55C | Bowl | 6.00 | 20.00 | 0.90 | 0 | 0 | 1650–1675 |
| 10C-136-29A-1 | Bowl | 9.40 | 25.10 | 0.90 | 0 | 0 | 1690–1800 |
| KM751E | Bowl | 7.10 | 27.20 | 0.60 | 0 | 0 | 1770–1850 |
| PG3/508B3CD8 | Bowl | 9.20 | 30.40 | 0.60 | 1 | 0 | 1700–1750 |
| CL118J,L,M | Bowl | 3.80 | 13.70 | 0.50 | 0 | 0 | 1770–1850 |
| 10C-104-20A18 | Porringer | 5.50 | 13.70 | n.d. | 0 | 0 | 1690–1800 |
| ER1570B-2P | Porringer | 10.90 | 20.40 | 0.60 | 0 | 0 | 1650–1825 |
| 10C-6-1A2 | Porringer | 8.30 | 16.30 | n.d. | 0 | 0 | 1700–1725 |
| CL118H,L,M | Porringer | 7.80 | 16.60 | 0.70 | 0 | 0 | 1770–1850 |
| KM312M-1 | Soup plate | 5.40 | 16.00 | 1.10 | 0 | 0 | 1670–1710 |

*(continued)*

**Table 2.** *(Continued)*

| Catalog Number[1] | Type | Height (cm) | Major Diameter (cm) | Wall Thickness (cm) | Charred | Spall | Date Range[2] |
|---|---|---|---|---|---|---|---|
| CC34/FEA6-1 | Pan | 6.30 | 34.30 | 0.70 | 0 | 1 | 1700–1800 |
| NH-62-10-6 | Pan | 6.60 | 30.00 | n.d. | 0 | 0 | 1730–1740 |
| ER243G-28D | Skillet | 16.20 | 18.30 | n.d. | 0 | 0 | 1770–1780 |
| BIN-65-80B | Cup | 11.00 | 12.00 | n.d. | n.d. | n.d. | 1670–1760 |
| BIN-65-80A | Cup | 7.50 | 10.00 | n.d. | n.d. | n.d. | 1670–1760 |
| 10C-58-10B | Cup | 9.20 | 10.00 | 0.60 | 0 | 1 | 1690–1800 |
| CC34/FEA6-2 | Jar | 13.30 | 14.80 | 0.55 | 0 | 0 | 1700–1800 |
| KM312M-2 | Jar | 20.40 | 23.00 | 0.90 | 0 | 0 | 1660–1700 |
| KM314A-1 | Jar | 20.20 | 23.80 | 1.60 | 0 | 0 | 1680–1710 |
| KM54G | Jar | 13.30 | 15.20 | 1.10 | 0 | 1 | 1680–1710 |
| KM55C-1 | Jar | 14.20 | 16.60 | 1.30 | 0 | 0 | 1650–1675 |
| ER797C-4B | Chamber pot | 11.70 | 20.00 | 0.70 | 0 | 0 | 1780–1825 |
| 17J4 | Chamber pot | 12.00 | 21.10 | 0.90 | 0 | 0 | 1650–1825 |
| ER1165-W.9N | Chamber pot | 13.90 | 20.00 | 0.70 | 0 | 0 | 1690–1800 |
| 10C-54-9D1 | Chamber pot | 13.20 | 23.40 | 0.70 | 0 | 0 | 1650–1825 |

Total number vessels = 50

[1]See Appendix 1 for key to catalog numbers.

[2]Interval includes time during which vessel was made and used.

**Table 3. Whole Colono Vessels from South Carolina**

| Catalog Designation[1] | Type | Height (cm) | Major Diameter (cm) | Wall Thickness (cm) | Volume (liters[2]) | Charred | Spall | Mark | Date Range[3] |
|---|---|---|---|---|---|---|---|---|---|
| 38GN2-72-23J | Bowl | 6.50 | 23.50 | 0.90 | 1.74 | 0 | 0 | 0 | 1670–1825 |
| 38CN7-1-254A | Bowl | 6.20 | 20.80 | 0.60 | 1.08 | 0 | 0 | 0 | 1670–1825 |
| 38BK160-8G-5 | Bowl | 5.30 | 24.00 | 0.80 | 0.72 | 0 | 0 | 0 | 1790–1805 |
| Stamped Vessel | Bowl | 9.00 | 26.00 | 0.70 | 1.92 | 0 | 0 | 0 | 1670–1825 |
| 38BK75B-F29-5 | Bowl | 7.00 | 20.80 | 0.60 | 1.74 | 0 | 1 | 0 | 1775–1800 |
| 38BK75B-F2-3 | Bowl | 3.70 | 9.70 | 0.50 | 0.12 | 0 | 0 | 0 | 1775–1800 |
| 38BK51-2-1 | Bowl | 11.60 | 18.20 | 0.90 | 1.71 | 0 | 0 | 1 | 1670–1825 |
| 38GN2-72-23H | Bowl | 7.10 | 21.60 | 0.80 | 1.92 | 0 | 0 | 0 | 1790–1810 |
| 38BK75-F31-1 | Bowl | 6.40 | 20.50 | 0.50 | 1.22 | 1 | 0 | 0 | 1775–1800 |
| 38BK76-F2-1 | Bowl | 6.80 | 15.80 | 0.50 | 0.53 | 0 | 0 | 0 | 1775–1800 |
| 38BK160-8D-9 | Bowl | 5.30 | 20.90 | 1.00 | 0.72 | 0 | 0 | 0 | 1790–1805 |
| 38BK75B-F2-13 | Bowl | 6.50 | 22.30 | 0.90 | 1.43 | 0 | 0 | 0 | 1775–1800 |
| Cooper River 1 | Bowl | 5.80 | 19.10 | 0.60 | 0.78 | 0 | 0 | 1 | 1670–1925 |
| 38CN7-1-109 | Bowl | 10.20 | 29.20 | 0.70 | 3.63 | 0 | 0 | 0 | 1670–1825 |
| ARL-200 | Bowl | 11.00 | 17.90 | 0.60 | 1.38 | 0 | 0 | 0 | 1700–1825 |
| 38BK62-69-20 | Bowl | 7.20 | 18.90 | 0.60 | 1.19 | 0 | 0 | 0 | 1670–1825 |
| 38BK48-WW-2 | Bowl | 6.40 | 17.10 | n.d. | 0.80 | 0 | 0 | 0 | 1670–1825 |
| 38BK62-68-22 | Bowl | 5.50 | 12.00 | 0.40 | 0.28 | 0 | 0 | 0 | 1670–1825 |
| 38BK75B-F29-6 | Bowl | 4.70 | 20.30 | 1.00 | 0.79 | 0 | 0 | 0 | 1775–1800 |
| 38CN7-1-254-B | Bowl | 6.20 | 16.90 | 0.60 | n.d. | n.d. | 0 | 0 | 1670–1825 |
| 38BK62-70-132 | Bowl | 6.40 | 17.20 | 0.65 | 0.75 | 0 | 0 | 0 | 1670–1825 |

| ID | Form | | | | | | | | Date |
|---|---|---|---|---|---|---|---|---|---|
| 38BK48-1-478 | Bowl | 6.40 | 20.10 | 0.50 | 1.14 | 0 | 0 | 1 | 1670–1825 |
| 38BK62-70-130 | Bowl | 6.80 | 17.10 | 0.60 | 0.76 | 0 | 0 | 0 | 1670–1825 |
| 38BK62-70-128 | Bowl | 6.00 | 17.20 | 0.65 | 0.75 | 0 | 0 | 0 | 1670–1825 |
| 38CN7-1-254-C | Bowl | 7.80 | 19.10 | 0.90 | 1.19 | 0 | 0 | 0 | 1670–1825 |
| 38BK160-8D-9 | Bowl | 6.90 | 18.10 | 0.50 | 1.10 | 1 | 0 | 0 | 1790–1810 |
| 38BK48-377 | Bowl | 8.90 | 17.50 | 0.70 | 1.02 | 0 | 0 | 1 | 1650–1850 |
| 38BK48-WW-1 | Bowl | 4.30 | 13.00 | n.d. | 0.19 | 0 | 0 | 0 | 1670–1825 |
| DH28QQ-2 | Bowl | 6.00 | 23.00 | 0.80 | 1.30 | 0 | 0 | 0 | 1700–1850 |
| 38GE57-79-4 (RB) | Bowl | 7.00 | 19.80 | 0.50 | 1.12 | 1 | 0 | 0 | 1740–1745 |
| Cooper River 2 | Bowl | 4.80 | 12.00 | 1.00 | 0.19 | 0 | 0 | 0 | 1650–1850 |
| 38DR15-200F-21 | Bowl | 6.40 | 32.40 | 0.90 | 2.23 | 0 | 1 | 0 | 1670–1715 |
| 38DR15-20A-56 | Bowl | 4.00 | 9.80 | 0.90 | 0.15 | 0 | 0 | 0 | 1670–1715 |
| 38BK48-378 | Bowl | 7.50 | 19.30 | 0.60 | 1.29 | 0 | 0 | 1 | 1650–1850 |
| 38GE62-2-1 | Bowl | 6.40 | 14.50 | 0.60 | 0.51 | 0 | 1 | 0 | 1670–1825 |
| DH28Q/IQ | Bowl | 5.40 | 20.90 | 0.65 | 1.04 | 0 | 1 | 0 | n.d.   n.d. |
| 38BK62-75-72 | Bowl | 9.60 | 26.00 | 0.60 | 1.72 | 0 | 0 | 0 | 1670–1825 |
| 38BK160-8E | Bowl | 7.10 | 18.20 | 0.50 | 0.96 | 0 | 0 | 0 | 1790–1805 |
| 38BK62-69-40 | Bowl | 5.00 | 14.60 | 0.65 | 0.52 | 0 | 0 | 0 | 1670–1825 |
| 38BK62-75-74 | Bowl | 5.70 | 20.20 | 0.60 | 0.93 | 0 | 0 | 1 | 1670–1825 |
| 38BK48-1-477 | Bowl | 7.40 | 16.50 | 0.80 | 0.70 | 0 | 0 | 0 | 1670–1825 |
| 38BK51-1-1 | Bowl | 7.90 | 22.20 | 0.70 | 1.66 | 0 | 0 | 0 | 1650–1850 |
| DH28QQ-1 | Pan | 3.70 | 21.00 | 0.50 | n.d. | 0 | 0 | 0 | 1700–1850 |
| DH41D | Pan | 3.00 | 13.40 | 0.60 | n.d. | 0 | 0 | 0 | n.d.   n.d. |
| 38CN7-1-196 | Pan | 6.00 | 31.60 | 0.60 | 0.96 | 0 | 0 | 0 | 1670–1825 |
| HWN #9 | Pan | 5.00 | 26.00 | 0.90 | 1.10 | 0 | 0 | 0 | 1760–1825 |

(continued)

**Table 3.** (*Continued*)

| Catalog Designation[1] | Type | Height (cm) | Major Diameter (cm) | Wall Thickness (cm) | Volume liters[2] | Charred | Spall | Mark | Date Range[3] |
|---|---|---|---|---|---|---|---|---|---|
| HWN #8 | Plate | 3.50 | 26.20 | 0.70 | n.d. | 0 | 0 | 0 | 1760–1825 |
| ARL-10-151 | Plate | 3.50 | 19.60 | 0.75 | n.d. | 0 | 0 | 0 | 1775–1810 |
| 38BK245A-A10 | Jar | 17.40 | 15.50 | 0.70 | 1.93 | 0 | 0 | 0 | 1775–1800 |
| 38BK62-69-39A | Jar | 15.60 | 14.50 | 0.60 | 1.17 | 1 | 0 | 0 | 1670–1825 |
| ARL-8630 (RB) | Jar | 15.50 | 18.90 | 0.75 | 2.59 | 1 | 0 | 0 | 1775–1810 |
| 38BK160-10C-4 | Jar | 11.60 | 13.50 | 0.50 | 0.92 | 1 | 0 | 0 | 1790–1805 |
| 38BK245-F6-2 | Jar | 15.40 | 14.90 | 0.80 | 1.44 | 1 | 0 | 0 | 1775–1800 |
| 38BK245A-A7 | Jar | 12.70 | 15.00 | 0.60 | 1.35 | 1 | 1 | 0 | 1775–1800 |
| 38GE57-1-37 | Jar | 19.80 | 22.90 | 0.80 | 4.64 | 1 | 0 | 0 | 1740–1750 |
| 38BK76-F14-1 | Jar | 11.50 | 19.00 | 0.75 | 2.03 | 0 | 0 | 0 | 1775–1800 |

| Catalog no. | Vessel | | | | Volume | | | | Interval |
|---|---|---|---|---|---|---|---|---|---|
| 38BK160-10B | Jar | 21.40 | 24.80 | 0.80 | 5.83 | 1 | 0 | 0 | 1790–1805 |
| 38CN7-1-254-D | Jar | 16.20 | 20.00 | 0.80 | 2.89 | 0 | 0 | 0 | 1670–1825 |
| 38BK62-69-39-B | Jar | 12.60 | 13.80 | 0.75 | n.d. | 1 | 1 | 0 | 1670–1825 |
| 38CH241-78B-1 | Jar | 13.70 | 15.90 | 0.52 | 1.55 | 1 | 0 | 0 | 1750–1780 |
| 38BK48-1-457 | Jar | 11.60 | 14.80 | 0.50 | 1.14 | 0 | 1 | 0 | 1670–1825 |
| 38BK48-322 | Jar | 11.90 | 13.00 | 0.65 | 0.94 | 0 | 1 | 0 | 1670–1825 |
| 38BK62-58-32 | Jar | 15.30 | 19.40 | 1.00 | 2.38 | 0 | 0 | 0 | 1670–1825 |
| 38BK38-323 | Jar | 13.50 | 17.70 | 0.65 | n.d. | 0 | 0 | 0 | 1670–1825 |
| Herbert Pitcher (RB) | Pitcher | 13.00 | 15.80 | 0.40 | 1.78 | 0 | 0 | 0 | 1790–1810 |
| ETN-124 (RB) | Pitcher | 13.50 | 11.60 | 0.60 | 0.79 | 0 | 0 | 0 | 1805 |
| 38CH241-77C-1 | Teapot | 12.30 | 14.90 | 0.69 | 1.08 | 0 | 1 | 0 | 1750–1780 |

Total number vessels = 67

[1]See Appendix 1 for key to catalog numbers

[2]Volumes calculated by Marion Smith

[3]Interval includes time during which vessel was made and used

**Table 4. Characteristics of South Carolina and Virginia Colono Ware Shapes**

| | Number | Average Thickness (cm) | STD[1] | Average Height (cm) | STD | Average Diameter (cm) | STD | Average Volume (liters) | STD |
|---|---|---|---|---|---|---|---|---|---|
| All SC Vessels | 67 | 0.68 | 0.15 | 8.68 | 4.21 | 18.77 | 4.71 | 1.36 | 0.98 |
| All VA Vessels | 50 | 0.80 | 0.24 | 8.70 | 3.89 | 20.02 | 6.60 | n.d. | n.d. |
| SC Vessels without River Burnished[2] | 61 | 0.70 | 0.15 | 8.57 | 4.17 | 19.07 | 4.69 | 1.38 | 1 |
| SC River Burnished | 6 | 0.56 | 0.11 | 9.75 | 4.42 | 15.82 | 3.90 | 1.2 | 0.79 |
| VA Vessels without Pettus & Utopia[3] | 41 | 0.69 | 0.16 | 7.54 | 3.01 | 19.47 | 6.27 | n.d. | n.d. |
| Pettus & Utopia, Types A&B[4] | 9 | 1.18 | 0.21 | 12.95 | 5.22 | 22.72 | 7.44 | n.d. | n.d. |
| SC Bowls | 42 | 0.68 | 0.21 | 6.72 | 1.70 | 19.15 | 4.57 | 1.10 | 0.67 |
| SC Bowls without River Burnished | 36 | 0.70 | 0.16 | 6.81 | 1.69 | 19.37 | 4.48 | 1.13 | 0.66 |
| SC River Burnished Bowls | 3 | 0.53 | 0.05 | 5.50 | 1.36 | 16.20 | 4.61 | 0.67 | 0.42 |
| VA Bowls[5] | 35 | 0.76 | 0.37 | 6.98 | 2.25 | 20.84 | 6.85 | n.d. | n.d. |

(*continued*)

**Table 4.** (*Continued*)

| | Number | Average Thickness (cm) | STD | Average Height (cm) | STD | Average Diameter (cm) | STD | Average Volume (liters) | STD |
|---|---|---|---|---|---|---|---|---|---|
| VA Bowls without Pettus & Utopia | 30 | 0.68 | 0.16 | 6.64 | 2.04 | 19.51 | 5.79 | n.d. | n.d. |
| VA Bowls, Pettus & Utopia | 6 | 1.14 | 0.16 | 8.48 | 2.78 | 25.80 | 8.74 | n.d. | n.d. |
| SC Jars | 16 | 0.70 | 0.13 | 14.73 | 2.86 | 17.10 | 3.35 | 2.20 | 1.39 |
| SC Jars without River Burnished | 15 | 0.69 | 0.13 | 14.68 | 2.95 | 16.98 | 3.43 | 2.17 | 1.44 |
| SC Jars, River Burnished | 1 | 0.75 | 0 | 15.5 | 0 | 18.90 | 0 | 2.59 | 0 |
| VA Jars | 5 | 1.09 | 0.36 | 16.28 | 3.30 | 18.68 | 3.91 | n.d. | n.d. |
| VA Jars without Pettus & Utopia | 1 | 0.55 | 0 | 13.30 | 0 | 14.30 | 0 | n.d. | n.d. |
| VA Jars, Pettus & Utopia | 4 | 1.23 | 0.16 | 17.03 | 3.29 | 19.65 | 3.79 | n.d. | n.d. |

[1]STD = standard deviation.
[2]River Burnished type (Ferguson 1990).
[3]Includes Henry's (1980) Types C, D, and E.
[4]Bowls include porringers.
[5]Includes Henry's (1980) Types A and B.

**Table 5. Characteristics of Field-Hand Slave Quarters, Kingsmill Tract near Williamsburg, Virginia**

| Site | Type of Foundation | Units | Chimney | Cellars | Room Dimen.[1] | Unit Addition | Porch Dimen. | Date Range |
|---|---|---|---|---|---|---|---|---|
| Bray Qtr. | Earthfast | Single | Stick & Clay? | 4 | 12 × 12 | none | 4 × 12 | 1740–1781 |
| Littletown Qtr., 1 | Earthfast | Single | Stick & Clay? | 1 | 12 × 16 | none | 6 × 16 | 1750–1781 |
| Littletown Qtr., 2 | Earthfast | Single | Stick & Clay? | 3 | 15 × 15 | none | 5 × 15 | 1750–1781 |
| Kingsmill Qtr., 1 | Brick | Double | Brick | 18 | 20 × 18 | 12 × 36 | none | 1760–1781 |
| Kingsmill Qtr., 2 | Brick | Single | Brick | 6 | 28 × 20 | none | none | ?–1780 |
| Hampton Bay | Earthfast | Single | Stick & Clay? | 5 | 28 × 24 | 14 × 12 | none | 1750–1781 |
| North Qtr. | Brick | Single | Brick? | 2 | 25 × 16 | none | none | 1775–1781 |

Average room size = 365 square feet

Average earthfast room size = 308 square feet

[1] All dimensions in feet

*Source:* Kelso 1984:102–129

**Table 6. Characteristics of Colonial South Carolina Slave Quarters**

| Site | Foundation Type | Units | Room Dimen. (ft) | Chimney | Date Range[1] |
|------|-----------------|-------|------------------|---------|---------------|
| Spiers Landing | Post | Single | 20 × 15.5 | S & C[2] | 1775–1830 |
| Yaughan 75B1 | Post | Single | 12.5 × 11 | S & C | ?–1810 |
| Yaughan 75B2 | Post & Trench | Single | 13 × 10 | S & C | 1790 |
| Yaughan 76C | Trench | Single | 21.5 × 11.5 | none | 1790 |
| Yaughan 76D1 | Trench | Single | 13.5 × 11 | none | 1750–1800 |
| Yaughan 76D2 | Trench | Single | 17 × 10.5 | none | 1750–1800 |
| Yaughan 76M | Post | Single | 13 × 11.5 | none | 1750–1800 |
| Yaughan 76E | Trench | Double | 13 × 11.5 | none | 1750–1800 |
| Yaughan 76F | Trench | Single | 18.5 × 12 | none | 1750–1800 |
| Yaughan 76G | Trench | Single | 14.5 × 9.8 | none | 1750–1800 |
| Yaughan 76A | Trench | Single | 13 × 9.5 | none | 1773 |
| Yaughan 76K | Trench | Single | 18.8 × 14 | none | 1750–1800 |
| Yaughan 76L | Trench | Single | 15.5 × 10 | none | 1788 |
| Yaughan 76B1 | Trench | Single | 18 × 12 | none | 1788 |
| Yaughan 76B2 | Post | Single | 18 × 18 | none | 1750–1800 |
| Curriboo 245B | Trench | Double | 14 × 20 | none | 1750–1800 |
| Curriboo 245D | Trench | Double | 13.5 × 20 | none | 1750–1800 |
| Curriboo 245E | Trench | Single | 15 × 10 | none | 1750–1800 |
| Curriboo 245F | Trench | ? | 16 × ? | none | 1750–1800 |
| Middleburg | Post | ? | 14 × 28 | ? | 1786–1825 |

Average Room Size = 209 square feet

[1]House stood sometime during these dates or date ranges.

[2]Stick & clay.

*Sources:* Spiers Landing    Drucker and Anthony 1979:90–119.
          Yaughan    Wheaton et al. 1983:98–212.
          Curriboo    Wheaton et al. 1983:98–212.
          Middleburg    Adams 1990:93, 113–119.

**Table 7. Marks on Colono Ware Bowls from South Carolina**

| Site & Artifact | Site Location | Base Type | Mark Location | Execution | Preservation |
|---|---|---|---|---|---|
| Pimlico 1 | uw | R | Ext | Post | Whole |
| Pimlico 2 | uw | R | Ext | Pre | Whole |
| Pimlico 3 | uw | F | Ext | Pre | Frag |
| Pimlico 4 | uw | ? | Int | Pre | Frag |
| Pimlico 5 | uw | R | Ext | Pre | Whole |
| Mepkin 1 | uw | R | Ext | Pre | Whole |
| Mepkin 2 | uw | R | Ext | Post | Whole |
| Mepkin 3 | uw | F | Ext | Post | Frag |
| Mepkin 4 | uw | R | Int | Post | Whole |
| Mepkin 5 | uw | F | Int | Pre | Frag |
| Mepkin 6 | uw | F | Int | Pre | Frag |
| Mepkin 7 | uw | Rnd | Int | Post | Frag |
| Mepkin 8 | uw | ? | Int | Pre | Frag |
| Middleburg-1 | ter | F | Int | Pre | Frag |
| Middleburg-2 | ter | F | Ext | Post | Frag |
| Middleburg-3 | ter | F | Int | Pre | Frag |
| Curriboo | ter | F | Int | Post | Frag |

Key: uw = underwater
ter = terrestrial
R = ring base
F = flat base
Rnd = rounded base
Ext = exterior
Int = interior
Post = post-firing
Pre = pre-firing
Frag = fragment of mark
Whole = whole mark

# Notes

**Prologue**

1. Wood 1974:142–155, 302.
2. A family bible records a baby born in the house at Middleburg in 1699, the first reference to this plantation name and house. According to Max L. Hill III, son of the present owner, the barns most likely were built in the early nineteenth century. The avenue of live oaks are probably those referred to in 1832 by A.E. Miller, who wrote of these trees being planted on Middleburg Plantation by J. Lucas. The servants' quarters were in such bad condition in the early 1980s that they were dismantled by the present owner with plans for rebuilding. The kitchen and one of the barns were lost in Hurricane Hugo, 1989.
3. Joseph 1987.
4. Banks on the East Branch of Cooper River contain approximately 500,000 cubic feet per river mile; the volume of the Cheops pyramid is about 91 million cubic feet. A measurement of approximately 500 miles of banked creeks and rivers indicates that the volume of the South Carolina rice bank system alone was nearly three times the volume of Cheops, the world's largest pyramid.
5. Jonathan Lucas's father, Thomas Lucas, adapted steam power to rice processing. One of the earliest rice mills as well as one of the earliest applications of industrial technology to agriculture, the mill at Middleburg probably dates from the first quarter of the nineteenth century. The effects that this change in the mode of

production may have had on the lives of Middleburg slaves is an interesting and unexplored topic.

6. Affleck 1990.

7. Briggs 1951:113.

8. Ibid.

9. These artifacts survived because of their stability. We didn't find pieces of clothing, fragments of wooden bowls, or kernels of rice or corn in the sifter screen. One can conceive of a continuum of probability of finding any given artifact based on chemical and organic stability. Rocks or bricks would be at the "preserved" end of the continuum, bones, shells, and most metals would be in the middle and materials like leather, cloth, or basketry would be at the "decayed" end. Nevertheless, under unusual conditions—where oxidation or bacterial action has been held to a minimum—even these latter materials may be recovered. Such conditions are most often found archaeologically in very dry or continuously wet conditions. In the southeastern United States there are situations where it is continuously wet—the muck in the bottom of rivers and marshes, in old privies, and in wells—and here we find excellent preservation.

10. Once a soil is disturbed by human activity such as digging a pit or building a house, archaeologists can usually detect it. Digging a neatly squared hole in virgin soil you would ideally see three obvious layers usually labeled as the A, B, and C horizons. "A" is a humus layer composed of decaying organic material. "B" is a second zone where decaying organic material is mixed with the inorganic soil below. "C" is a subsoil made up of inorganic sands and clays derived from the very slow deterioration of the earth's crust. When slave builders dug the original ditch at Middleburg to receive the upright posts, they dug through both the A and B horizons and dug up some of the bright yellow sandy subsoil that my students first encountered in the dark midden.

11. Nairne 1710:49.

### Introduction

1. Curtin 1969:216,264; Bean 1971:237; Klein 1978:14.

2. During the early years of settlement in the Carolina colony, many Native Americans as well as Africans were forced into slavery. Indian slavery was especially common during the first decade of the eighteenth century when the English colonists were raiding Spanish mission settlements in Florida. According to a census taken in 1708, approximately one-fourth of Carolina's 5,500 slaves were Indians. Lauber 1913:105–106; Petty 1943:21; Wood 1974:141–155.

3. These quotes are from Wood (1974:105), Vlach (1978:135), and Doar (1970:8) respectively.

4. For examples of slave narratives see Bayliss 1979; Blassingame 1977; Boney 1972; Bontemps 1969; Hurmence 1984, 1989; Lester 1968; and Rawick 1972.

5. King et al. 1977:30–31.

6. Fairbanks 1972, 1984.

7. Sea Island cotton was an especially fine variety of long-staple cotton, grown only on the Sea Islands of the southeastern coast of North America; for more information see Theodore Rosengarten (1986:68–76).

8. Some African American archaeology occurred sporadically before Fairbanks's work. In the 1930s, well-known prehistoric archaeologist James A. Ford (1937) excavated a sugar mill, presumably run by slaves, on the Georgia coast. Bullen and Bullen reported on their excavations of the site of Black Lucy's Garden in Andover, Massachusetts in 1945; this may have been the earliest excavation explicitly directed toward African Americans. Later Noël Hume (1966) excavated a slave trash dump in at Tutter's Neck in Virginia, and test excavations in Florida (Poe 1963) were aimed at finding a Negro fort on the Appalachicola River. However, these projects were not followed by a sustained program of African American studies, as Fairbanks's was (Fairbanks 1984:1).

9. Fairbanks's students John Otto (1984) and Theresa Singleton (1985) have published two of the few books on African American archaeology.

10. Fairbanks 1974:62. Archaeologist Lewis Binford, a prehistorian, was the leader of the "new archaeology" movement (Binford 1962, 1964, 1965). In historical archaeology this movement was encouraged by Stanley South (1977). See Thomas (1989:52–61) for a review of this effort by archaeologists to become more explicitly scientific.

11. King et al. 1977:30–31.

12. Raines et al. 1966. By the time Congress passed this bill in 1966, scholars had been writing and presenting African American history for more than one hundred years, and African American families and communities had been passing down their oral history from the earliest days of American colonization. While that history had become part of everyday African American life however, it had not become broadly recognized as part of American public history. According to historians Jeffrey C. Stewart and Fath Davis Ruffins (1986:307), African American history was excluded from this broader public history because it "chronicled the history of a community at odds with the American status quo."

13. The National Historic Preservation Act was preceded and supplemented by other legislation concerned with the preservation of historical and archaeological resources. Later legislation includes the National Environmental Protection Act of 1969, the Archaeological and Historical Preservation Act of 1974, and the Archaeological Resources Protection Act of 1979, but all their regulations base the evaluation of archaeological and historical significance on guidelines established by the National Historic Preservation Act.

14. Stanley South's *Method and Theory in Historical Archaeology*, published in 1977, is still one of the most rigorous treatments of American historical archaeology available. The book draws examples primarily from southern America during the colonial era, yet the index contains no citation for African Americans in any form.

15. See Ferguson 1977; South 1977.

16. Fairbanks 1972, 1976; Ascher and Fairbanks 1971; Ascher 1974.

17. See Ferguson 1987; for more detailed comments and criticism see Joseph (1989) and Orser (1988a, 1988b, 1989).

18. Ferguson 1988.

19. Within a few short years, sociologist Guion Griffis Johnson wrote *A Social History of the Sea Islands* (1930), black historian W. E. B. Dubois wrote of *Black Folk: Then and Now* (1939), cultural anthropologist Melville Herskovits debunked prevailing stereotypes in *The Myth of the Negro Past* (1941), and WPA folklorists collected stories from ex-slaves along the Georgia coast and published *Drums and Shadows* (1986, originally published in 1941). Meanwhile, well-known prehistoric archaeologist William C. McKern presented "The Midwestern Taxonomic Method as an Aide to [Prehistoric] Archeological Culture Study" in *American Antiquity* (1939); and James A. Ford and Gordon R. Willey published "An Interpretation of the Prehistory of the Eastern United States" in the *American Anthropologist* (1941). In the nascent field of historical archaeology, Arthur Woodward emphasized the value of European trade goods for Indian archaeology (1932), excavators were digging for house foundations in colonial Williamsburg (King et al. 1977:21), and Henry C. Forman was writing about *Jamestown and St. Mary's—Buried Cities of Romance* (1938).

20. See Leone (1973) for a discussion of the ways archaeological results are used to substantiate contemporary ideology. For an essay on the beginning of self-conscious archaeology in America see Mark Leone's introduction to *Research Strategies in Historical Archaeology* (1977b), edited by Stanley South. And for a provocative discussion of the association of archaeology with American foreign policy see Gero and Root's (1989) analysis of National Geographic Society articles on archaeology.

21. Brathwaite 1971.

22. Ibid.:xv–xvi. Creolization is similar to the familiar anthropological concept of acculturation; but in its developed form, creolization has a structural ingredient that acculturation lacks; and creolization does not have the taint of ethnocentrism that acculturation has acquired. Originally, acculturation simply identified mutual cultural exchange between people in contact (Redfield et al. 1936:149). However, in recent years acculturation has commonly come to mean, according to a recent dictionary, "the adoption of the traits or patterns of another group" (Stein and Su 1980:7). In social science this generally means the adoption of European traits or patterns by non-European people, in some cases *forced* on subordinates by a dominant group (See Haviland 1987:373; Ember and Ember 1988:458). Few anthropologists have ever described the acculturation of European colonists. The central idea of this modern "Eurocentric" view of acculturation is that either through choice or through force, non-European people in contact with Europeans give up their traditional ways and become like Europeans. Creolization, on the other hand, recognizes the free-will, imagination, and creativity of non-Europeans; creolization does not simply model cultural contact and exchange but describes the building of a new culture from diverse elements.

23. Joyner 1984.

24. Ibid.:xxi.

25. Otto 1984:61–69.

26. Orser 1988b:741–742, 1989:8–10. Following other scholars, Orser states (1988a:9) that "the distinction between *Marxian* studies—using the philosophical and socioeconomic concepts explained in Karl Marx's view of history—and *Marxist* studies—incorporating a belief in the political agenda of today's Marxist regimes—must be made explicit."

27. Stuckey 1987.

28. Hodder 1982:10.

29. Of course archaeologists are in daily contact with people in classrooms and museums, but there remains a wide gulf between professionals and the public. One of the most promising exceptions is the interactive archaeological program Mark Leone has developed in historic Annapolis, Maryland in recent years.

30. WPA 1986:179. This quote was originally written and published in "dialect," that is, white, WPA interviewers' attempts at rendering African American language. Unfortunately these interviewers were not trained linguists, and their attempts at dialect were often as much racial stereotype as linguistic description. For this reason I have translated the "dialect" in this quote, and others throughout the book, into contemporary style. I have been careful not to distort the meaning of the passages and to include all key words from the originals. Nevertheless, readers may want to compare my quotes with the sources.

31. For a variety of methodological discussions aimed at drawing meaning from the archaeological record see Leone and Potter (1988).

## Chapter 1, Handmade Pots

1. WPA 1986:166.

2. Rawick 1972:60, 198.

3. Noël Hume 1962:3.

4. Tabe 1972:13.

5. Since 1980 Colonial Williamsburg has been developing exhibits illustrating the role of African Americans in the history of the town.

6. South 1979.

7. Even though southwestern archaeologist Arthur Woodward recently received the Harrington Award for historical archaeology (*Historical Archaeology* 1987:1–2), his work and the work of other historical archaeologists in the Southwest have never drawn a large audience in historical archaeology.

8. Colonial Williamsburg Foundation 1972:xiii.

9. Noël Hume 1962:7.

10. Ibid.:5.

11. Fairbanks 1962; Baker 1972; Binford 1965; South 1976, 1977.

12. Of the 50,482 sherds from South Carolina listed in Appendix 3, Table 1, very few came from projects aimed primarily at researching the African American past. Seven thousand and thirty came from private, local, state, and federal projects focused on Anglo-American history. The bulk of the collection, 41,357 sherds or 82 percent, came from excavations required by the National Historic Preservation Act of 1966 and related acts. Thus, only 2,095 sherds or 4 percent of the collection tabulated in Appendix 3, Table 1 resulted from pre-planned, nonsalvage excavations of African American sites. No doubt, without federal preservation legislation requiring mitigation of damage to African American sites we would know less than 4 percent of what we presently know about this pottery and the early African American past in South Carolina.

13. See Connah 1981:76–98; Shaw 1978:37–59.

14. Polhemus 1977:314.

15. See South 1974:185–186; Baker 1972.

16. "Cool" in potters terms is usually less than 1,000 degrees Centigrade (Rye 1981:25).

17. Dale Rosengarten 1986.

18. Handler and Lange 1978:135–144; Handler 1963, 1964.

19. Elizabeth Farkas was participating in an archaeological field school in the West Indies when she bought the small pot from a woman potter on Nevis.

20. Calling the pottery a "ware," Noël Hume (1962) was clearly aware that he was not describing a "type."

21. See Thomas 1979:212–225.

22. Binford 1965.

23. Noël Hume 1962:12. Other archaeologists who worked carefully with this material also interpreted it in this way. For example, Steve Baker wrote (1972:3), "Noël Hume intended Colono-Indian to serve as a blanket descriptive term for Indian pottery of the colonial period that exhibits definite European influences in its manufacture."

24. Ferguson 1980.

25. Binford 1965.

26. Swanton 1911:62.

27. Evidence of plates comes from Mary Ellen N. Hodges, personal communication, 1980.

28. See Thomas 1979 for a discussion of spatial and temporal aspects of ceramic typology.

29. See Henry 1980:19–21; Henig 1823:350; Bushnell 1937:40–41.

30. Durand 1932:118, quoted in Henry 1980:20.

31. The same is true of aboriginal ceramics from sites like the Spanish town of Santa Elena, the English Fort Prince George in South Carolina (South 1983; Harmon 1986), Tellico Blockhouse in Virginia (Polhemus 1977) and Fort King George on the coast of Georgia (Kelso 1968). The fact that so-called aboriginal ceramics are present on these sites demonstrates the colonial influence on ceramic use.

32. In many cases native settlements were dramatically affected by European and African contact long before the people saw the intruders firsthand. As early as the first half of the sixteenth century, epidemic diseases (Dobyns 1983), introduced from across the Atlantic, decimated many Native American villages and forced relocation of Indian settlement.

33. Wood 1974:3–4.

34. Bourne 1973:3–4.

35. Merrell 1984:365. The Catawba's shunning of blacks for racial reasons was not well developed until the beginning of the nineteenth century; before that time their relations with blacks and whites, "fluctuated widely between intimate friendships and bitter hostility" (Merrell 1984:373).

36. Repositories included the South Carolina Institute of Archaeology and Anthropology, University of South Carolina; the Charleston Museum; the Virginia Research Center for Archaeology, Virginia Landmarks Commission; Colonial Williamsburg; the Department of Anthropology, College of William and Mary; the Research Laboratories of Anthropology, University of North Carolina; Archaeology Branch, North Carolina Department of Archives and History; the Florida State Museum, University of Florida; the St. Augustine Historical Society; Flowerdew Hundred, Incorporated; Carolina Archaeological Services, Incorporated; and Soil Systems Incorporated.

37. See Schuyler (1978) for a collection of papers on techniques for dating historic sites. Most of these techniques rely on known dates and predictable changes of industrially manufactured items like ceramics and pipe stems.

38. Braun 1983; see also Hally 1983; Posnansky and DeCorse 1986.

39. I originally presented these criteria in a paper presented to the 1979 Conference on Historic Sites Archaeology in Wilmington, North Carolina. Later I shared the criteria with Tom Wheaton and Patrick Garrow, who used them to show that pottery had been made at the Yaughan and Curriboo slave villages (Wheaton et al. 1983:225–250).

40. Rye 1981:114, 131.

## Chapter 2, North America's Slave Coast

1. See Joyner (1984:41–89) for a description of the South Carolina task system; see Kulikoff (1986:396–416) for a discussion of labor organization in the tobacco colonies.

2. Noël Hume 1962:12.

3. Carter Hudgins, personal communication, 1980.

4. See Otto 1984:83–84; Kelso 1979:95, 132–133; Adams 1987:179, 186).

5. Lowery 1959:156; Hoffman 1990.

6. South 1986.

7. Wright 1981:27.

8. Southeastern archaeologists might find, in the prehistoric record, occurrences of all the features exhibited by this post-contact pottery. However, this approach overlooks

the possibility that, rather than copying European or African ceramics, Indians may have been adjusting their own craft tradition to fit the new circumstances. Such changes are as much a product of the colonial situation as an Indian imitation of a Westerwald chamber pot, though more subtle.

9. Deagan 1983:31. Most information on Spanish Florida in this chapter comes from Deagan 1973 and 1983.

10. Deagan 1983:77, 191.

11. Ibid.:234.

12. Otto and Lewis 1974:109; Deagan 1983:123.

13. There is a significant difference between vessels with conoidal bases and elongated bodies and those with round bases and spherical bodies. Ralph Linton (1944) points out that among American Indian traditions elongated vessels with conoidal bases were used for cooking *in* fires while spherical vessels with round bottoms were used for cooking *over* them. The cooking vessels from St. Augustine are of the former type, while those from South Carolina are of the latter.

14. Smith 1948:315; Otto and Lewis 1974:95–96.

15. See Deagan 1983:29–34.

16. Landers 1988, 1989.

17. See South (1977:10–11) for a discussion of quantification; Shepard (1983:77) for St. Augustine data.

18. Smith 1624; Breen and Innes 1980:54.

19. Morgan 1975:308.

20. Cope 1973:24.

21. Morgan 1975:327.

22. Morgan (1975) and Kulikoff (1986) both give excellent discussions on the transformation from small farms relying on the labor of servants to larger plantations supported by black slave labor.

23. Lauber 1913:108, 130–132; Morgan 1975:330; Nash 1982:126.

24. Swanton 1946:175–176.

25. Kelso 1984:104; Henry 1980:163; Deetz 1988.

26. Kelso 1984.

27. Two of the nine whole vessels have spall fractures that probably occurred during firing.

28. See Henry 1980:116.

29. This pottery is categorized in Types A and B in Susan Henry's typology of Virginia Colono Wares (Henry 1980). Henry established five distinct types based on temper: Type A, fossil shell; Type B, untempered; Type C, no temper visible; Type D, shell flakes; Type E, sand. Types A and B are among the earliest found on colonial sites.

30. For examples see Sieber (1980) and Dark (1973) for African arts and crafts and Vlach (1978) for African American basketry, woodcarving, quilting, etc.

31. Newman 1974:17; Sieber 1980:246.

32. Noël Hume 1962:5.

33. This vessel is from James Deetz's excavations at Flowerdew Hundred Plantation across the James River from Williamsburg.

34. Binford 1965; Mary Ellen N. Hodges, personal communication, 1980; Speck 1928; Stern 1951; Henry 1980; Beaudry 1979; Jones 1983.

35. Nash 1982:286.

36. Swanton 1946:175–176. Groups like the Pamunkey still live on the Atlantic coastal plain and are commonly called "mixed-bloods" or, in anthropological jargon, "tri-racial isolates." I believe both of these terms are anchored in our legacy of racism. Both white and black Americans in the South are at least "tri-racial" groups with various admixtures of European, African, and Native American ancestry, yet they are usually referred to as either "white" or "black." Likewise, in the American West, Native Americans with white ancestry are identified and accepted as Indians. On the other hand, in the American South, communities known internally as Indian communities since at least the nineteenth century are called "tri-racial" groups. They say they are Indian, but outsiders, including many prominent scholars, noting their phenotypic black admixture insist they be called something else. In this way, Native Americans in the South have been subjected to double discrimination, that against blacks as well as that against Indians.

37. Stern 1951:49; Henry 1980:30.

38. Deetz 1988:365–366.

39. Henry 1979.

40. Emerson 1988.

41. Henry 1980:96–98, 133–136, 153–155.

42. Binford 1965:83–85; Henry 1980:130–133.

43. From Noël Hume 1962; Binford 1965; Henry 1980, as well as my own research.

44. Noël Hume 1962:91.

45. See Henry 1980:153.

46. Swanton 1946:554; Sieber 1980:246, 250. Vessel KM55C-1 from Pettus was definitely treated with infusion. Also, spill stains on vessel CL118H show that other vessels probably were infused, but through use, most of the infusion had worn away.

47. Mary Ellen N. Hodges, personal communication, 1980; Binford 1965.

48. Kelso 1984:102–103.

49. This argument is presented by Deetz (1988:366) and based on Upton (1982:44–57).

50. See Kelso 1984:18–23; Carson et al. 1988.

51. Information about the architecture at Kingsmill is taken from Kelso 1984:102–128.

52. McDaniel 1982:45–102.

53. Boney 1972:6.

54. McDaniel 1982:45–102; Vlach 1978:122–138.

55. In his description of slave houses McDaniel (1982:53–56) follows historian Bayly Ellen Marks (1979) who analyzed the size of all types of houses in St. Mary's County, Maryland for the period 1780 to 1841. Marks found that most late eighteenth-century slave quarters were log and most measured either 16 by 12 or 24 by 16 feet.

56. Kelso 1984:56–102.
57. Vlach 1978:136–138.
58. Kelso 1984:56–102; Carson et al. 1988.
59. Basing her arguments on written sources, Mechal Sobel (1987:100–126) suggests that the lightweight framing techniques used by Africans and African Americans evolved into the "scantling" architecture of colonial Virginia and, one might presume, ultimately into modern framing.
60. Kelso 1984:105.
61. Tattler 1850:162.
62. Kelso 1984:201.
63. Nichols 1988.
64. Wood 1974:132. Early history of Carolina is primarily from Wood (1974), Weir (1983), Nash (1982), and Meinig (1986). North Carolina was separated politically from the rest of the Carolina colony in 1710 (Fenn and Wood 1983:35).
65. Wood 1974; Greene and Harrison 1932.
66. Theresa Singleton (1985:1–2).
67. Wood 1974:13–34; Littlefield 1981.
68. Wright 1981:102–125. See Crosby (1972) and Dobyns (1983) for reviews of the Native American struggle with Old World disease.
69. Weir 1983:26.
70. Wood 1974:35–62; Littlefield 1981:74–114.
71. Amazingly, some of these coastal plain tribes survived. Descendants of colonial Indians are living in small towns and rural communities in both North and South Carolina today. The best known of these are the Lumbees of the eastern border area of the Carolinas, but there are many others including the Santees, Edistos, and Haliwas. See Berry (1963), Blu (1980), Ferguson (1985), Kasakoff and White (1986).
72. Meinig 1986:187.
73. Littlefield 1981:109; Wood 1974:95–130.
74. Doar 1970:8.
75. Ibid.:31.
76. Ibid.:33.

## Chapter 3, Carolina's African American Majority

1. Petty 1943:63–64.
2. Wheaton et al. 1983.
3. Natalie Adams 1990.
4. See architectural historian Lane Green's discussion of cob-wall construction in Wheaton et al. (1983, appendix D).
5. Merrens 1977:135.
6. Hamer and Rogers 1972:482.

7. Both planked and thatched roof-types were photographed on St. Helena Island, South Carolina, by Leigh Richmond Miner in the early 1900s (see Dabbs 1970). A travel guide for *Beaufort and the Sea Islands* (WPA 1938:12) included a picture of a rectangular earthfast stable with a gabled roof; the entire structure was thatched with palmetto fronds.

8. Wheaton et al. 1983:139, 158.

9. Ibid.:149, 194.

10. Structures 38BK75B1 and 38BK75B2 (Ibid.:113).

11. See Kelso 1984:18–33 and Carson et al. 1988:117–125.

12. Drucker and Anthony 1979:96.

13. Morgan 1977:48–49; Vlach 1978:123–128; Joyner 1984:117–126.

14. See Gluck 1968.

15. WPA 1986:166.

16. Ibid.:181.

17. Ibid.:179.

18. Vlach 1978:136; Montgomery 1908.

19. E. Franklin Frazier and Guy B. Johnson were "integrationists" who feared associating assimilated black Americans with Africa; on the other hand, Melville Herskovits and Lorenzo Dow Turner are examples of scholars who pursued African connections (Joyner in WPA 1986:xx–xxiv). See Stuckey (1987:59) for an example of Christian missionary effort to stop African-style dancing.

20. Mullin 1972:86, quoted in Vlach 1978:135.

21. Abbot 1819.

22. Smith 1985:20.

23. Nathanael Greene Papers, William L. Clements Library, University of Michigan 38, Item 21.

24. Hurmence 1989:30. In the South Carolina lowcountry, log cabins are usually called "pole houses." Poles are generally perceived as smaller than logs; perhaps in this warmer climate, building techniques did not call for the massive logs needed to insulate log houses to the north.

25. Carson et al. 1988:117–118.

26. Quoted in Gordon 1971:130.

27. See Hudson 1976:216–217 for description of "chickees."

28. Merrick Posnansky, personal communication, 1990.

29. Grimke 1839:43.

30. Jones 1987:72.

31. Grimke 1839:43; see also Gordon 1971:119.

32. Lester 1968:87.

33. Breeden 1980:125.

34. WPA 1986:162.

35. South 1971:102–105.

36. Lewis and Haskell 1980:102.

37. Wheaton et al. 1983:232; Zierden et al. 1986:7.49–7.50.

38. While there are twice as many whole vessels in the South Carolina collection there are three times as many examples of spalling. Unfortunately the number of spalled pieces from Virginia is so small that normal tests of statistical significance cannot be applied.

39. Lewis and Haskell 1980:64, 102; Wheaton et al. 1983:227, 232.

40. Wheaton et al. 1983:153.

41. Zierden et al. 1986; Ronald Anthony, personal communication, 1986.

42. Wheaton et al. 1983:233; Lewis 1978:62–65.

43. Lewis 1978:62–65.

44. Older lowcountry residents are still familiar with local clays. In a 1989 interview, Mr. Postell Smalls of Huger, South Carolina, described specific clays used for chinking walls, building chimneys, and even patching whiskey stills.

45. Wheaton et al. 1983:237. X-ray diffraction analysis was performed on Colono Ware and the subsoil clay from Lesesne Plantation near Charleston. These comparisons showed that the subsoil clay was not a likely source for the pottery found on that site (Zierden et al. 1986:7-24–7-25). However, this does not rule out other local clay sources either on land or in marine deposits. Such analyses and comparisons, more broadly based, are an important next step in determining the location of the raw materials and the distribution of pottery in the folk economy. In South Carolina, Colono Ware is either not tempered at all or tempered with sand, which is easily acquired.

46. Merrens 1977:197.

47. Wheaton et al. 1983; Ferguson 1990; Anthony 1986 (in Zierden et al. 1986).

48. Lees and Kimery-Lees 1979; Trinkley 1986:232–233; Wheaton et al. 1983:244.

49. Ferguson 1990.

50. Gregorie 1925:21.

51. Simms 1841:122.

52. Randolph 1984:34–35.

53. Turner 1969:199.

54. WPA 1986:144.

55. Pinckney 1972:97.

56. Grime 1979:184; Merrens 1977:101; see also Wagner 1981. Sorghum *(Sorghum vulgare* var. *saccharatum)* was originally classified as a "tropical millet" and Catesby identified it as *"Milium indicum,* bunched guinea corn." "Grown chiefly by Negroes" in the eighteenth century, sorghum became one of the important subsistence and cash crops of North America.

57. WPA 1986:167.

58. Hudson 1976:302–307.

59. Merrens 1977:99.

60. Joyner 1984:97–98.

61. Kaplan 1971:519; Hudson 1976:294.

62. Reitz et al. 1985.

63. Reitz 1986.

64. Land 1969:67. See Ascher and Fairbanks (1971), Doar (1970:27), and Smith (1985) for archaeological and historical accounts of slaves using firearms. In the Carolina lowcountry, slaves routinely were allowed to use guns to scare birds away from rice fields.

65. Deetz 1977:28–61.

66. Hudson 1976:309; Lawson 1967:36; Swanton 1946:557–558.

67. See Lewicki 1974; Bascom 1951a, 1951b; Fortes and Fortes 1936.

68. Deetz 1977:52–53, following Anderson 1971.

69. Deetz 1977:122–124; Anderson 1971:239.

70. Jones 1987:72.

71. Although "pound" is the word commonly used for this process, the pestle does not actually "pound" rice. The action is more gentle than implied by "pound." See Doar (1970) for a general description of rice agriculture including pounding and threshing machinery.

72. WPA 1986:193–194.

73. Wood 1974:110.

74. Knives, spoons, forks, and other metal utensils are found on slave sites, though in much lower frequency than on European-American sites. Fragments of basketry have been found in an eighteenth-century privy in Charleston (Dale Rosengarten 1986:16) and in a slave village on Yaughan Plantation (Wheaton et al. 1983:145). Additional pieces of basketry probably will be found as more waterlogged and charred features are excavated on plantations.

75. Wheaton et al. 1983; Drucker and Anthony 1979; Zierden et al. 1986. Most of the bottle fragments found on slave sites are fragments of wine bottles, but this does not mean that slaves had ready access to wine. On the colonial frontier, bottles were viewed differently than we see them. To us milk bottles hold milk, beer bottles hold beer, and wine bottles hold wine; when the contents are gone they are usually thrown away. In contrast, slave-village containers like wine bottles were probably brought home whenever they were available to be used again and again to hold water, milk, juice, and even alcoholic beverages.

76. Leith-Ross 1970; David and Hennig 1972:7–16; MacGaffey 1975:29.

77. Braun 1983:118–125.

78. Trinkley 1986:233.

79. See Gordon 1971:130; WPA 1986:179.

80. Joyner 1984:91.

**Chapter 4, Powerful Legacy**

1. Thompson 1983:110, 121.

2. For a more detailed discussion of these marked pieces, see Ferguson (in press).

3. One of these astute listeners was Wythe Dornan, then an undergraduate student at the University of Indiana. The other was an unknown member of the audience.

4. MacGaffey 1986:42–51; Thompson 1983:108–131; Laman 1953, 1957, 1962, 1968.

5. Thompson 1983:117.

6. MacGaffey 1986:42–46; Thompson 1983:108–109.

7. Stuckey 1987:11.

8. Ibid.:15, quoting Herskovits 1941:106–107.

9. The Civil Rights Movement demonstrated that the Christian church serves as a bulwark of strength and leadership in African American communities. Recently, historians Sterling Stuckey (1987), Patricia Jones-Jackson (1987) and Margaret Washington Creel (1988) have discussed how aspects of African religion and culture combined with Christianity in the colonial and antebellum South to form the modern African American church.

10. Grimke 1839:43.

11. Brown 1989.

12. Cabak 1990.

13. South 1983:72–75. The beads had been placed in a small pit filled with firewood and the wood burned until many of the beads were fused together. South suggests this may have been part of an African American ritual.

14. Klingelhofer 1987.

15. Lester 1968:87.

16. Creel 1988:322.

17. Orser 1988b.

18. Mann 1986:18–32.

# References Cited

Abbot, Abiel
    1819    Journey to Savannah: March 24–April 16, 1819. Manuscript, Essex Institute Library, Chelmsford, Great Britain.

Adams, Natalie P.
    1990    *Early African-American Domestic Architecture from Berkeley County, South Carolina*. Master's thesis, Department of Anthropology, University of South Carolina, Columbia.

Adams, William Hampton (editor)
    1987    *Historical Archaeology of Plantations at Kings Bay, Camden County, Georgia*. Reports of Investigations 5, Department of Anthropology, University of Florida, Gainesville.

Affleck, Richard M.
    1990    *Power and Space: Settlement Pattern Change at Middleburg Plantation, Berkeley County, South Carolina*. Master's thesis, Department of Anthropology, University of South Carolina.

Anderson, Jay Allan
    1971    *'A Solid Sufficiency': An Ethnography of Yeoman Foodways in Stuart England*. Ph.D. dissertation, University of Pennsylvania, Philadelphia.

Anthony, Ronald
    1986    Colono Wares. In *Home Upriver: Rural Life on Daniel's Island, Berkeley County, South Carolina*, by Martha A. Zierden et al., pp. 7.22–7.50. Carolina Archaeological Services, Inc., Columbia, South Carolina.

**161**

Ascher, Robert

1974 Tin*Can Archaeology. *Historical Archaeology* 8:7–16.

Ascher, Robert, and Charles Fairbanks

1971 Excavation of a Slave Cabin: Georgia, U.S.A. *Historical Archaeology* 5: 3–17.

Baker, Stephen G.

1972 *Colono-Indian Pottery from Cambridge, South Carolina with comments on the Historic Catawba Pottery Trade*, pp. 3–30. Institute of Archeology and Anthropology, Notebook 4. Columbia, South Carolina.

Bascom, William R.

1951a Yoruba Food. *Africa* 21:41–53.

1951b Yoruba Cooking. *Africa* 21:125–137.

Bayliss, John F.

1970 *Black Slave Narratives*. MacMillan Publishing Co., New York.

Bean, R.N.

1971 *The British Transatlantic Slave Trade, 1650–1775*. Arno Press, New York.

Beaudry, Mary C.

1979 *Excavations at Fort Christanna, Brunswick County, Virginia: 1979 Season*. College of William and Mary in Virginia, Williamsburg.

Berry, Brewton

1963 *Almost White*. MacMillan Publishing Co., New York.

Binford, Lewis

1962 Archaeology as Anthropology. *American Antiquity* 28:217–225.

1964 A Consideration of Archaeological Research Design. *American Antiquity* 29:425–441.

1965 Colonial Period Ceramics of the Nottoway and Weanock Indians of Southeastern Virginia. *Quarterly Bulletin of the Archaeological Society of Virginia* 19(4):78–87.

Blassingame, John W.

1979 *The Slave Community: Plantation Life in the Antebellum South*. Oxford University Press, New York and Oxford.

Blu, Karen I.

1980 *The Lumbee Problem: The Making of an American Indian People*. Cambridge University Press, New York.

Boney, F.N. (editor)

1972 *Slave Life in Georgia: A Narrative of the Life Sufferings and Escape of John Brown, a Fugitive Slave*. The Beehive Press, Savannah, Georgia.

Bontemps, Anna

1969 *Great Slave Narratives*. Beacon Press, Boston, Massachusetts.

Bourne, Edward G. (editor)

1973 *Narratives of the Career of Hernando de Soto in the Conquest of Florida*. The American Explorer Series, vol. 2. AMS Press, New York.

Brathwaite, Edward Kamau

1971    *The Development of Creole Society in Jamaica: 1770–1820*. Clarendon Press, Oxford.

Braun, David P.

1980    Experimental Interpretation of Ceramic Vessel Use on the Basis of Rim and Neck Formal Attributes, Appendix I. In *The Navajo Project Archaeological Investigations, Page to Phoenix 599KV Southern Transmission Line*, edited by Donald C. Fiero et al., pp. 171–221. Museum of Northern Arizona Research Paper 11. Flagstaff.

1983    Pots as Tools. In *The Hammer Theory of Archaeological Research*, edited by A. Keane and J. Moore, pp. 107–134. Academic Press, New York.

Breeden, James O. (editor)

1980    *Advice Among Masters: The Ideal in Slave Management*. Greenwood Press, Westport, Connecticut.

Breen, T.H., and Stephen Innes

1980    *"Myne Owne Ground": Race and Freedom on Virginia's Eastern Shore, 1640–1676*. Oxford University Press, New York and Oxford.

Briggs, Loutrell

1951    *Charleston Gardens*. University of South Carolina Press, Columbia.

Brown, Kenneth

1989    From Slavery to Wage Labor Tenancy: Structural Continuity in an Afro-American Community. Paper presented to a symposium entitled, "Digging the Afro-American Past," University of Mississippi, Oxford.

Bullen, Adelaide K., and P. Ripley Bullen

1945    Black Lucy's Garden. *Bulletin of the Massachusetts Archaeological Society* 6:17–28.

Bushnell, David I., Jr.

1937    *Indian Sites Below the Falls of the Rappahannock, Virginia*. Smithsonian Miscellaneous Collections 96(4). Washington, D.C.

Cabak, Melanie

1990    Searching for the Meaning of Blue Beads to Afro-American Slaves. Paper on file at the Department of Anthropology, University of South Carolina, Columbia.

Carrillo, Richard F.

1980    Green Grove Plantation: Archaeological and Historical Research at the Kinlock Site (38Ch109), Charleston County. Unpublished report prepared for the South Carolina Department of Highways and Public Transportation, Columbia.

Carson, Cary, Norman F. Barka, William M. Kelso, Gary Wheeler Stone, and Dell Upton

1988    Impermanent Architecture in the Southern Colonies. In *Material Life in America, 1600–1800*, edited by Robert Blair St. George, pp. 113–158. Northeastern University Press, Boston.

Colonial Williamsburg Foundation

1972    *Colonial Williamsburg: Official Guidebook and Map.* Williamsburg, Virginia.

Connah, Graham

1981    *Three Thousand Years in Africa: Man and Environment in the Lake Chad Region of Nigeria.* Cambridge University Press, Cambridge, Great Britain.

Creel, Margaret Washington

1988    *A Peculiar People: Slave Religion and Community Among the Gullahs.* New York University Press, New York.

Crosby, Alfred W.

1972    *The Columbian Exchange: Biological and Cultural Consequences of 1492.* Greenwood Publishing Co., Westport, Connecticut.

Curtin, Philip D.

1969    *The Atlantic Slave Trade: A Census.* University of Wisconsin Press, Madison.

Dabbs, Edith

1970    *Face of an Island: Leigh Richmond Miner's Photographs of Saint Helena Island.* The R.L. Bryan Co., Columbia, South Carolina.

Dark, Philip J.C.

1973    *An Introduction to Benin Art and Technology.* Oxford University Press, London.

David, Nicholas, and Hilke Hennig

1972    *The Ethnography of Pottery: A Fulani Case Seen in Archaeological Perspective.* McCaleb Module in Anthropology 21. Addison Wesley, Reading, Massachusetts.

Deagan, Kathleen

1973    *Mestizaje* in Colonial St. Augustine. *Ethnohistory* 20:55–65.

1983    *Spanish St. Augustine: The Archaeology of a Colonial Creole Community.* Academic Press, New York.

Deetz, James

1967    *Invitation to Archaeology.* Natural History Press, New York.

1977    *In Small Things Forgotten.* Doubleday, Garden City, New York.

1988    American Historical Archeology: Methods and Results. *Science* 239:362–367.

Doar, David

1970    *Rice and Rice Planting in the South Carolina Low Country.* Contributions from the Charleston Museum 8. Charleston, South Carolina.

Dobyns, Henry F.

1983    *Their Number Become Thinned: Native American Population Dynamics in Eastern North America.* University of Tennessee Press, Knoxville.

Drucker, Lesley M., and Ronald W. Anthony

1979    *The Spiers Landing Site: Archaeological Investigations in Berkeley County, South Carolina.* Carolina Archaeological Services, Inc., Columbia, South Carolina.

Dubois, W.E.B.

1939     *Black Folk Then and Now: An Essay in the Historical Sociology of the Negro Race*. H. Holt and Company, New York

Durand, du Dauphine

1932     *Un Francais en Virginie: Voyage d'u Francois Exile pour Religion, avec and Description de la Virginie and Marilan dans l'Amerique*. Historical Documents, Institute Francais de Washington, Cahier 5. Librairie E. Droz, Paris.

Ember, Carol R., and Melvin Ember

1988     *Anthropology*. Prentice Hall, Englewood Cliffs, New Jersey.

Emerson, Matthew C.

1988     *Decorated Clay Tobacco Pipes from the Chesapeake*. Ph.D. dissertation, Department of Anthropology, University of California at Berkeley. University Microfilms International, Ann Arbor, Michigan.

Fairbanks, Charles H.

1962     A Colono-Indian Ware Milk Pitcher. *The Florida Anthropologist* 15:103–105.

1974     The Kingsley Slave Cabins in Duval County, Florida, 1968. *The Conference on Historic Site Archaeology Papers 1972* 7:62–93.

1976     Spaniards, Planters, Ships and Slaves: Historical Archaeology in Florida and Georgia. *Archaeology* 29:164–172.

1984     The Plantation Archaeology of the Southeastern Coast. *Historical Archaeology* 18:1–14.

Fenn, Elizabeth, and Peter H. Wood

1983     *Natives and Newcomers: The Way We Lived in North Carolina before 1770*. The University of North Carolina Press, Chapel Hill.

Ferguson, Leland

1977     Historical Archaeology and the Importance of Material Things. *Historical Archaeology*, Special Publication No. 2.

1980     Looking for the "Afro" in Colono-Indian Pottery. In *Archaeological Perspectives on Ethnicity in America*, edited by Robert L. Schuyler, pp. 14–28. Baywood Farmingdale, New York.

1984     History from the Hands of Black Americans: A Methodological Proposal. In *Black Americans in North Carolina and the South*, edited by Jeffrey J. Crow and Flora J. Hatley, pp. 57–70. University of North Carolina Press, Chapel Hill.

1985     Contemporary Native Americans in South Carolina. In *Contemporary Native Americans in South Carolina: A Photo Documentation Covering the Years 1983–1985*, by Gene J. Crediford. South Carolina Endowment for the Humanities, Columbia.

1988     Review of *The Archaeology of Slavery and Plantation Life*, edited by Theresa A. Singleton. *American Antiquity* 55(1):195–196.

1990     Low Country Plantations, the Catawba Nation and River Burnished Pottery. In

Studies in South Carolina Archaeology: Essays in Honor of R.S. Stephenson, Anthropological Studies 8, edited by Albert C. Goodyear III and Glen T. Hanson. South Carolina Institute of Archaeology and Anthropology.

in press   "The Cross is a Magic Sign": Marks on Eighteenth-Century Bowls from South Carolina. In *Studies in African-American Archaeology*, edited by Theresa Singleton. University of Virginia, Charlottesville.

Fleetwood, Rusty

  1982   *Tidecraft: The Boats of Lower South Carolina and Georgia*. Coastal Heritage Society, Savannah, Georgia.

Ford, James A.

  1937   An Archaeological Report on the Elizafield Ruins. In *Georgia's Disputed Ruins*, edited by E. Coulter, pp. 191–225. University of North Carolina Press, Chapel Hill.

Ford, James A., and Gordon R. Willey

  1941   An Interpretation of the Prehistory of the Eastern United States. *American Anthropologist* 43:325–363.

Forman, Henry C.

  1938   *Jamestown and St. Mary's: Buried Cities of Romance*. Johns Hopkins Press, Baltimore, Maryland.

Fortes, Meyer, and Sonia Fortes

  1936   Food in the Domestic Economy of Tallensi. *Africa* 9:237–276.

Foss, Robert W., Patrick H. Garrow, and Silas P. Hurry

  1979   *Archaeological Investigations of the Edenton Snuff and Tobacco Manufacture*. North Carolina Archeological Council and the Archeology Branch, Division of Archives and History, Department of Cultural Resources, Raleigh.

Gero, Joan, and Delores Root

  1989   Public Presentations and Private Concerns: Archaeology in the Pages of *National Geographic*. In *Politics of the Past, Proceedings of the World Archaeological Congress, Southampton, England, September 1986*, edited by Peter Gathercole and David Lowenthal. Unwin Human Publishers, London.

Gluck, Julius F.P.

  1968   African Architecture. In *The Many Faces of Primitive Art: A Critical Anthology*, edited by Douglas Fraser, pp. 224–243. Prentice-Hall, Inc., Englewood Cliffs, New Jersey.

Gordon, Asa H.

  1971   *Sketches of Negro Life and History in South Carolina*. University of South Carolina Press, Columbia.

Green, E.B., and V.D. Harrison

  1932   *American Population before the Federal Census of 1790*. Columbia University Press, New York.

Gregorie, Anne K.

  1925   *Notes on Sewee Indians and Indian Remains of Christ Church Parish,*

*Charleston County, South Carolina*. Contributions from the Charleston Museum 5. Charleston, South Carolina.

Grime, William E.
1979  *Ethno-Botany of the Black Americans*. Reference Publications, Inc., Algonac, Michigan.

Grimke, Sarah
1839  *Slavery as It Is*. American Anti-Slavery Society, New York.

Gutman, Herbert
1977  *The Black Family in Slavery and Freedom*. Vintage Books, New York.

Hally, David J.
1983  Use Alteration of Pottery Vessel Surfaces: An Important Source of Evidence for the Identification of Vessel Function. *North American Archaeologist* 4:3–26.

Hamer, Philip, and George Rogers (editors)
1972  *The Papers of Henry Laurens, Volume III: Jan. 1, 1759–Aug. 31, 1763*. The University of South Carolina Press, Columbia.

Handler, Jerome
1963  Pottery Making in Rural Barbados. *Southwestern Journal of Anthropology* 19:314–334.
1964  Notes on Pottery-Making in Antigua. *Man* 64:150–151.

Handler, Jerome S., and Frederick W. Lange
1978  *Plantation Slavery in Barbados: An Archaeological and Historical Investigation*. Harvard University Press, Cambridge, Massachusetts.

Harmon, Michael A.
1986  *Eighteenth Century Lower Cherokee Adaptation and Use of Material Culture*. Master's thesis, Department of Anthropology, University of South Carolina, Columbia.

Haviland, William A.
1987  *Cultural Anthropology*. Holt, Rinehart and Winston, Fort Worth, Texas.

Hening, William Walter
1823  *The Statutes at Large: Being a Collection of all the Laws of Virginia*, vol. 2. Second edition. R & W Barton, New York.

Henry, Susan L.
1979  Terra-Cotta Tobacco Pipes in 17th Century Maryland and Virginia: A Preliminary Study. *Historical Archaeology* 13:14–37.
1980  *Physical, Spatial, and Temporal Dimensions of Colono Ware in the Chesapeake, 1600–1800*. Master's thesis, Department of Anthropology, Catholic University of America, Washington, D.C.

Herold, Elaine Bluhm
1981  *Historical Archaeological Report on the Meeting Street Office Building Site, Charleston, S.C.*. Charleston Museum.

Herskovits, Melville J.
1941  *The Myth of the Negro Past*. Beacon Press, Boston.

Hodder, Ian (editor)

1982    Theoretical Archaeology: A Reactionary View. In *Symbolic and Structural Archaeology*, pp. 1–16. Cambridge University Press, London.

Hoffman, Paul

1990    Focus, Buffer and Fulcrum: South Carolina and the Spanish Borderlands, 1521–1763. Paper presented to a symposium entitled "First Encounters in South Carolina: Native Americans and Early Spanish Exploration." South Carolina State Museum, Columbia.

Holmes, W.H.

1903    *Aboriginal Pottery of the Eastern United States*. Twentieth Annual Report of the Bureau of American Ethnology to the Secretary of the Smithsonian Institution: 1898–99, edited by J.W. Powell. Washington, D.C.

Holschlag, Stephanie L., and Michael J. Rodeffer

1977    *Ninety Six: Exploratory Excavations in the Village*. Star Fort Historical Commission, Ninety Six, South Carolina.

Hudson, Charles

1976    *The Southeastern Indians*. University of Tennessee Press, Knoxville.

Hurmence, Belinda (editor)

1984    *My Folks Don't Want Me to Talk about Slavery*. John F. Blair, Winston-Salem, North Carolina.

1989    *Before Freedom: When I Can Just Remember*. John F. Blair, Winston-Salem, North Carolina.

Hvidt, Kristian

1980    *Von Reck's Voyage*. Beehive, Savannah, Georgia.

Johnson, Guion Griffis

1930    *A Social History of the Sea Islands, with Special Reference to St. Helena Island, South Carolina*. University of North Carolina Press, Chapel Hill.

Jones, Donald G.

1983    Indian, African and European Influences in Colono Ware: Two Examples from Virginia. Unpublished paper, Archaeological Studies Program, Boston University.

Jones, George Fenwick

1987    The 1780 Siege of Charleston as Experienced by a Hessian Officer: Part Two. *South Carolina Historical Magazine* 88:63–75.

Jones-Jackson, Patricia

1987    *When Roots Die: Endangered Traditions on the Sea Islands*. University of Georgia Press, Athens.

Joseph, J.W.

1989    Pattern and Process in the Plantation Archaeology of the Lowcountry of Georgia and South Carolina. *Historical Archaeology* 23:55–68.

Joseph, Kathryn

1987    Agricultural Construction on the East Branch of Cooper River from 1780–

1825. Paper delivered to the Southeastern Archaeological Conference/Eastern States Archaeological Federation. Charleston, South Carolina.

Joyner, Charles
 1984    *Down by the Riverside: A South Carolina Slave Community*. University of Illinois Press, Urbana.

Kaplan, Lawrence
 1971    Archaeology and Domestication in American Phaseolus (Beans). In *Prehistoric Agriculture*, edited by Stuart Struever, pp. 516–533. The Natural History Press, Garden City, New York.

Kasakoff, Alice Bee, and Wesley White
 1986    Native Americans in South Carolina. Paper delivered to the annual meeting of the Southern Anthropological Society. Wrightsville Beach, North Carolina.

Kelso, William M.
 1968    *Excavation at the Fort King George Historical Site, Darien*. Georgia Historical Commission, Archaeological Research Series 1. Atlanta.
 1979    *Captain Jones's Wormslow: A Historical, Archaeological, and Architectural Study of an Eighteenth-Century Plantation near Savannah, Georgia*. University of Georgia Press, Athens.
 1984    *Kingsmill Plantations, 1619–1800*. Academic Press, New York.

Kimball, S. Fiske
 1966    *Domestic Architecture of the American Colonies and the Early Republic*. Dover Publications, New York.

King, Thomas F., Patricia P. Hickman, and Gary Berg
 1977    *Anthropology in Historic Preservation: Caring for Culture's Clutter*. Academic Press, New York.

Klein, H.S.
 1978    *The Middle Passage*. Princeton University Press, Princeton, New Jersey.

Klingelhofer, Eric
 1987    Aspects of Early Afro-American Material Culture: Artifacts from the Slave Quarters at Garrison Plantation, Maryland. *Historical Archaeology* 21(2):112–119.

Kulikoff, Allan
 1986    *Tobacco and Slaves: The Development of Southern Cultures in the Chesapeake, 1680–1800*. University of North Carolina Press, Chapel Hill.

Land, Aubrey
 1969    *Bases of the Plantation Society*. University of South Carolina Press, Columbia.

Landers, Jane
 1988    *Black Society in Spanish St. Augustine*. Ph.D. dissertation, Department of History, University of Florida, Gainesville.
 1989    African Presence in Early Spanish Colonization of the Caribbean and the Southeastern Borderlands. Paper delivered to a symposium entitled "Digging the Afro-American Past," Oxford, Mississippi.

Lauber, Almon Wheeler

1913    *Indian Slavery in Colonial Times within the Present Limits of the United States*. Columbia University, New York.

Lawson, John

1967    *A New Voyage to Carolina*. University of North Carolina Press, Chapel Hill.

Lees, William B.

1980    *Limerick, Old and In the Way: Archaeological Investigations at Limerick Plantation*. Anthropological Studies No. 5, Occasional Papers of the Institute of Archaeology and Anthropology. University of South Carolina, Columbia.

Lees, William B., and Kathryn Kimery-Lees

1979    The Function of Colono-Indian Ceramics: Insights from Limerick Plantation, South Carolina. *Historical Archaeology* 13:1–13.

Leith-Ross, Sylvia

1970    *Nigerian Pottery*. Ibadan University Press, Ibadan.

Leone, Mark

1973    Archaeology as the Science of Technology: Mormon Town Plans and Fences. In *Research and Theory in Current Archaeology*, edited by Charles Redman, pp. 125–150. John Wiley and Sons, New York.

Leone, Mark P., and Parker B. Potter, Jr. (editors)

1988    *The Recovery of Meaning: Historical Archaeology in the Eastern United States*. Smithsonian Institution Press, Washington.

Lester, Julius

1968    *To Be a Slave*. Dell Publishing Co., New York.

Lewicki, Tadeusz

1974    *West African Food in the Middle Ages According to Arabic Sources*. Cambridge University Press, Cambridge.

Lewis, Kenneth E.

1975    *Archeological Investigations at the Colonial Settlement of Long Bluff (38Da5), Darlington County, South Carolina*. Research Manuscript Series No. 67. Institute of Archaeology and Anthropology, University of South Carolina, Columbia.

1976    *Camden: A Frontier Town in Eighteenth Century South Carolina*. Anthropological Studies No. 2, Occasional Papers of the Institute of Archaeology and Anthropology. University of South Carolina, Columbia.

Lewis, Kenneth E., and Donald L. Hardesty

1979    *Middleton Place: Initial Archaeological Investigations at an Ashley River Rice Plantation*. Research Manuscript Series No. 148. Institute of Archaeology and Anthropology, University of South Carolina, Columbia.

Lewis, Kenneth E., and Helen Haskell

1980    *Hampton II: Further Archeological Investigations at a Santee River Rice Plantation*. Research Manuscript Series No. 161. Institute of Archaeology and Anthropology, University of South Carolina, Columbia.

Lewis, Lynne G.

1978    *Drayton Hall: Preliminary Archaeological Investigation at a Low Country Plantation*. National Trust for Historic Preservation, Charlottesville, Virginia.

Linton, Ralph

1944    North American Cooking Pots. *American Antiquity* 9:369–380.

Littlefield, Daniel C.

1981    *Rice and Slaves: Ethnicity and the Slave Trade in Colonial South Carolina*. Louisiana State University Press, Baton Rouge.

Lowery, Woodbury

1959    *The Spanish Settlements within the Present Limits of the United States*. Russell and Russell, New York.

Mann, Michael

1986    *Sources of Social Power*. Cambridge University Press, London.

MacGaffey, Janet

1975    Two Kongo Potters. *African Arts* 9:29–31, 92.

MacGaffey, Wyatt

1986    *Religion and Society in Central Africa: The Bakongo of Lower Zaire*. University of Chicago, Chicago.

McDaniel, George W.

1982    *Hearth and Home: Preserving a People's Culture*. Temple University Press, Philadelphia.

McKern, William C.

1939    The Midwestern Taxonomic Method as an Aide to Archeological Culture Study. *American Antiquity* 4:301–313.

Marks, Bayly Ellen

1979    *Economies and Society in a Staple Plantation System: St. Mary's County, Maryland, 1790–1840*. Ph.D. dissertation, University of Maryland.

Meinig, D.W.

1986    *The Shaping of America: A Geographical Perspective on 500 Years of History, Vol. 1, Atlantic America, 1492–1800*. Yale University Press, New Haven.

Merrell, James H.

1984    The Racial Education of the Catawba Indians. *The Journal of Southern History* 50:365–384.

Merrens, H. Roy (editor)

1977    *The Colonial South Carolina Scene: Contemporary Views, 1697–1774*. University of South Carolina Press, Columbia.

Montgomery, Charles J.

1908    Survivors of the Cargo of the Slave Yacht *Wanderer*. *American Anthropologist* 10:611–623.

Morgan, Edmund S.

1975    *American Slavery, American Freedom: The Ordeal of Virginia*. W.W. Norton and Company, New York.

Morgan, Philip D.

1977    *The Development of Slave Culture in Eighteenth Century Plantation America*.
Ph.D. dissertation, University College, London.

Mullin, Gerald W.

1972    *Flight and Rebellion: Slave Resistance in Eighteenth Century Virginia*. Oxford
University Press, London.

Nairne, Thomas

1710    *A Letter from South Carolina*. Printed for A. Baldwin, London.

Nash, Gary B.

1982    *Red, White and Black: The Peoples of Early America*. Second Edition.
Prentice-Hall, Englewood Cliffs, New Jersey.

Newman, Thelma R.

1974    *Contemporary African Arts and Crafts*. Crown Publishers, New York.

Nichols, Elaine

1988    *No Easy Run to Freedom: Maroons in the Great Dismal Swamp of North
Carolina and Virginia, 1677–1850*. Department of Anthropology, University
of South Carolina, Columbia.

Noël Hume, Ivor

1962    An Indian Ware of the Colonial Period. *Quarterly Bulletin, Archaeological
Society of Virginia* 17:1.

1966    *Excavations at Tutter's Neck in James City County, Virginia, 1960–1961*.
United States National Museum Bulletin 249, Contributions from the Museum
of History and Technology 53. Washington, D.C.

1970    *A Guide to Artifacts of Colonial America*. Alfred A. Knopf, New York.

Orser, Charles E., Jr.

1988a   *The Material Basis of the Postbellum Tenant Plantation: Historical Archaeology
in the Piedmont of S.C*. University of Georgia Press, Athens.

1988b   The Archaeological Analysis of Plantation Society: Replacing Status and Caste
with Economics and Power. *American Antiquity* 53:735–751.

1989    On Plantations and Patterns. *Historical Archaeology* 23:28–40.

Otto, John Solomon

1984    *Cannon's Point Plantation, 1794–1860: Living Conditions and Status Patterns
in the Old South*. Academic Press, New York.

Otto, John Solomon, and Russell Lamar Lewis, Jr.

1974    A Formal and Functional Analysis of San Marcos Pottery from Site SA-16-23,
St. Augustine. Florida Department of State, *Bureau of Historic Sites and
Properties Bulletin* 4:95–117.

Outlaw, Mercy Abbitt, Beverly A. Bogley, and Alain C. Outlaw

1979    Rich Man, Poor Man: Status Definition in Two Seventeenth Century Ceramic
Assemblages from Kingsmill. Manuscript on file, Department of Historic Resources, Richmond, Virginia.

Petty, Julian

1943     *The Growth and Distribution of Population in South Carolina*. State Council for
          Defense, Industrial Development Committee, Columbia.

Pinckney, Elise (editor)
1972     *The Letterbook of Eliza Lucas Pinckney, 1739–1762*. University of North
          Carolina Press, Chapel Hill.

Poe, Stephen R.
1963     *Excavations at Fort Gadsden, Florida*. Notes in Anthropology, No. 8. Depart-
          ment of Anthropology, Florida State University, Tallahassee.

Polhemus, Richard R.
1977     Archaeological Investigation of the Tellico Blockhouse site (40MR50): A
          Federal Military and Trade Complex. Unpublished report submitted to the
          Tennessee Valley Authority.

Posnansky, Merrick, and Christopher R. DeCorse
1986     Historical Archaeology in Sub-Saharan Africa—A Review. *Historical Archae-
          ology* 20:14.

Raab, L. Mark, and Albert C. Goodyear
1984     Middle Range Theory in Archaeology: A Critical Review of Origins and Appli-
          cations. *American Antiquity* 49:255–268.

Raines, Albert, et al.
1966     *With Heritage So Rich: A Report of a Special Committee on Historic Preservation
          Under the Auspices of the U.S. Conference of Mayors with a Grant from the Ford
          Foundation*. Random House.

Randolph, Mary
1984     *The Virginia House-Wife*. University of South Carolina Press, Columbia.

Rawick, George P. (editor)
1972     *The American Slave: A Composite Autobiography, South Carolina Narratives,
          Parts 1 and 2*. Greenwood Publishing Company, Westport, Connecticut.

Redfield, Robert, Ralph Linton, and Melville Herskovits
1936     Memorandum on the Study of Acculturation. *American Antiquity* 37:149–152.

Reitz, Elizabeth J.
1986     Urban/Rural Contrasts in Vertebrate Fauna from the Southern Atlantic Coastal
          Plain. *Historical Archaeology* 20(2):47–58.

Reitz, Elizabeth J., Tyson Gibbs, and Ted A. Rathbun
1985     Archaeological Evidence for Subsistence on Coastal Plantations. In *The Ar-
          chaeology of Slavery and Plantation Life*, edited by Theresa A. Singleton, pp.
          163–191. Academic Press, New York.

Rosengarten, Dale
1986     *Row Upon Row: Sea Grass Baskets of the South Carolina Lowcountry*.
          McKissick Museum, University of South Carolina, Columbia.

Rosengarten, Theodore
1986     *Tombee: Portrait of a Cotton Planter*. William Morrow and Company, New
          York.

Rye, Owen S.

    1981    *Pottery Technology: Principles and Reconstruction*. Taraxacum, Washington, D.C.

Schuyler, Robert L.

    1978    *Historical Archaeology: A Guide to Substantive and Theoretical Contributions*. Baywood Publishing Co., Farmingdale, New York.

Shaw, Thurston

    1978    *Nigeria: Its Archaeology and Early History*. Thames and Hudson, London.

Shepard, Steven J.

    1983    The Spanish Criollo Majority in Colonial St. Augustine. In *Spanish St. Augustine: The Archaeology of a Colonial Creole Community*, by Kathleen Deagan, pp. 65–67. Academic Press, New York.

Sieber, Roy

    1980    *African Furniture and Household Objects*. Indiana University Press, Bloomington.

Simms, William Gilmore

    1841    Loves of the Driver. *The Magnolia: Or Southern Monthly* 3:122. Savannah, Georgia.

Singleton, Theresa A. (editor)

    1985    *The Archaeology of Slavery and Plantation Life*. Academic Press, New York.

Smith, Hale G.

    1948    Two Historical Archaeological Periods in Florida. *American Antiquity* 13:313–319.

Smith, John

    1624    *The Generall Historie of Virginia, New-England and the Summer Isles*. Facsimile reproduction by the World Publishing Company, Cleveland, Ohio.

Smith, Julia Floyd

    1985    *Slavery and Rice Culture in Low Country Georgia, 1750–1860*. University of Tennessee Press, Knoxville.

Sobel, Mechal

    1987    *The World They Made Together: Black and White Values in Eighteenth Century Virginia*. Princeton University Press, Princeton, New Jersey.

South, Stanley

    1971    *Archaeology at the Charles Town Site on Albemarle Point, South Carolina*. Research Manuscript 10. South Carolina Institute of Archaeology and Anthropology, University of South Carolina, Columbia.

    1974    *Palmetto Parapets*. Anthropological Studies 1, Occasional Papers of the Institute of Archaeology and Anthropology. University of South Carolina, Columbia.

    1976    *An Archeological Survey of Southeastern Coastal North Carolina*. The Institute of Archaeology and Anthropology Notebook 8. University of South Carolina, Columbia.

1977a    *Method and Theory in Historical Archaeology.* Academic Press, New York.

1977b    *Research Strategies in Historical Archaeology* (editor). Academic Press, New York.

1979    *The Search for Santa Elena on Parris Island, South Carolina.* Research Manuscript Series 165. South Carolina Institute of Archaeology and Anthropology, University of South Carolina, Columbia.

1983    *Revealing Santa Elena.* Research Manuscript Series 88. South Carolina Institute of Archaeology and Anthropology, Columbia.

Speck, Frank G.

1928    *Chapters on the Ethnology of the Powhattan Tribes of Virginia.* Indian Notes and Monographs 1(5). Heye Foundation, New York.

Stein, Jess, and P.Y. Su (editors)

1980    *The Random House Dictionary.* Ballantine Books, New York.

Stern, Theodore

1951    *Pamunkey Pottery Making.* Southern Indian Studies 3. Chapel Hill, North Carolina.

Stewart, Jeffrey C., and Fath Davis Ruffins

1986    A Faithful Witness: Afro-American Public History in Historical Perspective, 1828–1984. In *Presenting the Past,* edited by Susan Porter Venson, Stephen Brier, and Roy Rosenzweig, pp. 307–336. Temple University Press, Philadelphia.

Stuckey, Sterling

1987    *Slave Culture: Nationalist Theory and the Foundations of Black America.* Oxford University Press.

Swanton, John R.

1946    *The Indians of the Southeastern United States.* Bureau of American Ethnology, Bulletin 137. Smithsonian Institution, Washington, D.C.

Tattler

1850    Management of Negroes. *Southern Cultivator* 8:162–164.

Tabe, Thad

1972    *The Negro in Eighteenth Century Williamsburg, Virginia.* Colonial Williamsburg Foundation.

Thomas, David Hurst

1979    *Archaeology.* Holt, Rinehart, and Winston, New York.

Thompson, Robert Farris

1983    *Flash of the Spirit: African and Afro-American Art and Philosophy.* Random House, New York.

Thompson, Robert Farris, and Joseph Cornet

1989    *The Four Moments of the Sun: Kongo Art in Two Worlds.* National Gallery of Art, Washington.

Trinkley, Michael (editor)

1986    *Indian and Freedmen Occupation at the Fish Haul Site (38BU805), Beaufort*

County, South Carolina. Research Series 7. Chicora Foundation, Columbia, South Carolina.

Turner, Lorenzo Dow
  1969    *Africanisms in the Gullah Dialect*. Arno Press, New York.

Vlach, John Michael
  1978    *The Afro-American Tradition in Decorative Arts*. Cleveland Museum of Art, Cleveland, Ohio.

Wagner, Mark
  1981    The Introduction and Early Use of African Plants in the New World. *Tennessee Archaeologist* 6:112–123.

Weir, Robert M.
  1983    *Colonial South Carolina: A History*. KTO Press, Millwood, New York.

Wheaton, Thomas R., Amy Friedlander, and Patrick H. Garrow
  1983    *Yaughan and Curriboo Plantations: Studies in Afro-American Archaeology*. Soil Systems, Atlanta, Georgia.

Wheaton, Thomas R., and Patrick H. Garrow
  1985    Acculturation and the Archaeological Record in the Carolina Lowcountry. In *The Archaeology of Slavery and Plantation Life*, edited by Theresa Singleton, pp. 239–259. Academic Press, New York.

Wood, Peter H.
  1974    *Black Majority*. Alfred A. Knopf, New York.

Woodward, Arthur
  1932    The Value of Indian Trade Goods in the Study of Archaeology. *The Pennsylvania Archaeologist* 3: 8, 9, 16–19.

Work Projects Administration (WPA)
  1938    *Beaufort and the Sea Islands*. The Clover Club, Savannah, Georgia.
  1986    *Drums and Shadows: Survival Studies among the Georgia Coastal Negroes*. University of Georgia Press, Athens and London.

Wright, J. Leitch, Jr.
  1981    *The Only Land They Knew: The Tragic Story of the American Indians in the Old South*. The Free Press, New York.

Zierden, Martha, Suzanne Buckley, Jeanne Calhoun, and Debi Hacker
  1987    *Georgian Opulence: Archaeological Investigations of the Gibbes House*. The Charleston Museum, Archaeological Contributions 12. Charleston, South Carolina.

Zierden, Martha A., Lesley M. Drucker, and Jeanne Calhoun
  1986    *Home Upriver: Rural Life on Daniel's Island, Berkeley County, South Carolina*, vol. 1. Carolina Archaeological Services and the Charleston Museum, Columbia and Charleston.

Zierden, Martha, and Kimberly Grimes
  1989    *Investigating Elite Lifeways through Archaeology: The John Rutledge House*. The Charleston Museum, Archaeological Contributions 21. Charleston, South Carolina.

# Index

**177**

Archaeologists (*cont.*)
87; Ralph Linton, 154; William C. McKern, 150; Elaine Nichols, xxx, 58, 72; Ivor Noël Hume, 6, 10, 47–48, 52, 149; Charles Orser, xliii, 119; John Otto, 149, xlii; Richard Polhemus, 9–10, 83–84; Merrick Posnansky, 80; Delores Root, 150; Theresa Singleton, 60, 149; Stanley South, 7, 9, 10, 82, 116–17, 149 150, 151; Thomas Wheaton, 63; Gordon R. Willey, 150; Arthur Woodward, 150, 151

Archaeology: African American, xxv–xl; effect of National Historic Preservation Act on, 152; legislation, 149; program at Annapolis, Maryland, 151; and resistance to slavery, 118–20

Architecture: African, 68–69; Native American, 80; in South Carolina, 63–82; in Virginia, 55–59

Artifacts, as symbols, xliv

Ascher, Robert (archaeologist), xl

Ashley River, South Carolina, 82, 87

Authority, slave master's, 75

Babson, David W. (archaeologist), xxviii

Bacon's Rebellion, 43–44

Bakongo religion, 110–16

Ball, Charles (ex-slave), 81, 118

Barbados, as origin of slaves, 82

Bark, for roofing and sheathing, 66

Barrels, 100

Baskets, coiled, 12–15

Bauer, Carl (observed slave houses), 80, 98

Beads: and African American ritual, 116–17, 160; for babies, xxii; on slave ships, 92

Beef, as principle lowcountry food, 96

Beer, made in large jars, 103

Bestwick, Edward (Virginia settler), 42

"Big house," xxiii, 83

Binford, Lewis (archaeologist), 7, 18, 47, 149

Black, Maggie (ex-slave), 2

Blassingame, John (historian), xl

Bluff Plantation, South Carolina, 11

Boards, for houses, 81

Bogley, Bly (curator), 46

Bottles, use, 159

Bowls: African American use of, xliii, 55, 106–7; delftware, 4; gourd, 106; Indian, 42; poorly made, 87; remembered by ex-slaves, 2; ritual use of, 109–16; in South Carolina, 105–6; in St. Augustine, 38–40; in Virginia, 48, 52, 54; wooden, 100, 106. *See also* Colono Ware

Brathwaite, Edward Kamau (poet and historian), xix, xli–xlii

Braun, David (archaeologist), 24, 105

Bread: corn, 95; sorghum, 94

Brick: chimney, 77; foundations, 79; hearths, 105

Britain, as source of culture, 69

British West Indies, as origin of blacks in Charles Towne, 82

Brown, Ben (from St. Helena Island), 34

Brown, John (runaway slave), 56–57

Brown, Kenneth (archaeologist), 116

Bucket, in slave household, 98

Burnishing, 52, 90–92; on bowls at Charles Towne, 82

Cabins: clay, 79; weather-boarded, 81

Cakes, boiled grain, 94

Calabash, 97

Cannon's Point Plantation, Georgia, xlii

Canoe, dugout, xxvi

Carolina colony, population of, 59

Carolina, Albert (ex-slave), 2–3

Catawba Indians, 90, 107, 153

Catesby, Mark (naturalist), 94–95

Great Dismal Swamp, North Carolina, 58
Green, Lane (architectural historian), 156
Green, Rebeccah (of St. Helena Island), 68, 99
Greene, General Nathanael, 77
Grimke, Sarah (abolitionist), 81
Grits, hominy, 95
"Ground house," 75
Guinea corn, 94
Gullah, 93
Gutman, Herbert (historian), xl

Halidon Hill Plantation, South Carolina, xxviii
Haliwa Indians, 156
Hall, Shad (ex-slave), 1–3, 74, 94
Hampton Plantation, South Carolina, 84–87
Hand mill, 98–99
Hands, eating with, 97, 100, 106
Hearths, 80, 66–67; at Newington Plantation, 83; slaves cooking on, 100; of three stones, 105
Heat, effect on earthenware, 103–104
Heider, Karl (anthropologist), 12
Henry, Susan (archaeologist), 49–50, 154 (typology for Virginia Colono Ware)
Herskovits, Melville (anthropologist), xl, 115, 150, 157
Heyward-Washington House, Charleston: bowls from, 87; coiled basketry from, 15
Hill III, Max L. (Middleburg owner), 147
Historian, architectural (Lane Green), 156
Historians: Margaret Washington Creel, 118, 160; Wyth Dornan, 160; W.E.B. Dubois, 150; Patricia Jones-Jackson, 160; Charles Joyner, xliii; Daniel Littlefield, 61; Bayly Ellen Marks,

155; Edmund S. Morgan, 42; Gary Nash, 49; Fath Davis Ruffins, 149; Mechal Sobel, 156; Jeffrey C. Stewart, 149; Sterling Stuckey, xliii, 115, 160; Robert Weir, 60; Peter Wood, 16, 61; J. Leitch Wright, 38
Historians, art: Sylvia Leith-Ross, 15; Roy Sieber, 106; Robert Farris Thompson, 110
History, European American, 5–6
Hodder, Ian (archaeologist), xliv, 119
Hodges, Mary Ellen N. (archaeologist), 152
Hoes, 43
Home, slave, xxi
Hominy, 95
Hominy grits, 95
Honey, in *saraka*, 94
Horn spoons, 97
Houses: account of, xxii; African, 1, 74; African-style, 75; built by Okra, xlv, 75; clay-walled, 79–82; earthfast, 37; fictional, xxi–xxiii; Jamaican, 66; in South Carolina, 63–82; in Virginia, 55–59
Huguenin, Thomas and Mary (plantation owners), xxviii
Hunting, for subsistence, 96
Hut, 75, 80, 98

Ideology, Georgian, 52–54
Indian. *See* Native American
Individualism, 97
Individualistic, slaves not, 81
Ingenuity, of African Americans, 87

Jamaica, as creole society, xlii
Jamaican house, 66
Jamestown, Virginia, 5
Jars, Colono Ware, 25, 28, 84, 85, 86, 102–5
Johnson, Guion Griffis (sociologist), 150

Johnson, Guy B. (anthropologist), 157
Jones-Jackson, Patricia (historian and folklorist), 160
Joyner, Charles (historian and folklorist), xliii
Jug, Colono Ware, 10–11

Kelso, William (archaeologist), 44, 57–58, 67, 118
Kettles, 98
Kingsley Plantation, xxxvi–xxxvii
Kingsmill Plantation, Virginia, 44, 56, 57–59, 67, 117
Klingelhofer, Eric (archaeologist), 117
Knives, as part of English foodways, 98
Knowledge, African American, 92

Laurens, Henry (planter and merchant), 61, 66
Leaves, for serving food, 97
Legislation, for archaeology, xxxviii, 149
Legumes, 95
Leith-Ross, Sylvia (art historian), 15–16
Leone, Mark (archaeologist), 150
Lesesne Plantation, South Carolina, 87, 158
Lewis, Lynne (archaeologist), 87
Linguist: Lorenzo Dow Turner, 157
Linguistics, applied to creolization, xlii
Littlefield, Daniel (historian), 61
Locks and keys, for control of slaves, 47
Log cabin 77–81, 157
Lowcountry, Carolina, as African American region, 60–61
Lucas, Jonathan (planter), xxiii, 147
Lucas, Thomas, 147
Lumbee Indians, 156
Lye, wood-ash, 95
Lynches River, South Carolina, 77

Macy, Rueben L. (Quaker), 81
Maize. See Corn

Marion, General Francis, 77
Marks, on Colono Ware, 10, 26, 110–16
Marks, Bayly Ellen (historian), 155
Marks, cutlery, 25, 54, 106
Maroons, 58
Marxian theory, xliii, 119; contrasted to Marxist theory, 151
Material culture, African American, 118–19
Maxwell, Susan (ex-slave), 93
McKern, William C. (archeologist), 150
McLeod, Jake (ex-slave), 77
Meal, boiled, 94
Meat, as food, 94–97
Meherrin Indian village, 18
Mexico (New Spain), 37–38
Middleburg Plantation, South Carolina, xxiii–xxxi, 72, 147
Miller, A.E. (nineteenth-century writer), 147
Millet, 94
Miner, Leigh Richmond (photographer), 157
*Minkisi*, 114–16
Missions, Spanish, 84
Mode of production, xliii
Morgan, Edmund S. (historian), 42
Mortar and pestle, wooden, 100
Mortars, for pounding rice, 98–99
Mose, Gracia Real de Santa Teresa de, 41
Mud, for walls, 75
Mugs, European-style, 104
Mulberry Plantation, South Carolina, 79
Mush, cornmeal, 95

Nairne, Thomas (Carolina settler), xxxi
Nash, Gary (historian), 49
National Historic Preservation Act, xx–xviii, 152
Native American peoples: Catawba, 90, 107, 153; Creek, 80; Edisto, 156;

Population, slave (*cont.*)
84; related to Virginia Colono Ware,
50
Porcher, Phillip (lowcountry informant), 90
Porches, 67
Posnansky, Merrick (archaeologist), 80
Possum Point, Georgia, 93
Post-and-beam houses, 55–56
Posts, for foundations, 64–67, 75, 81
Pots: 39, 102–7; charred earthenware,
83–84; for cooking relishes, 97; iron,
94, 97, 103–4, 107, 110; called
*mosojo*, 82; round-bottomed, 84; shape
of, 39, 48, 52, 105
Pottery: friable, 87; Native American,
10–11, 20–21, 39, 49–50, 82–83,
89–90, 92; River Burnished, 90–93;
San Marcos, 39–40, 48; sherds, xx-
xvi, 8, 39; wall thickness of, 87,
136–43. *See also* Colono Ware;
Colono-Indian Ware; Ceramics; Pots;
Bowls; Jars
Potting clay, 88–89
Power, social, 119–20
Prejudice, 47, 69, 104, 121–23
Preservation, 102, 148
Protein, 94
Pumpkins, 94
Purcell, Joseph (map maker), xxx

Quarters. *See* Houses
Quinby Plantation, South Carolina, 77–
78

Racial labeling, 155
Racism, emergence in Virginia, 43
Randolph, Mary (cookbook author), 105
Randolph, Shadwick (ex-slave), 100
Rappahannock River, Indian village on,
20
Recipe for okra soup, 90
Red painting on bowls, 84

Religion, African American, 114–16,
160
Relishes, 94, 97, 104
Renaissance, 82, 97
Revolutionary War, 77, 80–81
Rice, 60; in Africa, 61, 94; as food in
early South Carolina, 93–94; with
okra soup, 90; pounding, 100; as slave
food, 94, 98; threshing, xxv
Rice banks, xxiv–xxv
Rice fields, xxiv–xxv
"Rice Kingdom," 94–95
Rice plantations, xxi–xxxii, 59–62
Rims, everted on jars, 104
River Burnished pottery, 90–93
Roofs: for houses, 66; flat, 75; high-
pitched, 79; holes for smoke in, 81
Room size: in Africa, 73; of Okra's
house, 75; in South Carolina and Vir-
ginia, 72–73, 144–45
Rooms, partitioned, 77
Root cellar, 58, 67
Root, Delores (archaeologist), 150
Ruffins, Fath Davis (historian), 149
Runaway slaves, 41, 56, 58, 118

San Marcos pottery, 16, 39–40, 48
San Miguel de Guadalupe, 37
Santa Elena (in South Carolina), 6, 37,
152
Santee River, 67; and itinerant Catawba
Indians, 90
Sapelo Island, Georgia, xlv, 1, 37, 74
Sauces, 94; in bowls, 105–6; prepared
in small jars, 104; vessels for 104–5
Sea Islands, xxxvi, 79, 149
Sealing wax, 90
Senegal, West Africa, 115
Servant, 42
Servants, compared to slaves, 77
Settlement pattern, in Carolina and Vir-
ginia, 59–60

Turner, Nat (slave insurrectionist), 49
Tuscarora Indians, 60
Tutters Neck site, Virginia, 149

Use-wear, on Colono Ware, 27, 106. *See also* Cutlery marks; Charring
Utensils, in slave household, 98
Utopia site, Virginia, 48–50, 88

Vegetables: as African food, 94–95, 97; infusion made from, 28, 54
Vessels. *See* Bowls; Ceramics; Colono Ware; Colono-Indian Ware; Gourds; Jars; Jug; Mug; Plates; Pots; Pottery
Virginia: architecture in, 55–59, 133–35; Colono Ware from, 44–55, 128–29, 136–47, 142–43; early settlement in 41–44; lifeways contrasted with South Carolina, 33–37
Vlach, John (folklorist), 57

Waccamaw Neck, South Carolina, xlii
Washington, Adelaide (of St. Helena Island), 14
Waster, pottery, 84
Water: storage of, 103; in West African cosmology, 115–16
Wattle-and-daub, 56, 64
Weanock Indians, 55

Weir, Robert (historian), 60
West Africa: cobbed walls in, 64; craft specialization in, 47–48; crafts, 51–52; food, 94–95; houses, 73–75; influence on architecture, 37
West Indies, 16–17, 82
Wetherburn's Tavern, Williamsburg, 53
Wheaton, Thomas (archeologist), 63
Willey, Gordon R. (archaeologist), 150
Williamsburg, Virginia, 3–7, 33, 44, 50, 53
Wine, palm, 106
Women: as potters, 40–41; role of in St. Augustine, 39–40
Wood, Peter (historian), xl, 16, 61
Woodcarving, 100–2
Woodward, Arthur (archaeologist), 150, 151
Works Project Administration, xl, 1
Wright, J. Leitch (historian), 38

Yamassee Indians, 60
Yaughan Plantation, South Carolina, 66, 67, 87, 106, 153
Yeomans Hall Plantation, South Carolina, 66

Zaire, Central Africa, 114